The
GUILTLESS
Gourmet

200 recipes from top international chefs show you
how to eat what you like without gaining weight

DAVID MABEY

MITCHELL BEAZLEY

Editor Leonie Hamilton
Art Editor Eljay Crompton

Executive Editor Susan Egerton-Jones
Picture Research Brigitte Arora
Production Peter Phillips

Illustrator Barbara Karban

Edited and designed by
Mitchell Beazley International Limited
14-15 Manette Street
London W1V 5LB

Filmsetting by Hourds Typographica Ltd.
Reproduction by Chelmer Litho Reproductions
Printed and bound in Great Britain by
Clark Constable, Edinburgh, London, Melbourne

Acknowledgments
The author and publishers would like to thank the following for
their help and advice: Stephen Bull, Barbara Deane, Jonathon
Hayes, Somerset Moore, Rosie Shields.

Picture credits
Caterer and Hotelkeeper, Consumer Industries Press p. 106; Chef,
Consumer Industries Press pp. 33, 52, 88, 174, 191; Christian
Teubner jacket; Clive Streeter pp. 34, 87, 124, 192; Anthony Blake
pp. 51, 105; Mike Kirkup pp. 69, 70; Bay Books pp. 123, 173.

The GUILTLESS *Gourmet*

Contents

Foreword

It is as easy to eat badly as it is to eat well. Samuel Johnson was right when he said that anyone who does not mind what he puts in his belly probably does not mind about anything else. Food that is not good for you is probably not good food at all. Even if the ingredients are fresh, the chef who swamps his fish with a pint of double cream is not really *cooking* creatively. Such recipes were devised for the days when fish was almost certainly going to be old, dried out and quite possibly off. It needed to be served with a thick sauce to make it semi-palatable. The real art of the cook is to organize and prepare those ingredients that are available into an attractive and nutritious meal.

What we eat shapes both the way we live as well as the way our bodies function. Gourmet or not, the buying of food, its preparation and consumption are things we all have to do every day. And in the last decade, we have seen the emergence of a new generation of chefs, many featured in these pages, who have evolved a radical new style of cooking, much as Escoffier, Câremme and Soyer did in London 100 years ago. It is not *nouvelle cuisine* as such, although that played its part in the early days, but a new approach.

The food should taste of itself, and with this in mind, only the finest ingredients at the peak of ripeness will do. As chefs have ventured forth from their kitchens in search of better raw materials, a marked change has come over their menus, which is almost a morality.

For instance, anyone who has spent a day or two on a modern chicken farm is unlikely to feel like cooking or eating chicken the same night. If we are to eat meat, surely the animals have a right to a life of some freedom and enjoyment, instead of being locked up in concentration camps for a short, unnatural existence. This instinctive reaction has brought with it more fish and more vegetarian dishes. The food also tastes a great deal better.

The fact that battery chickens have little taste is insidious because we are encouraged to eat them as if it did not matter. But it does matter, and it is through the use of free-range birds that we learn to have respect for the birds both at the table and as animals.

The new cooking found strong allies among nutritionists. Suddenly areas that had formerly been regarded as purely matters of personal taste started to marry with ideas on healthy eating. Cooks rejected the use of tinned vegetables. The taste had been emaciated by the additives that had been put in to preserve them. It was those same additives that worried the nutritionists, who were fearful of possible side-effects. The nutritionists also objected to vegetables being overcooked, because fibre and vitamin values were lost. The cooks objected because the taste and texture were destroyed. Most potent of all, the nutritionists gave the cooks a reason to abandon the old heavy cream sauces that anchored diners to their chairs: namely, coronaries. So it was that between the two camps a persuasive doctrine emerged.

The climate too was right for change. In Britain chefs were not shackled to any great culinary tradition. Their experiments, using whatever was available from day to day, found an appreciative and ready audience. And, as an importing nation, the world was anxious to sell us its produce to supplement the vagaries of what our national agriculture could produce. Markets and shops became filled with fruits and vegetables from across the globe, which opened new possibilities.

So here at last is an alternative to the fast foods and processed produce of the 1950s, '60s and '70s, with their glamour image, TV advertising, cynical morality, and skeletons in the cupboard – usually ground and recycled into "pure meat" sausages. The new style of cookery is reflected in the recipes in this book; the emphasis is on fresh fish and vegetables, on poultry and game rather than red meat, on desserts based largely on fresh fruit, and on light cooking methods, such as grilling and steaming, which

preserve the nutrients in food.   *Drew Smith*

Introduction

Good food has acquired a bad reputation. We like to eat well, but the prospect of enjoying good food has been too often associated with becoming overweight and unhealthy. Fortunately that is now changing. There is enormous interest in healthy food and a new generation of chefs is at work creating a lighter style of cookery that takes full account of natural quality, flavour, health and nutrition without sacrificing anything or putting restrictions on what we eat.

This book is not about dieting or losing weight; it is a celebration of the pleasures of good food and adventurous cooking. It also shows that it is possible to enjoy eating what you like without *putting on* weight or affecting your well-being. Its message is that we should be expanding rather than constricting our diet, not laying down hard-and-fast rules which limit what we eat, but exploring new ingredients, new flavours and new cooking techniques.

Some people do have to stick to a rigid diet for medical reasons, but most of us can live and eat quite happily without dieting at all. All we need to do is to judge our food using a new set of guidelines, adjust our diet in favour of more natural ingredients, revise our cooking techniques, and above all apply a sense of balance to what we eat. Instead of blacklisting ingredients such as cream and butter, we should use them with discretion to enhance rather than swamp dishes and when we do allow ourselves an occasional bout of indulgence, we should know how to compensate.

The chefs who have contributed to this book are enthusiastically taking up the challenge and many are champions of the new style of cooking. They are well aware that restrictions and regimes limit good cooking and they know that when there is a real concern for natural flavour and quality, the results are often naturally healthy too. And that's encouraging news for everyone who wants to eat well *and* stay in good shape.

THE BALANCE RATINGS

To help readers eat in a balanced way, each recipe is given a rating of 1, 2 or 3, using the ⟍symbol. These ratings don't simply relate to calorie counts, but allow for ingredients, nutritional value and style of cooking.

What the ratings mean

Dishes that have little or no added fat or sugar. They tend to be quite simple, but highly nutritious, and many are low in calories (where the calorie count is high, it normally relates to protein rather than fat). Anyone pursuing a healthy and weight-reducing diet should set their sights on these dishes.

Average, well-balanced dishes which may contain moderate amounts of fat, but are nevertheless imaginative and good to eat. These dishes are unlikely to cause weight gain.

Rich, indulgent dishes which may include cream and other ingredients that are high in fat and calories. These are dishes for special treats, but they may safely be enjoyed provided they are combined with lower-rated dishes.

How the ratings work

Working on the basis of a three-course meal, a good overall balance rating to aim for is 6 (for example 3 + 2 + 1 or 2 + 2 + 2), ideally one dish rated 1 should be included in each meal. There is room for plenty of flexibility in this system to suit personal preference. The sample menus below show how the ratings work in practice.

MENU A
Fish Consommé with Brown Shrimps   1
Roast Mallard with Kumquat Sauce   2
Guava and Lime Syllabub   3
Total   6

MENU B
Parcels of Smoked Salmon with Yogurt Cream Sauce   3
Baked Loin of Pork garnished with Melon and Limes   2
Fruit Terrine with a Coulis of Mango   1

MENU C
Monkfish and Spinach Terrine   2
Petit Paillettes of Turbot with Mange-tout and Mussels   2
Hot Apple Tartlets   2

For a three-course meal, you could have overall ratings ranging from 3 to 9, as follows:

3 For enthusiastic healthy eaters, where every dish reflects the principles of health and diet.

4–5 Still healthy. Could contain one or two dishes rated 1.

6 An average meal for the guiltless gourmet. A balance of good eating and good health, enjoying what you like without restrictions.

7–8 Based on dishes rated 2 or 3. Acceptable as an occasional treat, but the overall balance is slightly tipped the wrong way.

9 Throwing caution to the wind, and likely to contain too much fat for healthy eating.

By simply changing one dish in a meal you can dramatically alter its overall rating. For example:

MENU A opposite is rated 6 as it stands. However if you substitute Parcels of Smoked Salmon (3) for Fish Consommé (1) the rating then goes up to 8 and the menu becomes unbalanced, with quite large amounts of fat at the beginning and end of the meal.

Variations on the theme

The choice of a three-course meal is a useful standard to work from, but there are plenty of variations on the theme. Sometimes you might want only one course, and there are numerous recipes in the book which will fit the bill. Some of the hors d'oeuvre and first courses would make good lunchtime snacks and a few recipes might even brighten up breakfast time. So keep an eye on the ratings, but allow yourself to be flexible.

Hidden extras

The balance ratings (and calorie counts) for each dish do not take into account many of the extras that usually go to make up a complete meal, so it is worth keeping an eye out for some of the more obvious traps.

Bread

This is likely to be part of any meal (particularly at the beginning); it will often be eaten with butter and will contribute to the overall picture.

Vegetables

Many of the main dishes in the book will naturally be served with vegetables. In their own right these are rated low, but the way they are cooked will affect their rating. Raw, steamed, blanched and lightly boiled vegetables are all fine, although if they are subsequently drenched in butter the results are not so good. Avoid fried or deep-fried vegetables with dishes that are already high in fat. They will boost the overall rating of the dish considerably, and too many calories contained in one course is bad planning.

Cheese

Many people like to finish off a meal with cheese (often with biscuits and butter as well), which needs to be fitted into your overall scheme, bearing in mind that many of our finest and most common cheeses are high in fat. If you want to eat sensibly, try to avoid eating a dessert followed by high-fat cheese.

Drinks

Beverages of one kind or another tend to be a natural part of most meals and can have a significant effect on balance ratings, calories and health. Drinking three or four glasses of red wine is not unlike having a second piece of gâteau, so drink carefully as well as eating carefully. The virtues and vices of alcohol have been well aired, but as a general rule, you should not drink too much too regularly. Black tea with Chinese meals, unsweetened fruit juices, mineral water and other non-alcoholic drinks have little or no effect on the rating of a meal, but consider what you are doing when you add cream to coffee. (The charts on pages 201-6 give specific details about the calories and nutrients in different types of food and drink.)

Calories per serving

The figures at the end of each recipe are very approximate guides to the calorie count of the dish. A great deal depends on the size of the portion and the quantity of various ingredients (how big the chicken breast is, or how much sauce is spooned on to the plate, for example). However I have made a few assumptions to make the figures as useful as possible. Portions of meat, fish, etc. are taken as 4 oz (120 g) per person, unless the recipe specifically states otherwise. I have also calculated the figures on small helpings of sauces (where these are served separately), generally allowing 1–2 tbs per person.

It's worth noting that most of the dishes in this book are quite low in calories. For instance, few of the main courses are more than 500 Calories, which compares favourably with a large cheese and tomato sandwich, which is 530 Calories, or steak and kidney pie with chips, which is 1,150.

Food value

The notes on food value are very general guidelines to the main nutrients in each dish, in particular, protein, fibre, vitamins and minerals. I have tended to disregard most carbohydrates, such as sugars and starches, as these are simply sources of energy. However they are listed in the nutritional charts on pages 201–6.

Fat is classified in various ways:

No fat.

No added fat. This refers to dishes where fat is not a specific ingredient, but may appear in, say, meat or fish.

Low fat. These dishes have noticeable, but not high amounts of fat in one
10   form or another.

Moderate fat. These dishes contain significant amounts of fat, which also represents a large percentage of the total calories. Alternative low-fat ingredients might be considered for these recipes.

By looking at the balance rating, ingredients, calories and food value of each recipe, you will have a good basis for planning a balanced meal.

INGREDIENTS

Choosing the right ingredients is an important part of eating well, and it goes without saying that fresh food is best. Try to avoid processed foods of all kinds, not only because their quality and flavour is not particularly good, but also because they often contain additives and sugar, animal fat and salt in unnecessarily high quantities.

Even frozen food is best kept to a minimum. Of course it is convenient and the techniques used nowadays are very sophisticated, but it still doesn't bear comparison to the best fresh food and may also have lost some nutrients, as well as flavour. Freezing also robs us of the pleasure of eating food in its true season.

More details about meat, fish, vegetables, fruit and so on will be found in the introduction to each recipe section, but there are a number of general points to bear in mind about specific foods – especially when considering useful low-fat and low-calorie alternatives for cooking.

Butter*

Although good for cooking, butter is a concentrated source of saturated animal fat. It is advisable to use a top-quality polyunsaturated margarine as an alternative. There is no difference in the fat content, but margarines of this type contain polyunsaturated vegetable fats which are less likely to cause health problems. Whichever you use, try to reduce the amount to a minimum. Margarines advertised as "low-fat" cannot be used for cooking as they contain too much water.

Cream

Like butter, cream is a concentrated source of animal fat, but used sparingly, with skill and care, it can enhance and enrich dishes to perfection. Used carelessly, it can completely swamp the natural flavour of a fine piece of fish or meat.

Once again, try to keep the quantities to a minimum, and use single cream rather than double if you want to cut down on fat. Also investigate the possibilities of sour cream, quark, *fromage blanc* and low-fat natural yogurt as alternatives. (The term "cream" in recipes refers to single cream, unless otherwise specified.)

Milk

To reduce fat substitute skimmed milk for gold top.

*Asterisked throughout to indicate that polyunsaturated margarine can be used as a substitute.

Oil
Many dishes require oil, either for cooking or in dressings and sauces. Use soya oil or groundnut oil for cooking if possible, and more interesting varieties, such as walnut or hazelnut oil, for dressings. Avoid low-quality blended vegetable oils which often have an unpleasant taste, and keep quantities to a minimum.

Sugar
Refined sugar is pure carbohydrate and a concentrated source of energy, but is considered by most nutritionists to be unhealthy, and should be kept to a minimum. Enterprising cooks make more use of both honey and the natural sweetness of fruit, vegetables and even herbs such as sweet cicely.

Salt
While this has no direct bearing on calories or weight gain, it is an ingredient that we tend to use too freely. One of the marks of a good cook is subtle seasoning, and the salt cellar should be used with discretion. The natural flavour of vegetables, in particular, can be ruined by over-salting.

COOKING TECHNIQUES

The way we cook food affects not only its flavour and texture, but also its nutritional value. In the West, there is still a strong emphasis on cooking in fat (in some countries it is a way of life). Obviously there is a place for techniques like sautéeing in butter or deep-frying in oil. However, methods of cooking which don't involve fat, such as steaming, poaching and grilling, not only improve the quality and natural flavour of our food, but can make it more healthy and less of a threat to the waistline. Dry sautéeing without fat (see the recipe for Sautéed Scallops with Chive Sauce on page 94) is also well worth trying. These techniques are helping to change the whole emphasis and complexion of our cooking towards really healthy eating.

Cooking times, like cooking methods, are also changing. There is still a tendency to overcook food, especially fish and vegetables, which dulls their flavour and texture as well as making them less nutritious (most vitamins, in particular, are lost during long cooking). We should take a tip from cooks in the East, who have reduced cooking times to a minimum for a great many of their dishes, with marvellous results: vegetables are crisp and full of real flavour, fish is soft and succulent, and all types of meat, poultry and game are juicy and tender.

Cooking in the West, at least much of *haute cuisine*, has been dominated by a repertoire of rich sauces, thickened with flour and enriched with large quantities of cream and butter. But this too is changing. In the new era of lighter, healthier food, sauces are increasingly based on reduced stock and pan juices, perhaps whisked up with a small amount of butter or laced with a little alcohol. The way sauces are presented is also changing.

12

Quantities of sauce, however delicious, simply poured over the food, completely swamps its true flavour. Today sauces are used more sparingly, the food is usually placed *on* the sauce or beside it. The result of this is not only dishes that look and taste better, but sauces that are less of a hazard for anyone who wants to eat sensibly. (See for example the recipes for Roast Guinea Fowl with Limes on page 139 and Sweetbreads with Chicory and Malaga on page 42).

TIPS FOR GOOD EATING

By taking note of these tips and guidelines you can be sure of good eating and good health. They are positive suggestions rather than restrictions.
1) Make better use of fresh ingredients of all kinds, particularly fruit, vegetables and fish.
2) Eat more fish, poultry and game in place of red meat.
3) Think of red meat as an ingredient to be used with and balanced by other ingredients, rather than as the focal point of a dish.
4) Cut down on all types of fat. Get to know the fat content of cheeses; try using skimmed instead of full-fat milk; find alternatives to double cream, such as sour cream and yogurt; use polyunsaturated margarine instead of butter for cooking.
5) Make better use of honey and the natural sweetness of fruit. Cut down on refined sugar.
6) Use the salt cellar with care.
7) Try out new cooking techniques, especially steaming, grilling and poaching rather than cooking in fat as a matter of course.
8) Steam, blanch and lightly cook vegetables.
9) Make stocks from carcasses and bones, rather than relying entirely on stock cubes.
10) Experiment with new sauces made from reduced stock and pan juices.
11) Remember that natural flavour comes first and that balance is the secret of good eating.

GLOSSARY
of cooking terms

Aiguillette
The breast of any kind of poultry.

Bain-marie
Also known as a water bath, this consists of a large pan such as a roasting tin filled with water, in which reduced saucepans or bowls containing food are set (ideally on a special trivet). Its most useful purpose is to ensure that dishes, especially sauces, cook at a constant low temperature without drying out or scorching. A *bain-marie* can also be used to keep cooked food warm and moist.

Beurre blanc
A reduced mixture of white wine, wine vinegar and finely chopped shallots, into which butter is whisked to make a smooth sauce.

Beurre noisette
A sauce made with butter, cooked until just brown, lemon juice and seasoning.

Blanch
A term meaning to immerse food briefly in boiling water to soften it, to remove its skin or to remove excess salt.

Clarify
To free fats, especially butter for cooking, stocks and consommés from impurities.

Coulis
A French word for a sauce made from puréed vegetable or fruits and without a thickening agent such as flour or cream.

Croustade
A small pastry case in which chopped meat, poultry or game is served.

Curd
The coagulated substance that is produced in milk when it is soured.

Deglaze
To scrape browned solidified cooking juices off the bottom of a saucepan with the help of liquid such as wine or stock, when making sauces or gravy.

Forcemeat
A mixture of minced meat, vegetables or bread used as a stuffing.

Glaze
Coating food with a sugar syrup, aspic, beaten egg or milk to make it shiny.

Julienne
Thin strips of vegetables normally used as a garnish.

Noisette
A good cut of lamb or venison taken from the best end of neck, trimmed and tied with string into a small boneless round.

Paillettes
Thin slivers usually of meat or fish.

Papillote
Papillote is literally French for curl-papers, and food *en papillote* is cooked, and often served, in a paper or other type of case.

Pâte feuilletée
The French word for puff pastry.

Quenelles
Lightly cooked dumplings made from finely chopped fish or meat.

Reduce
To concentrate or thicken a liquid by rapid boiling. To reduce by half means to boil until half the liquid has evaporated.

Roulade
A rolled slice of meat or pastry with a filling.

Stir-fry
A method of cooking favoured by the Chinese, in which finely chopped ingredients are quickly stirred and tossed in a little oil over a high heat, ideally in a wok.

Zest
The oily outer part of citrus skin, used for flavouring.

SOUPS
Introduction

Back in 1765, a French soup vendor named Boulanger began to describe his wares as *restaurants* or restoratives and, if *Larousse Gastronomique* is to be believed, coined our word "restaurant" in the process. Soups have always had restorative powers whether thick vegetable purées or delicate clear broths and there's hardly an ingredient that has not been used in a soup.

STOCK

The base of almost every soup is stock and, for the best results, this should be the real thing: the full-flavoured liquid obtained from simmering and straining bones, carcasses and vegetables. The aim is to extract as much goodness and flavour as possible from the ingredients without cooking them for so long that the stock loses body. When the strained stock has cooled, excess fat can be skimmed off, leaving a stock with few calories.

Stock cubes are useful and convenient, but if you take cooking seriously, you might think about organizing a stockpot. It's easy, cheap and avoids wasting bones and carcasses; and the stock can be used not only for soups, but for sauces and many other dishes as well.

The most refined version of stock – and one which will reveal the consummate skill of a good chef – is consommé. A transparent, subtle, yet strong flavoured soup, it needs patience, dedication and experience to perfect, and real consommé is a rare sight on today's restaurant menus.

FLOUR AND CREAM

Most of the classic, traditional soups are rich and substantial, thickened with flour and enriched with quantities of cream and often butter as well. The *crèmes* and *veloutés* of French *haute cuisine* are only now beginning to lose some of their original appeal as a new generation of chefs begins to devise lighter soups which emphasize the natural flavour of ingredients.

Cream is still used in many soups, of course, and when handled with restraint it can enhance and enrich a soup perfectly. Flour, however, is fast disappearing as a thickener for soups, and sieved and liquidized ingredients are taking over to provide the required body and substance. The result is a style of soup-making that is rich, elegant and sophisticated.

SOUPE DE MOULES
à la fleur de thym

The addition of fresh thyme at the very last moment gives this richly flavoured soup a wonderful fragrance.

INGREDIENTS

4 pts (2 litres) mussels
  (in shells)
1 pt (½ litre) dry white
  wine
2 pts (1 litre) fish stock
5 oz (150 g) carrots
1 medium onion
2 cloves garlic
4 dsp olive oil
2 dsp tomato purée
pinch of saffron
1 small bouquet garni
10 fl oz (300 ml) double
  cream
salt and pepper
1 sprig of fresh thyme

SERVES 4

METHOD

Sort through the mussels, scrub them well, remove their beards and throw out any that are damaged or open. Wash in several changes of fresh water to clean them.

Put the mussels into a large saucepan with the dry white wine and fish stock and cook briskly with the lid on until the shells are just open. Drain off the juice and keep separate.

Peel and finely chop the carrots, onion and garlic. Warm the olive oil in a separate saucepan and sweat the vegetables for about 10 minutes over a low heat (with the lid on). Add the juice from the mussels, then the tomato purée, saffron and bouquet garni. Cover and cook gently for 30-40 minutes. Meanwhile remove the mussels from their shells and keep hot.

When the carrots and other vegetables are cooked, stir in the cream and simmer gently for 10-15 minutes. Season with salt and pepper.

To serve, put the mussels into four soup plates, sprinkle with fresh thyme, then pour the hot soup over the top.
Pierre Chevillard, Chewton Glen Hotel

Calories per serving: 525
Food value: Protein, minerals and vitamins. Moderate fat.
Note: Mussels are not only a good source of protein, but lack the saturated fat associated with red meat, for example.

FISH CONSOMMÉ
with brown shrimps

For the best results make this soup from the bones of "white" fish that are high in natural gelatine, such as brill or turbot.

INGREDIENTS

2-3 lb (1-1½ kg) fish bones
1 onion
2-3 tomatoes
1 bay leaf
pinch of saffron
salt and pepper

GARNISH
brown shrimps

SERVES 4

METHOD

Put all the fish bones into a large pan and add the peeled and sliced onion and the chopped tomatoes, together with the bay leaf and the saffron (previously soaked in a little water). Season with salt and pepper.

Cover with water, bring to the boil, then turn down the heat and simmer gently for about 1 hour. During simmering, remove any scum as it forms and rises to the surface.

Allow the stock to cool, during which time any particles will settle. Ladle off the clear liquid and strain through muslin to ensure that the soup is completely clear. Leave to get cold.

Serve the consommé cold in individual bowls with a few brown shrimps scattered over the surface.

Somerset Moore, Flitwick Manor

Calories per serving: 70
Food value: Protein, minerals and vitamins. No added fat.
Note: The classic method of clearing a consommé by using egg whites isn't essential in this particular recipe.

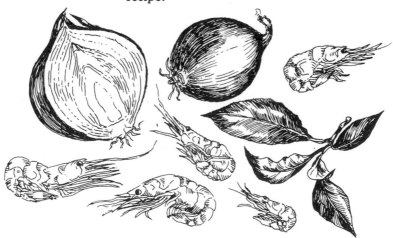

PEKING LAMB AND CUCUMBER SOUP

A light, simple and delicately flavoured soup that requires a minimal amount of cooking. Use a lean leg of lamb for the best results.

INGREDIENTS

8 oz (240 g) leg of lamb
1 tbs soya sauce
1½ tsp sesame oil
5-6 in (10-15 cm) cucumber
2 pts (1 litre) chicken stock
salt and pepper
1 chicken stock cube
1¼ tbs vinegar

SERVES 4-5

METHOD

Cut the lamb with a sharp knife into very thin, small slices. Sprinkle and rub with soya sauce and sesame oil. Leave to marinade for 10-15 minutes. Cut the cucumber into similar very thin slices.

Heat the stock in a saucepan. Season and add the stock cube. Bring to the boil. Add the lamb to poach in the stock for 1 minute, then remove. Add the cucumber, bring to the boil, then simmer for 2 minutes. Add the vinegar, return the lamb to the pan, bring the contents to the boil, and serve.

Kenneth Lo and Kam-Po But, Ken Lo's Memories of China

Calories per serving: 130
Food value: Protein and vitamins. Low fat.

GAME AND CHERRY SOUP

The basis of this soup is rich game stock made from carcasses and root vegetables, which must be prepared in advance.

INGREDIENTS

3 pts (1½ litres) game stock
8 oz (240 g) cooked wild duck (or other game)
8 oz (240 g) cherries
3 tbs medium sherry
½ celeriac
salt and pepper

SERVES 6-8

METHOD

Prepare the game stock, starting off with 6 pts (3 litres) and reducing it down to 3 pts (1½ litres).

Remove all skin, fat and sinew from the cooked game and cut into thin strips. Wash the cherries, remove the stalks and take out the stones. Liquidize half and put the rest to one side. Add the cherry purée and sherry to the stock, mix well and simmer. Peel the celeriac, cut into strips and blanch; then refresh in cold water. Add the meat, cherries and celeriac to the soup, season and serve very hot.

Barbara Deane and Jonathon Hayes, The Perfumed Conservatory

Calories per serving: 130
Food value: Protein, fibre, vitamins and minerals. No added fat.

POTAGE AUX FLAGEOLETS

A rich, but highly nutritious soup, combining flageolet beans, chicken livers and leeks, originally conceived by the best-known brothers in modern French cooking, Jean and Pierre Troisgros.

INGREDIENTS

5 oz (150 g) dried
  flageolet beans
3 leeks
1 oz (30 g) butter*
8 oz (240 g) chicken livers
2½ pts (1¼ litres) chicken
  stock
salt and pepper
3 fl oz (90 ml) cream

GARNISH
croutons

SERVES 4

METHOD

Wash the beans well and cook them in plenty of unsalted water for about 10 minutes. Cover the pan, remove from the heat and allow to stand for 1 hour. Then re-boil and continue to simmer until the beans are soft. Strain off any excess water and put the beans aside.

Wash and trim the leeks and cut them into thin slices. Sauté lightly in melted butter, then add the chicken livers (well trimmed). Continue to cook until the livers feel firm. Pour in the chicken stock, season with salt and pepper to taste, and simmer for a further 15-20 minutes.

Add the cooked and strained beans to the soup. Blend well, cook for a few minutes, then pass through a liquidizer. Finally, sieve until very smooth. Return the soup to the pan, stir in the cream and bring to simmering point again.

Adjust the seasoning if necessary, then serve in individual bowls with croutons.

Colin White, White's Restaurant

Calories per serving: 300
Food value: Protein, fibre, vitamins and minerals. Moderate fat.
Note: You can reduce the calories of this soup by leaving out the cream as a main ingredient, and simply using a little as a final garnish swirled on top of each serving.

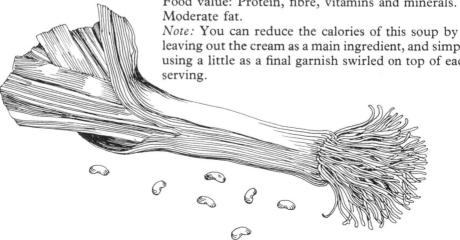

ALMOND SOUP

A full-bodied soup based on a 16th-century English recipe. It must be made from real chicken stock which provides a delicate flavour that a stock cube simply does not possess.

INGREDIENTS

3½ lb (1¾ kg) chicken
2 carrots
2 leeks
1 stick of celery
1 onion, stuck with cloves
handful of mixed herbs
4 oz (120 g) ground
 almonds
4 oz (120 g) white
 breadcrumbs
sea salt and white pepper
pinch of grated nutmeg
1 tsp sugar (optional)

GARNISH
heart-shaped croutons
chopped parsley, chervil
 or tarragon
swirl of cream (optional)

SERVES 6-8

METHOD

Put the fresh chicken in a large pan with the chopped carrots, sliced leeks, celery, whole onion and herbs. Cover with water, bring to the boil and simmer for about 1¼ hours, adjusting the level of liquid with extra water from time to time. Strain off the stock, allow to cool and skim off any excess fat.

Meanwhile, take all the meat off the chicken, discarding any gristle, fat and skin as well as the bones. Reduce the meat with the ground almonds and breadcrumbs in a food processor. (This can be done by hand using a pestle and mortar, but it is a time-consuming task.)

Add the resulting paste to about 3 pts (1½ litres) of chicken stock, season with sea salt, white pepper, a pinch of grated nutmeg and a teaspoon of sugar if you want to give the soup a little extra sweetness. Simmer for about 25 minutes.

Serve in hot bowls, and garnish with heart-shaped croutons sprinkled with some freshly chopped herbs. A swirl of cream makes the soup richer and more attractive to look at.

Victoria Stephenson, Bradfield House Restaurant

Calories per serving: 350
Food value: Protein, fibre, vitamins and minerals. Moderate fat.
Note: Both the almonds and the breadcrumbs provide a high percentage of calories, as well as body, texture and colour.

"Always buy the best. For first class results you need first class ingredients."
Victoria Stephenson

CHILLED BROAD BEAN SOUP
with summer savory

Summer savory is the ideal herb to complement broad beans and this recipe combines the two perfectly.

INGREDIENTS

2-3 lb (1-1½ kg) very
  young broad beans
1 pt (600 ml) chicken stock
1 tbs finely chopped
  summer savory
juice of ½ lemon
salt and pepper

GARNISH
crème fraiche
goat's yogurt
finely chopped summer
  savory
2-3 broad beans

SERVES 4

METHOD

Remove the beans from their pods, keeping two or three intact for garnishing. Bring the chicken stock to simmering point, then add the beans and a couple of empty pods for extra flavour. Cook gently for 5 minutes. Liquidize, then sieve. Add summer savory and lemon juice, then season to taste.

Chill the soup for at least 4 hours, then garnish with a swirl of *crème fraiche* mixed with an equal amount of goat's yogurt. Finally sprinkle on some fresh savory and chopped broad bean.

Melanie de Blank, Shipdham Place

Calories per serving: 125
Food value: Protein, fibre, vitamins and minerals. Low fat.

COLD RED PEPPER SOUP

An attractive cold soup made even more colourful with a garnish of finely chopped fresh tarragon.

INGREDIENTS

4 red peppers
1 onion
knob of butter*
2 pts (1 litre) chicken
  stock
4 sheets gelatine
salt and pepper

GARNISH
1 tsp chopped fresh
  tarragon

SERVES 4

METHOD

Split the peppers in half, remove the stalks and seeds and chop roughly. Peel and slice the onion. Melt the butter in a large pan, add the onions and sweat for 1-2 minutes. Stir in the red peppers and chicken stock, and cook slowly for 20-30 minutes.

When the soup has cooled, liquidize, and stir in the gelatine until dissolved. Pass through a fine sieve, season, pour into a bowl and allow to set.

To serve, stir with a fork to break up the jelly, spoon into bowls and sprinkle with fresh tarragon.

Richard Sandford, Milton Sandford Restaurant

Calories per serving: 50
Food value: Protein and vitamin C. No added fat.

WILD MUSHROOM SOUP
with garlic and thyme

Both garlic and thyme have an affinity with mushrooms, and this soup is a good way of combining them.

INGREDIENTS

2 tbs garlic oil
  (see Method)
3 oz (90 g) dried ceps
1 large horse mushroom (or
  large flat cultivated
  mushroom)
2 pts (1 litre) duck stock
½ tsp dried thyme
1 clove garlic
1 tsp fresh tarragon
salt and black pepper

GARNISH
1 tsp fresh thyme leaves
swirl of double cream

SERVES 4

METHOD

Make up a batch of garlic oil by steeping 3-4 cloves of garlic in 10 fl oz (300 ml) groundnut oil.

Warm some of the oil in a pan, add the roughly chopped mushrooms (the horse mushroom should be wiped clean with a damp cloth), plus the stock and dried thyme. Simmer for about 30 minutes. Blend in a crushed clove of garlic, then pass the soup through a medium-size sieve. Add the lightly chopped tarragon and season with salt and pepper.

Simmer again, then serve garnished with fresh thyme leaves and a swirl of lightly whipped cream.
James Kempston, Stone Green Hall

Calories per serving: 80
Food value: Protein, fibre and minerals. Low fat.

PUMPKIN AND SAFFRON SOUP

Wild duck stock is the best base for this soup, although any strong meat or game stock will produce good results.

INGREDIENTS

1 medium onion
1 oz (30 g) butter*
1 lb (½ kg) pumpkin
2 pts (1 litre) stock
¼ tsp saffron
salt and pepper

GARNISH
croutons

SERVES 4

METHOD

Peel and chop the onion and cook gently in butter for 10 minutes until soft and transparent. Prepare the pumpkin and chop the flesh into small cubes. Add to the onion. Stir well, then pour in the heated stock and the saffron (previously soaked in stock).

Cook gently over a low heat for about 15 minutes (or until the pumpkin is soft) and add salt and pepper to taste. When the soup is ready, liquidize and then sieve. Serve very hot with crisp croutons.
Patricia Hegarty, Hope End Country House Hotel

Calories per serving: 75
Food value: Protein and vitamins. Low fat.

WATERCRESS AND PEAR SOUP

A richly flavoured soup, made in the traditional manner, in which the delicate sweetness of pears and the pungency of watercress blend perfectly together.

INGREDIENTS

2 shallots
2 bunches watercress
3 oz (90 g) butter*
2 oz (60 g) flour
2 pts (1 litre) chicken
 stock
4 pears
10 fl oz (300 ml) double
 cream
salt and pepper

SERVES 4-6

METHOD

Peel and chop the shallots, wash and shred the watercress, and sauté in butter until soft. Stir in the flour and add the chicken stock, a little at a time, blending well. Peel two pears, chop into pieces and add to the soup. Bring to the boil, then simmer for no longer than 5 minutes. Put the soup through a liquidizer, return to the pan and stir in the double cream. Simmer gently and season with salt and pepper.

Meanwhile, peel the two remaining pears and chop into very small cubes. Sauté lightly in a little butter and use to garnish the soup.

Francis Coulson, Sharrow Bay Hotel

Calories per serving: 400
Food value: Protein, vitamins and minerals.
Moderate fat.

GREEN PEPPER AND FENNEL SOUP

The combination of green peppers and fennel produces a subtle flavoured soup which makes a particularly good choice for vegetarians.

INGREDIENTS

1 large green pepper
8 oz (240 g) bulb fennel
1 small onion
1 oz (30 g) butter*
1½ oz (45 g) ground
  almonds
½ tbs caster sugar
1 pt (600 ml) vegetable
  stock
sea salt and black pepper

GARNISH

4 sprigs of fennel leaves

SERVES 4

METHOD

Choose a large firm green pepper, wash it well, remove the stalk and pips and chop it into small pieces. Wash and trim the fennel, put aside a few feathery leaves for the garnish and chop the remainder. Peel and chop the onion. Heat the butter in a heavy saucepan over a low heat and sweat the vegetables slowly for about 5 minutes until the onion is transparent. Add the ground almonds, caster sugar and vegetable stock, and the sea salt and black pepper to taste. Bring to the boil, then lower the heat and simmer uncovered for 30 minutes.

Liquidize the soup, then sieve until it is very smooth. Taste and adjust the seasoning if necessary. Serve the soup in hot bowls, each one garnished with a sprig of fennel.

Lin Scrannage, The Market Restaurant

Calories per serving: 140
Food value: Fibre, vitamins and minerals. Low fat.
Note: This soup can be enriched by garnishing each bowl with a swirl of double cream just before serving, but this will increase the overall fat content (and calories) of the dish.

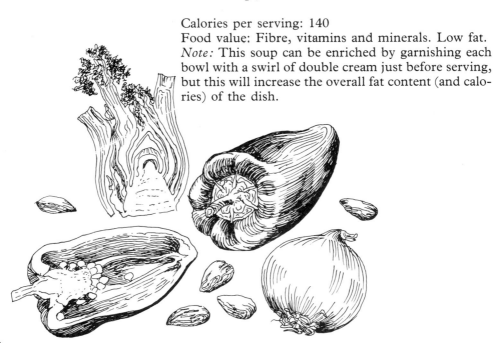

TOMATO AND APRICOT SOUP
with cumin

A delicate vegetable-based soup that is served garnished with creamy apricot purée. The apricots must be fresh, not dried.

INGREDIENTS

2 lb (1 kg) tomatoes
1 small onion
2 oz (60 g) butter*
1½ pts (900 ml) vegetable
  stock
6 fresh apricots
½ tsp ground cumin
juice of 1 orange
salt and pepper

GARNISH

2 fresh apricots
3 fl oz (90 ml) double
  cream
¼ tsp ground cumin
1 dsp finely chopped
  parsley

SERVES 6

METHOD

Roughly chop the ripe tomatoes and peel and slice the onion. Melt the butter in a saucepan and lightly cook the onion until soft but not brown. Add the tomatoes, together with the vegetable stock, apricots (halved and stoned) and ground cumin. Simmer for 20 minutes.

Remove from the heat and allow to cool slightly, then liquidize and pass through a sieve until really smooth. Return to a clean saucepan, add the orange juice and season with salt and pepper to taste. Allow to warm through.

To make the garnish, halve and stone two apricots, chop and pass through a sieve. Lightly whip the double cream and blend with the apricot purée. Season with ground cumin.

Heat the soup and ladle into heated bowls. Top each one with a spoonful of apricot cream and a sprinkling of freshly chopped parsley.

Carol Trevor-Roper, Knights Farm

Calories per serving: 150
Food value: Fibre and vitamins. Low fat.

TARATOR

*A refreshing yogurt-based soup that has its origins in
Bulgaria, but exists in various forms throughout Eastern
Europe and the Middle East.*

INGREDIENTS

1 cucumber
10 fl oz (300 ml) low-fat
  yogurt
5 fl oz (150 ml) single
  cream
1 small clove garlic
1 tbs tarragon vinegar
1 tbs finely chopped mint
salt and pepper

SERVES 4-6

METHOD

Coarsely grate the unpeeled cucumber into a large
bowl. Stir in the yogurt (home-made is best) and the
cream. Then add the crushed garlic, the tarragon
vinegar and the finely chopped mint leaves. Mix
together thoroughly and season to taste. Allow the
soup to infuse for at least 6 hours, then chill in the
refrigerator. Serve the soup in well-chilled bowls.
Tim Cumming, The Hole in the Wall

Calories per serving: 100
Food value: Vitamins and minerals. Low fat.
Note: It is possible to make this soup without the
addition of cream, which naturally reduces its richness
and calorie count. Finely chopped nuts (preferably
walnuts) can be added.

HORS D'OEUVRE AND APPETIZERS
Introduction

People who like to eat adventurously relish the prospect of hors d'oeuvre and appetizers, because they are often the most enterprising elements of a meal. Chefs are frequently at their most creative and imaginative when devising first courses, in keeping with the trend towards lighter food, smaller portions and greater artistry in the kitchen.

Hors d'oeuvre provide such a range of flavours and delights, that it isn't surprising that at least one restaurant, Ménage à Trois in London (see page 200) offers only starters and desserts on its highly individual menu.

TYPES OF HORS D'OEUVRE
There seems to be no limit to the kind of dishes that can be served as first courses. Prawn cocktail and egg mayonnaise may have their place, but it pays to be adventurous and take advantage of the new types of hors d'oeuvre being devised by today's chefs.

Cooks in the West are being influenced by the traditions of Oriental cuisine, and are beginning to refine the art of presentation, emphasizing colour, shape and texture. Ingredients are changing too; raw and marinated meat and fish are appearing on more menus, together with light imaginative salads and unexpected vegetable dishes that might also be served with main courses.

STARTERS AS MAIN COURSES
Many hors d'oeuvre can also be served as main courses. Sometimes the dish will be suitable as a snack without any adjustment of the recipe, but if you want to make a more substantial meal out of a starter, simply increase the quantities of the main ingredients in proportion. In some cases, for instance where the dish includes a sauce, it may not be necessary to increase all the ingredients, as the quantities given in the original recipe will be sufficient.

The virtue of many of the most interesting hors d'oeuvre is that they are dishes in miniature and their character derives from the fact that they are served in small quantities to whet the appetite and sharpen the palate. So, be selective when adapting recipes.

AVOCADO AND BACON IN PASTRY
with leek and walnut sauce

The contrast of avocado with smoked bacon and the unexpected flavour of the sauce make this an exciting starter.

INGREDIENTS

2 avocado pears
juice of 1 lemon
4 rashers rindless
  smoked bacon
4 very long, thin strips of
  puff pastry
1 beaten egg

SAUCE
1 small onion
2 leeks
4 fl oz (120 ml) white
  wine
10 fl oz (300 ml)
  vegetable stock
2 egg yolks
5 fl oz (150 ml) double
  cream
salt and pepper
2 oz (60 g) chopped
  walnuts

GARNISH
12 walnut halves
bay leaves (fresh)

SERVES 4

METHOD

First prepare the sauce. Peel and chop the onion, wash and thinly slice the leeks, then add to the wine and vegetable stock in a pan. Bring to the boil and simmer until reduced by half. Liquidize and pass through a sieve.

Whisk in the egg yolks and cream until thickened, over a very low heat, making sure that the sauce does not boil. Season to taste and finally stir in the chopped walnuts.

Cut the avocados in half, remove the stones, peel and rub with lemon juice to prevent discoloration. Using a spiral movement, wrap each half of avocado with a rasher of bacon, place on a greased baking tray and put in a hot oven for a few minutes to seal the bacon. Take out and allow to cool.

Brush the pastry strips with beaten egg and wrap, spiral fashion, around each avocado and bacon. Place on the greased baking tray once more, brush again with egg and bake in a hot oven at 400°F (200°C), Gas Mark 6 until golden brown.

Spread individual plates with a little of the sauce, set the pastry to one side and decorate the other side with three walnut halves and a few bay leaves (fresh if possible).
Anthony Rudge, Salisbury House

Calories per serving: 750
Food value: Protein, fibre, vitamins and minerals. Moderate fat.

AVOCADO AND WATERCRESS
with strawberry vinaigrette

An intriguing hors d'oeuvre that makes a delightful and colourful beginning to a summer meal.

INGREDIENTS

2 avocado pears
1 bunch watercress

DRESSING
1 tbs olive or sunflower oil
3 tbs white wine
2 tbs strawberry pulp

GARNISH
4 whole strawberries
4 lemon wedges
sprigs of fresh parsley

SERVES 4

METHOD

Peel the ripe avocados and slice in wedges lengthways. Arrange on individual plates with short clusters of cleaned watercress between each slice.

Prepare a light vinaigrette by blending together the oil and white wine. Purée some fresh strawberries in the liquidizer and add about 2 tbs of the pulp to the dressing. Shake well.

Pour a little of the dressing over each avocado and decorate each plate with a whole strawberry, a wedge of lemon and a sprig of fresh parsley.

Nicholas Ryan, Crinan Hotel

Calories per serving: 300
Food value: Fibre, vitamins and minerals. Low fat.

AVOCADO AND PRAWN SOUFFLÉ

A rich, easy-to-make soufflé which should be served very hot.

INGREDIENTS

2 large avocado pears
1 clove garlic
1 tsp wine vinegar
1½ oz (45 g) butter*
4 oz (120 g) peeled
 prawns
2 tbs basic white sauce
2 eggs, separated
2 oz (60 g) grated cheese
salt and black pepper

SERVES 4

METHOD

Split the avocados in half, remove the stones and rub the cavities with crushed garlic. Add the vinegar, then pour it away and put a knob of butter in each one. Fill the avocados with peeled prawns.

Melt the rest of the butter in a pan and whisk in the white sauce (made by the roux method). Add the egg yolks and half the cheese, then season to taste. Cook until the sauce is hot, but not boiling.

Whisk the egg whites until stiff, then fold into the mixture. Pour over the avocados, sprinkle with the remaining cheese and bake at 425°F (220°C), Gas Mark 7 for 10 minutes until golden brown.

Martin Hoefkens, Tarn End Hotel

Calories per serving: 460
Food value: Protein, vitamins and minerals.
Moderate fat.

29

WARM COCKTAIL OF VEGETABLES
with a cold aubergine mousse

This is a very attractive dish, in which the skin of the aubergines is cut into strips and used to decorate the mousse.

INGREDIENTS

6 medium sized aubergines
1 shallot
1 clove garlic
9 sheets gelatine
16 fl oz (480 ml) double
  cream
salt and pepper
12 fl oz (360 ml) cold
  jellied meat or game stock
4 egg whites
salt and paprika
6 fl oz (180 ml) walnut oil
  dressing

GARNISH
vegetables, trimmed or
  sliced and blanched:
  choose from
  cauliflower, broccoli,
  asparagus, tomatoes,
  mange-tout, French
  beans, carrots, cucumber,
  courgettes, artichokes

SERVES 4

METHOD

Peel the aubergines and keep the skin. Roughly dice the flesh, and cook it in a very little water with the chopped shallot and garlic for about 20 minutes or until soft enough to go into the food processor or liquidizer. Purée until smooth.

Meanwhile soften seven sheets of gelatine in a third of the cream and add them to the warm purée. Strain through a fine sieve. Season and allow to cool. Soften the remaining gelatine in cold water.

Simmer the aubergine peel in jellied stock with the two sheets of gelatine for about 8–10 minutes. Reserve the stock, keeping it at room temperature so it cools but does not set. Line four moulds with the aubergine peel and chill.

Whip the remaining cream to soft peaks. In a separate bowl whip the egg whites to a similar consistency. Fold first the whipped cream and then the whipped egg whites into the purée. Spoon the mixture into moulds and allow to set in the refrigerator for 2 hours.

After 2 hours dip the moulds in hot water for 10 seconds and turn them out on to a rack. Coat the cold mousses with the stock.

Warm the vegetables in the dressing, tossing them gently to ensure that they are glazed all over. Season. Place a mousse in the centre of each of the four plates and arrange the vegetables around them. Serve immediately.

Antony Worrall-Thompson, Ménage à Trois

Calories per serving: 750
Food value: Fibre, vitamins and minerals.
Moderate fat.
Note: Details of the walnut oil dressing can be found on page 47.

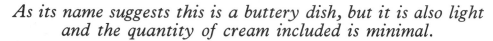

ARTICHOKES AND ASPARAGUS
in cider butter sauce

As its name suggests this is a buttery dish, but it is also light and the quantity of cream included is minimal.

INGREDIENTS

6 small artichoke hearts
1lb (½ kg) asparagus
2 oz (60 g) butter*
1 oz (30 g) shallots
2 oz (60 g) streaky bacon
1 fl oz (30 ml) white wine
1 fl oz (30 ml) cider
5 fl oz (150 ml) chicken
 stock
2 small tomatoes
2 sprigs of fresh basil
1 tbs double cream

GARNISH
sprigs of fresh chervil

SERVES 4

METHOD

Cook the artichokes in boiling water for about 20 minutes, allow to cool and remove the hearts. Also cook the asparagus in an upright bunch until just soft. Drain and allow to cool.

Melt half the butter in a pan and sweat the finely chopped shallots and the streaky bacon (cut into strips). Quarter the artichoke hearts and add to the pan, with the white wine. Pour in the cider, reduce by half, then add the chicken stock. Cook for a further 5 minutes, then remove the artichokes and reduce the liquor by half again.

Finally return the artichokes to the pan, together with the asparagus (cut into short lengths), the blanched and diced tomato flesh and the roughly chopped basil. Bring to the boil, whisk in the remaining butter and cream.

Serve into soup plates, garnish with sprigs of chervil and eat with warm brioche bread to mop up the sauce.
Michael Croft, The Royal Crescent Hotel

Calories per serving: 210
Food value: Vitamins and minerals. Moderate fat.

GLOBE ARTICHOKES
stuffed with mussels and prawns

The combination of artichokes with piquant marinated shellfish produces a delicious and well-balanced starter.

INGREDIENTS

4 globe artichokes
2 tbs white wine vinegar
20 mussels
1 clove garlic
3 tbs olive or sunflower oil
juice of ½ lemon
4 oz (120 g) peeled
  prawns (or shrimps)
salt and pepper

SERVES 4

METHOD

Trim the artichokes, cut off the stalks close to the base of the leaves and put into a large pan of salted water to which 1 tbs of wine vinegar has been added. Bring to the boil, then simmer for about 30 minutes until the artichokes are tender. (Test an outer leaf from time to time.) Drain upside down in a colander and allow to cool.

Clean the mussels, remove their beards and steam briskly in a covered pan with the chopped garlic until the shells open. (Discard any that stay shut.)

Make up a French dressing with 1 tbs wine vinegar, the oil and lemon juice. Remove the mussels from their shells and add to the dressing, along with the peeled prawns or shrimps. Allow to marinate for a short while.

When the artichokes are cold, pull out a few of the centre leaves from each one and scrape off the hairy "choke" using a pointed teaspoon. Fill the cavity with some of the shellfish, pour over a little of the dressing and serve.

Nicolas Ryan, Crinan Hotel

Calories per serving: 180
Food value: Protein, vitamins and minerals. Low fat.

WARM OYSTERS
with red wine vinegar and shallots

INGREDIENTS

1 small carrot
1 small leek
2 oz (60 g) unsalted
  butter*
24 oysters
2 medium mauve shallots
2 fl oz (60 ml) red wine
  vinegar

GARNISH
rock salt
seaweed
leaves of chervil

SERVES 4

METHOD

Cut the carrot and the white part of the leek into
julienne and sweat in butter. Open the oysters and
reserve their juices.

Finely chop the shallots, put into a pan with the
vinegar and reduce. When nearly dry add the oyster
juices and the vegetables.

Warm the oysters on a tray for 2–3 minutes in the
oven, place on a bed of rock salt and arrange seaweed
around the shells. Coat each oyster with the sauce and
decorate with chervil.
Robert Mabey, Hintlesham Hall

Calories per serving: 150
Food value: Protein, vitamins and minerals. Low fat.

SEAFOOD CUP

INGREDIENTS

12 scallops
2 oz (60 g) clarified butter*
1 piece root ginger
1 clove garlic
salt and white pepper
10 fl oz (300 ml) fish stock
4 tbs cream
white wine (or vermouth)
chopped chives and dill
2 pinches of saffron
8 spears asparagus
4 pastry cases
2 red peppers
8 oz (240 g) mange-tout

GARNISH
Chinese mushrooms
flowers and lemon balm
* leaves*

SERVES 4

METHOD

Bake the scallops gently in clarified butter with the ginger, garlic, salt and pepper. Allow to cool. Add a quarter of the stock and half the cream, plus a dash of wine to the liquor in the pan. Blend and add chives, dill and a pinch of saffron.

Steam the asparagus, keep the tips and discard the stalks. Make the pastry cases (see recipe opposite).

De-seed the peppers and poach in the rest of the stock for 20 minutes. Liquidize, sieve and add the rest of the cream and saffron. Lightly steam the mange-tout, warm the scallops in herb sauce and fill the pastry cases with the scallops on a bed of mange-tout. Place on top of the pepper purée and garnish with asparagus, lightly cooked Chinese mushrooms, edible flowers and lemon balm leaves.
Barbara Deane and Jonathon Hayes, The Perfumed Conservatory

Calories per serving: 450 (including pastry case)
Food value: Protein, vitamins and minerals. Low fat.

HOT SHRIMPS EN CROUSTADE

This is a very simple but impressive first course consisting of shrimps with a cream and parsley sauce served in a shell of shortcrust pastry.

INGREDIENTS

8 oz (240 g) shortcrust pastry
1 oz (30 g) shallots
1 oz (30 g) fresh parsley
2 oz (60 g) butter*
12 oz (360 g) shrimps
salt and pepper
4 fl oz (120 ml) fish stock
4 fl oz (120 ml) white wine
4 fl oz (120 ml) fish demi-glaze
8 fl oz (240 ml) double cream
1 fl oz (30 ml) cognac

GARNISH
chopped parsley

SERVES 4

METHOD

Roll out the pastry very thin, divide into four and use to line lightly greased individual pie dishes. Make the left-over pastry into "handles" for the croustades. Bake blind in the oven at 400°F (200°C), Gas Mark 6, until brown and crisp.

Sauté the chopped shallots and parsley in butter with 1 oz (30 g) peeled shrimps. Season and cook until golden. Pour in the stock and wine and reduce by two-thirds. Add the fish demi-glaze, cream and cognac, and blend well.

Stir in the rest of the shrimps, simmer for a few minutes, then pour into the pastry shells. Arrange a pastry "handle" on each croustade, sprinkle with chopped parsley and serve.

Baba Hine, Corse Lawn House Hotel

Calories per serving: 790
Food value: Protein, vitamins and minerals. Moderate fat.

PASTRY CASE FOR SEAFOOD CUP

INGREDIENTS

2 cups plain flour
1 tsp salt
3 eggs
cup of cornflour for dusting
oil for deep frying

METHOD

Sieve the flour and salt on to a large working surface. Mix with your fingers, forming a hollow, into which you break the eggs. Knead to form a stiff, dry dough (add water if necessary). Continue to knead thoroughly.

Place the pastry on a clean corn-dusted surface and roll out to a very thin, almost transparent sheet. Cut into two 10 in (25 cm) squares and dust liberally with sifted cornflour.

To cook, you need slightly smoking deep oil and two ladles, one large and one medium-size. Cut each pastry square in half, and place inside the large ladle, with the smaller ladle on top. Dip in the oil for 1½ minutes, then remove and drain upside down.

SEAFOOD WITH FRESH PASTA

It is important to use fresh pasta for this dish and to cook the mussels, mixed seafood and pasta simultaneously in three pans for the best results.

INGREDIENTS

2 pts (1 litre) mussels (or clams)
3 cloves garlic
15 fl oz (450 ml) white wine
salt and pepper
12 oz (360 g) fresh tagliatelle
12 oz (360 g) firm-fleshed seafood, e.g.
   scallops, lobster, monkfish
1 oz (30 g) butter*
12 prawns in their shells
5 fl oz (150 ml) cream

SERVES 6

METHOD

Scrub the mussels, remove their beards and discard any that are damaged or open. Put into a large pan with the chopped garlic, white wine and seasoning. Cover.

Heat a large pan of salted water (with a drop of oil in it) for the pasta. Slice the mixed seafood and melt the butter in a third pan.

Begin to cook the mussels; add the pasta to the salted water when boiling; and gently sauté the mixed seafood at the same time. As the mussels open remove them, one by one, and keep warm. Strain off the pasta when just cooked, but still *al dente*, and moisten with a knob of butter. Mix the mussels and sautéed seafood together.

To serve, arrange the pasta at the bottom of individual dishes, top with the seafood and two prawns in their shells, and keep warm.

Add the mussel liquor to the juices from the sautéed seafood, boil hard and reduce slightly. Adjust the seasoning if necessary and finally stir in the cream. Increase the heat and pour the hot sauce over the seafood and pasta.

Judy Knock, The Gentle Gardener

Calories per serving: 350
Food value: Protein, fibre, vitamins and minerals. Low fat.
Note: Other kinds of pasta can be used instead of tagliatelle and cooked accordingly.

RAMEKIN OF PRAWNS
in aspic with cucumber

A fine example of the delicacy and lightness of hors d'oeuvre and the way in which they can be adapted to provide richness.

INGREDIENTS

1 cucumber
1 tbs caster sugar
2 tbs white wine vinegar
4 sheets gelatine
5 fl oz (150 ml) hot water
5 fl oz (150 ml) dry white
  wine (or vermouth)
8 oz (240 g) peeled
  prawns
1 tsp chopped parsley

GARNISH
4 sprigs of fennel or dill

SERVES 4

METHOD

Slice the cucumber thinly and soak in the mixture of caster sugar and wine vinegar for about 30 minutes. When ready, arrange a few slices of cucumber at the bottom of each ramekin dish to give a flower-like effect when turned out.

Dissolve the gelatine in the mixture of hot water and wine and allow to cool. Meanwhile dust the peeled prawns with finely chopped fresh parsley, mix together and pack into the ramekin dishes. Top up with the aspic jelly and allow to set in the refrigerator.

Arrange some more slices of cucumber in a circular pattern around each plate, turn out the ramekin and place in the centre. Finally garnish with a sprig of fresh fennel or dill.

Anthony Rudge, Salisbury House

Calories per serving: 125
Food value: Protein, vitamins and minerals. No added fat.
Note: As it stands, this is a low-calorie dish with a rating of 1. A different effect, with a higher rating, can be achieved by setting the cucumber and prawn ramekins on a little horseradish cream (made by adding some grated horseradish root to 5 fl oz (150 ml) whipped cream).

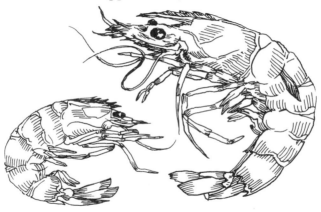

SOLE MOUSSELINE WITH MUSSELS
in light curry sauce

*In this dish there is a delicate balance between the smooth,
subtle flavour of the fish and the spiciness of the sauce.*

INGREDIENTS

2 pts (1 litre) mussels
*5 fl oz (150 ml) white
wine*

MOUSSELINE
9 oz (270 g) sole
1 egg
1 egg white
salt and pepper
pinch of grated nutmeg
*15 fl oz (450 ml) double
cream*

SAUCE
*5 fl oz (150 ml) dry white
wine*
1 shallot
10 fl oz (300 ml) cream
salt and pepper
1 tbs ground coriander
1 tsp turmeric
½ tsp ground cumin
¼ tsp cayenne pepper
¼ tsp ground fenugreek
lemon juice (optional)

GARNISH
watercress

SERVES 6

METHOD

Fillet the fish and remove any skin and bones. Purée
the flesh in a liquidizer until very smooth, then
transfer to a stainless steel bowl. Set this over a pan of
ice or iced water and gradually beat in the egg and egg
white. Add the salt and other seasonings and continue
to beat (using a wooden spoon). Finally incorporate
the cream a little at a time, again beating well. Keep the
mousseline cool until needed.

Clean the mussels, remove their beards and discard
any that are open or damaged. Put in a pan with the
white wine, cover and cook until they are just open.
Remove the mussels from their shells and leave in the
cooking liquor.

To make the sauce, reduce the wine with the finely
chopped shallot. Add the cream and reduce again until
the mixture has a good consistency. Pour in a little of
the strained mussel liquor and simmer for a few
seconds. Season, then add the curry spices (pounded
together) and a little lemon juice if you wish. Blend
and simmer, then strain through a fine sieve.

Butter six individual moulds and put a piece of
buttered paper at the bottom of each one. Fill with
mousseline, cover with parchment and chill until
ready to cook. Bake in a *bain-marie* in a moderate oven
at 350°F (180°C), Gas Mark 4 for about 20 minutes
until just set.

Unmould the mousselines on to shallow dishes,
pour some of the sauce around and garnish with
mussels (gently warmed in their liquor) and some
watercress.
Ian Weeks, Weeks Restaurant

Calories per serving: 500
Food value: Protein, vitamins and minerals.
Moderate fat.

MEDALLIONS OF MONKFISH
with orange and avocado

Serve the marinated monkfish with a fresh tomato sauce, to which a little orange juice and olive oil have been added.

INGREDIENTS

2 lb (1 kg) monkfish
salt and pepper
2 tbs olive oil

MARINADE
6 fl oz (180 ml) orange juice
6 fl oz (180 ml) lemon juice
6 fl oz (180 ml) olive oil
1 medium onion, diced
2 fl oz (60 ml) vermouth
Angostura bitters

GARNISH
1 large avocado
2 oranges

SERVES 4–6

METHOD

Remove all skin and bones from the fish and cut into small medallions. Season and leave for 30 minutes. Then quickly seal the fish in hot olive oil.

Prepare the marinade by heating the citrus juices with the oil and diced onion. Simmer for a few minutes then add the vermouth and a few drops of bitters. Pour over the fish and chill for several hours. (This dish will keep for up to 2 days.)

Drain the medallions, arrange on fresh tomato sauce and garnish with diced avocado and orange segments.
Ian Weeks, Weeks Restaurant

Calories per serving: 220
Food value: Protein, vitamins and minerals. Low fat.

THAI PRAWNS

Try substituting courgettes for cucumber and honey for sugar.

INGREDIENTS

6 tbs prepared cucumber
2 dsp white wine vinegar
2 dsp lemon juice
1–2 dsp light soya sauce
  (Japanese)
1–1½ dsp sugar
2 cloves garlic
1 hot jalapeno pepper
2 good sprigs of apple mint
4 tbs large Norwegian
  prawns (shelled)

SERVES 1

METHOD

Peel, de-seed and dice the cucumber into small cubes. Mix together the vinegar, lemon juice and soya sauce, and stir in the sugar until dissolved. Add the finely chopped garlic and sliced chilli pepper.

Sort the mint, putting aside some good leaves and flowering tops. Add the old stems and leaves to the sauce and leave for 30 minutes. Strain, add the cucumber and leave for 10 minutes. Stir in the prawns and garnish with mint leaves and a flowering top.
James Kempston, Stone Green Hall

Calories per serving: 150
Food value: Protein, vitamins and minerals. No fat.

CEVICHE OF MONKFISH
with coriander

Ceviche is a method of marinating or pickling raw fish in various kinds of citrus juices.

INGREDIENTS

juice of 1 lemon
juice of 2 limes
1½ oz (45 g) caster sugar
1 heaped tsp crushed
  coriander seeds
salt
12 oz (360 g) skinned
  monkfish

GARNISH
chopped chives
coriander leaves

SERVES 4

METHOD

Mix together the lemon and lime juice with the caster sugar, coriander seeds and salt to taste. Blend well, and allow to stand for a few minutes, making sure that the sugar has dissolved.

Cut the monkfish into very thin slices, flattening with a wide-bladed knife if necessary. Lay the fish carefully in a wide shallow dish and pour over the marinade. Leave for 2–6 hours in a cool place.

Serve on individual plates. Sprinkle the fish with finely chopped chives and decorate with a few fresh coriander leaves.
Stephen Bull, Lichfield's

Calories per serving: 100
Food value: Protein, vitamins and minerals. No fat.

SALMON TARTARE

This dish provides a marvellous introduction to the pleasures of eating raw fish. The salmon must, of course, be very fresh.

INGREDIENTS

14 oz (420 g) fresh
  salmon
salt and freshly ground
  pepper
lemon juice
pinch of cayenne pepper
1 small onion, chopped
  finely
1 oz (30 g) chives,
  chopped finely
lettuce or young spinach
  leaves
1 tbs Beluga caviar or
  salmon roe (optional)

SERVES 4

METHOD

Remove the bones and skin from the salmon. Season the salmon with salt, pepper, a little lemon juice and a pinch of cayenne pepper to taste, and then chop very finely. Mix the fish carefully with the finely chopped onion; taste and season again if necessary. Form small balls of the mixture and roll them in the chives.

If using the caviar or roe, arrange it in the middle of a serving plate before covering the plate with the lettuce or spinach leaves. Arrange the salmon balls on the leaves. Serve with slices of toasted French bread.
Anton Mosimann, The Dorchester

Calories per serving: 180
Food value: Protein, vitamins and minerals. No added fat.

PARCELS OF SMOKED SALMON
with yogurt cream sauce

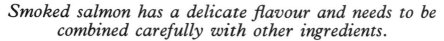

Smoked salmon has a delicate flavour and needs to be combined carefully with other ingredients.

INGREDIENTS

8 slices of smoked salmon

MOUSSE
3 oz (90 g) smoked salmon
  trimmings
1 oz (30 g) smoked trout
  fillet
5 fl oz (150 ml) double
  cream

SAUCE
5 fl oz (150 ml) double
  cream
5 fl oz (150 ml) low-fat
  yogurt
juice of 1 lemon
sugar to taste
salt and pepper

GARNISH
sprigs of fresh dill
chopped tomato flesh

SERVES 4

METHOD

First prepare the mousse. Liquidize the smoked salmon trimmings and the smoked trout fillet and force through a very fine sieve. Place the purée in a basin and set over crushed ice. Gradually beat in the double cream with a wooden spoon until the mixture has the consistency of a light mousse.

Make the sauce by carefully mixing together the cream, yogurt and lemon juice. Add a little sugar if you want some extra sweetness, and season with salt and pepper.

Place a spoonful of mousse in the centre of each slice of smoked salmon and fold over to form a neat parcel. Pour some of the sauce on to four individual plates and arrange two parcels on each. Garnish with sprigs of fresh dill and a little chopped tomato flesh.

Allan Holland, Mallory Court

Calories per serving: 400
Food value: Protein, vitamins and minerals.
Moderate fat.
Note: Although this dish is perfectly constructed as it stands, you can reduce its fat, calories and balance rating by halving the quantity of cream in the mousse and using a mixture of yogurt and sour cream for the sauce. The results are different, but just as enjoyable.

SWEETBREADS WITH CHICORY
and Malaga sauce

A dish which successfully combines the smooth texture and richness of sweetbreads with the crispness and bitter flavour of chicory.

INGREDIENTS

1 lb (½ kg) sweetbreads
½ oz (15 g) butter*
½ onion
1 clove garlic
5 fl oz (150 ml) pork stock
2 fl oz (60 ml) Malaga
salt and pepper
1 large (or 2 small)
  chicory heads

SERVES 4

METHOD

Prepare the sweetbreads by soaking them in milk or water; then blanch and pick off any membrane and fat. Strain and allow to cool.

Melt a knob of butter in a pan and lightly sauté the chopped onion and garlic until soft and transparent. Thinly slice the sweetbreads and add to the pan. Cook for a couple of minutes, then add the pork stock and Malaga. Deglaze the pan and continue to poach the sweetbreads in this liquid for a few minutes until they are firm but still slightly soft to the touch. Adjust the seasoning and allow the liquid to reduce until you have a concentrated, well amalgamated sauce.

Slice the raw chicory into thin strips and toss briefly in a separate pan with a little butter and pepper. To serve, pour the sweetbreads and sauce on to the plate and arrange some strips of chicory on top.

John Kenward, Kenwards Restaurant

Calories per serving: 175
Food value: Protein, vitamins and minerals. Low fat.
Note: This recipe shows how easily a sauce can be made using simply reduced stock, pan juices and a dash of alcohol.

"Aim for flavours, textures and colours that provide contrasts of bitterness and richness, crunchy brittleness and smoothness, bright colour with subdued."
John Kenward

FILLETS OF DUCKLING AND PIGEON
in orange jelly

The combination of duckling and pigeon produces the best results in this recipe, although any cooked meat can be used.

INGREDIENTS

5 fl oz (150 ml) dry white
wine
10 fl oz (300 ml) chicken
stock
1 tbs Madeira
½ oz (15 g) gelatine
3 tbs water
8 oz (240 g) cooked duck
and pigeon
1 tsp chopped chives
black pepper
3 oranges

GARNISH
chopped lettuce

SERVES 6

METHOD

Boil the wine, stock and Madeira in a large pan. Soak the gelatine in water and when soft, mix with the stock and wine, stirring until dissolved.

While the liquid is cooling, prepare the meat. Make sure that all skin and fat is removed, then slice the lean meat into a bowl. Toss in a sprinkling of chives and season with a little pepper. Peel the oranges, remove the pith and pips, cut into segments and mix well with the meat.

Lightly grease six ramekin dishes and fill each one with a portion of the meat and orange mixture. Pour over the cool jelly so that the meat is covered and allow to set in the refrigerator. Serve on small plates, garnished with chopped lettuce.
Ann Long, The Count House Restaurant

Calories per serving: 130
Food value: Protein, vitamins and minerals. No added fat.

PIGEON BREAST SALAD

You can vary the ingredients in this unusual cold starter.

INGREDIENTS

8 quail's eggs
4 oz (120 g) extra fine
French beans
4 pigeon breasts, cooked
1 iceberg lettuce
1 small radicchio
2 tbs mayonnaise
1 tsp Dijon mustard
4 tomato roses

SERVES 4

METHOD

Hard-boil the quail's eggs, shell and slice. Blanch the beans and refresh under cold water; cut into even lengths. Slice the pigeon breasts and shred the lettuce.

Arrange radicchio leaves around the plate and put a spoonful of lettuce in the centre, topped with a spoonful of mustard mayonnaise. Arrange the pigeon breast and beans in little heaps around it, and decorate with quail's eggs and a tomato rose.
Robert Jones, Ston Easton Park

Calories per serving: 175
Food value: Protein, fibre, vitamins and minerals. Low fat.

RAW FILLET OF BEEF
Japanese-style

A variation on the theme of sashimi, the Japanese method of serving raw fish. In fact the meat is not completely raw.

INGREDIENTS

6–8 oz (180–240 g) fillet
  of beef
2 tbs sunflower oil

MARINADE
2 dsp sesame oil
2 dsp soya sauce
2 dsp saké or dry sherry
1 dsp sunflower oil
2 dsp water

GARNISH
3 oz (90 g) carrot
2 oz (60 g) spring onion
2 oz (60 g) celery
¾–1 oz (20–30 g) root
  ginger
1 oz (30 g) radish
wasabe (green
  horseradish) or any
  strong horseradish

SERVES 4

METHOD

Choose a piece of beef 2–5 days old, preferably from the tail end of the fillet. Heat a little sunflower oil in a hot pan and seal the meat quickly on all sides. Then plunge into iced water for about 30 seconds to prevent any further cooking. Remove, dry on absorbent paper and put in the refrigerator to chill.

Mix together all the ingredients for the marinade in a large bowl. Check the saltiness of the mixture and add a little water if necessary (particularly if you are using Chinese soya sauce). Peel and trim the carrot, spring onion and celery and, with the root ginger, cut into very fine matchsticks. Toss in the marinade and leave in the refrigerator for 1 hour, stirring occasionally.

To serve, slice the meat as thinly as possible and lay in an overlapping circle around the outside of the plate. Heap the vegetables in the centre, sprinkle 1 dsp of marinade over the meat and decorate with a little finely chopped radish. Provide some *wasabe* and marinade for dipping.
Christopher Bradley, Mr Underhill's Restaurant

Calories per serving: 180
Food value: Protein, fibre, vitamins and minerals. Low fat.
Note: Japanese ingredients are best for the marinade, although Chinese versions produce perfectly adequate results.

PAPER-THIN RAW BEEF
with rock salt and Colchester oysters

The attraction of this dish, according to Antony Worrall-Thompson, is the texture of the raw ingredients.

INGREDIENTS

12 oz (360 g) Scotch beef
  fillet, divided into four
  equal pieces and flattened
rock salt
12 Colchester oysters,
  shelled
strained oyster juices
6 fl oz (180 ml) dill
  mayonnaise (see below)

MAYONNAISE

1 egg
juice of 2 lemons
1 tsp sugar
1 tsp Dijon mustard
2 tbs dill weed, chopped
salt and pepper
5 fl oz (150 ml) olive oil

GARNISH

peel of 2 lemons, julienned
  and blanched
sprigs of dill weed

SERVES 4

METHOD

To make the mayonnaise, blend all the ingredients except the oil in a liquidizer. Keep the machine running and add the oil gradually until the desired consistency is reached. The more oil is used, the thicker the mayonnaise will be.

Spread the paper-thin pieces of beef on four cold plates. Sprinkle with salt crystals. Place three oysters on each piece of beef, and sprinkle with a little strained oyster juice. Decorate the oysters with lemon peel and dill sprigs. Serve the dill mayonnaise separately.

Antony Worrall-Thompson, Ménage à Trois

Calories per serving: 185 + 300 for the mayonnaise.
Food value: Protein, vitamins and minerals.
Moderate fat.
Note: In the absence of Scotch beef and Colchester oysters, choose the best alternatives available. The mayonnaise contributes a large number of calories and is the main source of fat in this dish.

DUCK LIVER AND VEGETABLES
with cider vinegar sauce

A sophisticated starter that highlights the flavours of autumn, including wild mushrooms, chard and apples.

INGREDIENTS

4 baby onions
4 baby carrots
a few yellow French beans
1 apple
1 duck liver
2 fl oz (60 ml) cider
  vinegar
5 fl oz (150 ml) chicken
  stock
2 fl oz (60 ml) duck glaze
salt and pepper
handful of chard
knob of butter*
a few girolles
1 shallot
sprigs of fresh coriander

SERVES 1

METHOD

Peel and trim the onions, carrots and yellow beans and blanch in boiling water. Immediately cool on ice and put to one side. Peel and core the apple and chop into small oblong shapes.

Pan-fry the duck liver quickly until sealed but still pink inside and keep warm. Mix the pan juices with the cider vinegar, chicken stock and duck glaze. Taste and adjust the seasoning. Pass the mixture through a sieve and keep warm.

Cook the chard leaves in a large saucepan with a knob of butter. Pan-fry the girolles with the chopped shallot and season to taste. Roast the apple. Glaze the vegetables and add the freshly chopped coriander.

To serve, lay the chard leaves over the plate and arrange the duck liver, vegetables, wild mushrooms and apple on top to give a colourful visual effect. Spoon the sauce around the liver.

René Gaté, Les Semailles

Calories per serving: 230
Food value: Protein, fibre, vitamins and minerals. Low fat.
Note: René Gaté recommends using "old" or well-matured vinegar for this dish because ordinary vinegar is too sharp and lacks flavour.

CHICKEN AND LOBSTER SALAD
with walnut oil dressing

The combination of delicate smoked chicken and luxurious lobster makes this a very sophisticated salad.

INGREDIENTS

½ cucumber, peeled, seeded
  and cut into sticks
julienned cucumber peel
4 spring onions, cut into
  sticks
1 chicory head, julienned
3 tomatoes, peeled, seeded
  and julienned
julienne of blanched lemon
  rind
1 smoked chicken breast,
  skinned, boned and
  julienned
1 lb (½ kg) lobster tail,
  cooked, shelled and diced
6 fl oz (150 ml) walnut oil
  dressing (see below)
salt and white pepper

DRESSING

4 fl oz (100 ml) walnut oil
4 fl oz (100 ml) peanut oil
½ tsp Dijon mustard
1 shallot, finely chopped
1 clove garlic, chopped
juice of 1 lemon
3 tbs champagne vinegar
1 bay leaf
1 sprig of tarragon
salt and black pepper
½ tsp sugar

GARNISH

1 pear, peeled and poached
corn salad leaves
2 tomatoes, peeled, seeded
  and diced

SERVES 4

METHOD

To make the dressing, blend all the ingredients with a hand whisk. Leave to settle for up to 24 hours. Pass through a fine sieve. Whisk before using.

Sprinkle salt over the cucumber sticks. After 30 minutes, drain and rinse the cucumber to remove excess salt. Dry on absorbent paper.

Toss the main ingredients in the walnut oil dressing. Season, and divide between four small bowls.

Quarter and core the cooked pear. Slice and arrange around the plate with the corn salad leaves (dipped in dressing) and the diced tomato.

Antony Worrall-Thompson, Ménage à Trois

Calories per serving: 350
Food value: Protein, vitamins and minerals. Low fat.
Note: Antony Worrall-Thompson suggests using a julienne of smoked ham if smoked chicken is unobtainable. He also recommends experimenting with different dressings.

Like many salads, this one is essentially a combination of low-calorie, low-fat ingredients with a high-calorie, high-fat dressing. By using the dressing sparingly, you can easily cut down the overall number of calories in the dish.

RIGATONI AMATRICIANA

The short, thick, ribbed macaroni known as rigatoni makes an excellent base for this popular pasta dish which contains ham, tomatoes and oregano.

INGREDIENTS

8 oz (240 g) rigatoni

SAUCE
1 tbs vegetable oil
1 small onion
2 cloves garlic
2 oz (60 g) Parma ham
1 tsp dried oregano
8 oz (240 g) tomatoes,
 fresh or tinned
salt and pepper

GARNISH
freshly chopped parsley

SERVES 4

METHOD

Put the rigatoni into a pan containing plenty of boiling slightly salted water and cook briskly.

Put a little oil in a frying pan and lightly sauté the thinly sliced onion and garlic until soft and transparent. Add the strips of ham, dried oregano, chopped tomatoes and a little seasoning. Cook slowly, stirring well to prevent burning, until the sauce is amalgamated and thick.

When the rigatoni is cooked, but still firm and slightly resistant, strain well and immediately put into a hot buttered dish. Top with the sauce and garnish with freshly chopped parsley. Eat at once.

Vincenzo Iannone, La Fiorentina

Calories per serving: 290
Food value: Protein, fibre, vitamins and minerals. Low fat.
Note: The quantities given above will be adequate if you want to serve this dish as a starter or a snack. For a main course, allow 3–4 oz (90–120 g) rigatoni per person and increase the quantity of sauce to match.

PÂTÉS AND TERRINES
Introduction

Despite the enormous variety of pâtés and terrines, they are all based on a very simple principle – that of pounding or mincing assorted ingredients and baking the mixture in a mould. The idea couldn't be more straightforward, yet the different combinations, textures and flavours that can be achieved are extraordinary.

Traditionally a pâté is baked in pastry (*pâte*), while a terrine is cooked in a special mould which gives the dish its name. But these distinctions have become blurred and the two terms are used quite freely nowadays.

INGREDIENTS
The choice of ingredients for pâtés and terrines is almost limitless. The most familiar are liver of all types and coarsely minced pork, but any kind of meat, poultry and game can be used to good effect. In fact, pâtés can be flavoured with anything from herbs and nuts to more unusual ingredients, such as water chestnuts, which provide a contrast to the meat in both flavour and texture. Fish is used increasingly for pâtés by contemporary chefs, who have also created recipes for exquisite vegetable terrines. While we tend to think of these dishes as starters, they can also be used for desserts (see the recipe for Fruit Terrine with a Coulis of Mango on page 176).

It's a mistake to think that all pâtés and terrines are automatically fatty and high in calories. Certainly a number do have a percentage of fat (mainly from meat) and some require cream and butter, but these can be drastically reduced without affecting the overall quality of the pâté. While the coarse, fatty pâtés, which are a mainstay of traditional French cooking, have their place, the trend is towards lighter, more subtle dishes that highlight the flavour of their ingredients.

Whether pâtés are rich and strong or mild and delicate, they are best eaten in modest quantities. This will allow you to enjoy all their qualities to the full without affecting your diet.

MONKFISH AND SPINACH TERRINE
with tomato and basil sauce

This is a classic recipe, but it is possible to reduce the amount of cream by half without losing the texture.

INGREDIENTS

4 oz (120 g) spinach
pinch of grated nutmeg
8 oz (240 g) monkfish
2 large egg whites
1 tsp sea salt
4 fl oz (120 ml) double
  cream

SAUCE

4 large ripe tomatoes
1 clove garlic
sea salt and black pepper
1 tbs olive or sunflower oil
4 fresh basil leaves

SERVES 4

METHOD

Strip the spinach of stems, wash the leaves well and cook gently without any added water until soft. Purée in a food processor with a pinch of grated nutmeg.

Detach the skin, bones and any discoloured bits from the monkfish and chop the flesh into small squares. Process with the egg whites until smooth. Add the sea salt and double cream and process again until the cream is well amalgamated. Be careful not to overdo this stage as the mixture can curdle.

Brush a small terrine or loaf tin with oil. Divide the fish mixture into three and mix one portion with the puréed spinach. Spread one layer of fish over the bottom of the terrine, then the spinach layer, followed by the remaining fish. Cover and bake in a *bain-marie* for about 15 minutes at 300°F (160°C), Gas Mark 2, or until set. Cool thoroughly in the refrigerator before turning out.

To make the sauce, cut the tomatoes into six pieces each, cook quickly for 3 minutes and then sieve. Crush the garlic with a little sea salt and cook in the olive oil over a moderate heat for half a minute. Add the sieved tomato, more salt if necessary and a little black pepper. Allow to cool, and just before serving, stir in the basil leaves torn into two or three pieces.

To serve cut the terrine into thick slices and put on individual plates with a little of the sauce poured around each slice.

Patricia Hegarty, Hope End Country House Hotel

Calories per serving: 230
Food value: Protein, vitamins and minerals. Low fat.

"The basis of eating well is to live on a diet of good fresh ingredients all the time and to present them in a balanced way."

LOBSTER TERRINE
with smoked salmon and sole

INGREDIENTS

14 oz (420 g) sole fillet
 (or other white fish)
2 oz (60 g) smoked salmon
3 egg whites
1 dsp chopped chives
15 fl oz (450 ml) double
 cream
2 medium-size lobsters
cayenne pepper

GARNISH
sprigs of watercress

SERVES 6–8

METHOD

Blend the sole fillet, smoked salmon, one egg white, the chives and 5 fl oz (150 ml) cream in a food processor until well processed but not puréed.

Ask your fishmonger to kill fresh lobsters for you. Remove the meat from the shell. Blend the lobster meat with two egg whites, 10 fl oz (300 ml) cream and the cayenne pepper (only process briefly otherwise the mixture may curdle).

Line a terrine with greaseproof paper. Spoon in the sole mixture, followed by the lobster mixture, cover with foil, and place the terrine in a *bain-marie*. Cook in a pre-heated oven at 350°F (180°C), Gas Mark 4 for 1½ hours.

Remove the terrine and skewer test to check that it is cooked through. Cut the terrine into slices, garnish with watercress and serve as above.

Calories per serving: 580
Food value: Protein, vitamins and minerals.
Moderate fat.

51

TERRINE OF SCALLOPS
with squat lobsters and chive sauce

INGREDIENTS

2 lb (1 kg) clean scallops
  with corals
3 egg whites
1 lb (½ kg) spinach leaves
beurre noisette
20 fl oz (600 ml) double
  cream
salt and cayenne pepper
42 squat lobsters

SAUCE

2 pts (1 litre) fish stock
6 fl oz (180 ml) Muscadet
6 fl oz (180 ml) double
  cream
bunch of fresh chives

SERVES 6

METHOD

Remove the corals from the scallops. Discard the coral bases, blanch the rest, dice and refrigerate. Liquidize the scallops and egg whites, sieve and rest on ice. Blanch the spinach, toss in hot *beurre noisette*, then cool. Line a terrine with the spinach.

Stir the cream into the scallop purée, season and whisk. Mix in the coral and pour into the terrine. Cover with buttered greaseproof paper and a lid. Cook in a *bain-marie* at 450°F (250°C), Gas Mark 9 for 40 minutes. Then leave to rest for 30 minutes.

Clean the lobsters, poach in salted water. Leave six lobsters whole; remove and peel the tails of the rest, and toss in butter before serving. Serve the terrine in a reduction of the fish stock, wine, cream and chopped chives, decorated with the lobsters as above.

François Huguet, Inverlochy Castle

Calories per serving: 800
Food value: Protein and vitamins. Moderate fat.

GÂTEAU OF SALMON AND HALIBUT
with mint and yogurt sauce

An interesting feature of this dish is the strip of whole salmon running through the middle of it.

INGREDIENTS

1 oz (30 g) butter*
12 oz (360 g) fillet of salmon
1 lb (½ kg) halibut
10 fl oz (300 ml) dry white wine
salt and pepper
8 oz (240 g) leaf spinach
4 oz (120 g) cream cheese
4 oz (120 g) mixture of cooked peas, French beans and parsley
8 sheets gelatine
1 oz (30 g) red pepper
1 oz (30 g) cucumber
½ oz (15 g) green peppercorns
10 fl oz (300 ml) double cream
2 egg whites

SAUCE
2 tbs mint jelly
5 fl oz (150 ml) low-fat yogurt
5 fl oz (150 ml) semi-whipped cream

GARNISH
lemon wedges
French beans
mange-tout
parsley

SERVES 6–8

METHOD

Butter two earthenware dishes, place the salmon in one and the halibut in the other. Add half the white wine to each dish and season. Cover and cook for 20 minutes at 400°F (200°C), Gas Mark 6.

Strip the spinach from its stalks, wash well, then blanch in boiling salted water for 1 minute. Cool rapidly, drain well and line the inside of a large rectangular mould with some of the leaves.

When the salmon is cool, slice it in half lengthways, then wrap in spinach. Put to one side. Liquidize the halibut and blend with the cream cheese. Remove half the mixture and put into a stainless steel bowl. Add the peas, beans and parsley to the fish still in the liquidizer, blend and put into another bowl.

Soften the gelatine in warm water and when dissolved, add half to the fish and cream cheese. Blend in the finely diced red pepper and cucumber and green peppercorns, then add 5 fl oz (300 ml) cream. Adjust the seasoning, then fold in one stiffly whipped egg white. Spoon this mixture into the mould so that it is about half full. Lay the piece of salmon on top and push down so that half of it is submerged.

Add the rest of the gelatine to the halibut and vegetable mixture, with the rest of the cream and the other whipped egg white. Fill the mould to the top with this mixture. Place in the refrigerator for at least 4 hours.

To make the sauce, warm the mint jelly until melted, cool, then blend with the yogurt and cream.

To serve, place the mould in hot water for 10 seconds, turn upside down on to a large plate and cut into slices. Surround each slice with sauce and decorate with lemon wedges, French beans, mange-tout and parsley.

Robert Thornton, The Moss Nook Restaurant

Calories per serving: 370
Food value: Protein, fibre, vitamins and minerals. Moderate fat.

53

SCALLOP PÂTÉ
with green peppercorns

To help set this delicate pâté, use good white fish like brill or turbot that are rich in natural gelatine.

INGREDIENTS

½ onion
1 tbs butter*
1 lb (½ kg) scallops
6 oz (180 g) white fish
5 fl oz (150 ml) cream
1 tbs dry white wine
1 tbs green peppercorns

GARNISH
seaweed
4 wedges of lemon
sprigs of parsley

SERVES 4

METHOD

Finely chop the onion and sweat in butter until soft and transparent. Trim the scallops and chop the white fish into pieces. Add to the pan and cook gently until just opaque. (Don't overcook or the flavour and texture will be impaired.)

Stir in the cream and white wine and mix well. Liquidize, put into a large dish and chill. Finally stir in the green peppercorns to taste. Serve in scallop shells surrounded by seaweed and garnished with wedges of lemon and fresh parsley.

Somerset Moore, Flitwick Manor

Calories per serving: 240
Food value: Protein, vitamins and minerals. Low fat.

POTTED HAM
with rosemary

A delicious example of the traditional English method of potting all kinds of meat, fish and game.

INGREDIENTS

10 oz (300 g) cooked ham
2 oz (60 g) butter*
6 rosemary leaves
black pepper
pinch of grated nutmeg
butter or lard for sealing

GARNISH
slices of Ogen melon

SERVES 4

METHOD

Mince the ham twice and put into a bowl with the softened butter. Add the finely chopped rosemary leaves and season with freshly ground black pepper and a little nutmeg. Blend well in a food processor.

Pack the seasoned meat into a dish, making sure that there are no air pockets. Melt some butter or lard and gently pour over the surface to seal. As the fat begins to set you can lightly inscribe a pattern on it with the tip of a knife.

Serve with a fan of Ogen melon slices and wholemeal bread.

Jean Butterworth, White Moss House

Calories per serving: 290
Food value: Protein and vitamins. Low fat.

HOT RABBIT PÂTÉ EN BRIOCHE

This pâté of rabbit, apricots, belly of pork, fresh herbs and garlic is enclosed in light brioche dough, cooked in individual moulds and eaten hot.

INGREDIENTS

BRIOCHE
½ oz (15 g) yeast
½ tsp sugar
5 fl oz (150 ml) milk
2 eggs
2 oz (60 g) butter*
10 oz (300 g) flour
pinch of salt

PÂTÉ
1 large rabbit
2 oz (60 g) dried apricots
5 fl oz (150 ml) white
  wine
8 oz (240 g) belly of pork
1 fl oz (30 ml) brandy
fresh parsley and thyme
1 clove garlic
salt and pepper
1 egg

SERVES 8

METHOD

First prepare the brioche. Blend the yeast with the sugar and warm the milk to blood temperature. Mix together, then beat in the eggs.

Rub the butter into the sifted flour and add a pinch of salt. Beat in the egg and milk mixture and allow to rise for 1 hour. Put the dough into a plastic bag and leave in the refrigerator overnight. (Do not seal the bag too tightly because the dough will continue to rise.)

To make the pâté, remove all the meat from the rabbit, and cut the saddle into thin strips. Slice the apricots into similar strips and marinate both in white wine.

Mince the remainder of the rabbit and the belly of pork and mix with the brandy. Stir in the herbs and crushed garlic, season and leave overnight.

The next day, divide the pastry into eight pieces, roll out and put into well greased individual moulds allowing plenty of spare dough to overlap the top. Strain off the marinade from the fillets and apricots and mix it with the minced meat, beating in an egg at the same time.

Half fill each mould with minced meat, then arrange some strips of rabbit and apricot to make a separate layer. Finish off with the remainder of the minced meat. Draw the excess dough (which is very pliable) over the top of the pâté, seal and trim off any surplus. Leave in a warm place for 1 hour until the dough is soft and puffy. Brush with beaten egg and bake in a hot oven at 425°F (220°C), Gas Mark 7 for 15 minutes. Then reduce the heat to 350°F (180°C), Gas Mark 4 for a further 25 minutes, covering the pastry with foil if it starts to become too brown.

Judy Knock, The Gentle Gardener

Calories per serving: 370
Food value: Protein, fibre, vitamins and minerals.
Low fat.
Note: One advantage of this recipe is that most of the work can be done the day before serving.

PORK, VEAL AND PRUNE TERRINE

In this terrine, the softness of the prunes, which are soaked in white wine overnight, contrasts with the more solid texture of the minced meat and liver.

INGREDIENTS

8 oz (240 g) veal
12 oz (360 g) shoulder of
  pork
12 oz (360 g) belly of pork
4 oz (120 g) calf's liver
¼ onion
3 peppercorns
2 cloves garlic
½ tbs brandy
2 tbs dry white wine
fresh marjoram and
  thyme, finely chopped
4 oz (120 g) prunes
6 rashers fat bacon

SERVES 8–10

METHOD

Mince or roughly chop the meat and onion and mix well. Liquidize the peppercorns and garlic with the brandy and wine, and mix with the marjoram and thyme. Steep the meat in this marinade overnight; also soften the prunes overnight in white wine.

Line a large terrine with bacon and pack in half the meat mixture. Stone the prunes and form a layer of them on top of the meat. Pack in the rest of the meat, cover with bacon, butter papers and a lid.

Put the terrine into a *bain-marie* and bake in the oven at 350°F (180°C), Gas Mark 4 for 55 minutes. Cool with a weighted board on top. Serve in slices.
Bronwen Nixon and Jane Binns, Rothay Manor

Calories per serving: 260
Food value: Protein, fibre, vitamins and minerals. No added fat.

DUCK LIVER PÂTÉ
with water chestnuts

INGREDIENTS

1 onion
1 clove garlic
1 rasher bacon
2 oz (60 g) butter*
1 lb (½ kg) duck livers
2 tbs brandy
juice of 1 orange
grated rind of 2 oranges
1 tsp Dijon mustard
1 tsp mixed spice
salt and pepper
4 oz (120 g) water
  chestnuts (tinned)

SERVES 4

METHOD

Finely chop the onion, crush the garlic and cut the bacon into small pieces (discard the rind). Fry gently in butter. Add the cleaned and trimmed duck livers and cook until sealed, then liquidize.

Add the brandy to the pan, mixing well with the juices. Blend in the orange juice and rind, mustard, mixed spice and seasoning. Liquidize well and seive.

Drain and chop the water chestnuts and fold into the pâté. Pack into ramekin dishes and seal with melted butter. Leave for at least 24 hours. Serve with orange salad or Cumberland sauce.
Jean Butterworth, White Moss House

Calories per serving: 370
Food value: Protein, vitamins and minerals. Low fat.

DUCK TERRINE
with brandied raspberry compote

This terrine is stuffed into the skin of a duck before being cooked, and the "sausage" is cut into slices when cold.

INGREDIENTS

1 large duck
1 lb (½ kg) lean pork
5 tbs brandy
1 tsp mixed herbs
1 pinch each of nutmeg,
  allspice and cayenne
  pepper
salt and pepper
1 egg
8 oz (240 g) chicken or
  duck livers

COMPOTE
1 lb (½ kg) raspberries
5 fl oz (150 ml) red wine
  vinegar
4 oz (120 g) caster suger
2 tbs brandy

SERVES 8–10

METHOD

Carefully skin the duck and remove all the lean meat from the bones. Put the skin to one side and chop the meat into small cubes. Finely mince the pork and mix with the duck.

Mix the meat with the brandy and leave for 2 hours. Then add the mixed herbs and spices, season with salt and pepper and bind with the beaten egg.

Lay the duck skin flat and place half the meat mixture in the centre. Then add a layer of chicken or duck livers and finally the remainder of the forcemeat. Pull the skin together into a large sausage shape and sew up.

Grease a large terrine lightly and press the duck "sausage" into it. Cover with foil and place the dish in a *bain-marie*. Cook in the oven for about 1½ hours at 350°F (180°C), Gas Mark 4. Allow to chill overnight.

To make the compote, simmer the raspberries in the wine vinegar for 5 minutes. Stir in the sugar and brandy and simmer for a further 5 minutes until the mixture is well amalgamated and the sugar completely dissolved. Allow to cool.

Serve the terrine in slices accompanied by the fruity compote.

Peter and Betty Saville, The Weavers Shed Restaurant

Calories per serving: 390
Food value: Protein, fibre, vitamins and minerals.
No added fat.

VEGETABLE TERRINE

This terrine is essentially a colourful arrangement of vegetables bound together with a light mousseline of chicken, and ideally served with a tomato coulis and hot toast.

INGREDIENTS

2 chicken breasts
1 egg white
15 fl oz (450 ml) double cream
salt and pepper
8 oz (240 g) large leaf spinach
4 oz (120 g) button mushrooms
4 oz (120 g) broccoli florets
4 oz (120 g) cauliflower florets
8 oz (240 g) courgettes
8 oz (240 g) French beans
½ red pepper

SERVES 6–8

METHOD

Clean and trim the chicken breasts and purée in a liquidizer. Rub through a fine sieve to remove any sinew. Put the purée into a stainless steel bowl and place this over a second bowl containing ice. Beat the egg white into the purée thoroughly. Slowly add the cream, mixing well, season and allow to rest in the refrigerator for 30 minutes.

Trim and wash all the vegetables. Cut the courgettes into six lengthways; skin and purée the red pepper. Blanch all except the pepper in boiling salted water, then refresh under cold water.

Lightly butter a large terrine mould. Line the bottom with some of the spinach leaves (keep some for the top). Spread a thin layer of mousseline on the spinach. Arrange the vegetables colourfully in layers, using the *minimum* amount of mousseline as a binding agent between each layer. Finish with the rest of the spinach leaves. Cover and place in a *bain-marie*, then cook in the oven at 350°F (180°C), Gas Mark 4 for 45–60 minutes.

Insert a skewer into the terrine, wait for 10 seconds, then test placing on the back of the hand. If it feels hot, the terrine is cooked.

Remove the terrine, lightly press with a weighted board until cold. Cut into slices and serve with a tomato coulis and hot toast.
Russell Allen, The English Garden

Calories per serving: 300
Food value: Protein, fibre, vitamins and minerals. Moderate fat.
Note: It is important to use the mousseline very sparingly so that it does not mask the natural flavour of the vegetables. The mousseline also provides almost all the calories in this dish.

The choice of vegetables can be varied, but aim for as much colour and contrast as possible.

CHEESE AND EGG DISHES
Introduction

CHEESE

One of our basic and most nutritious foods, cheese is produced in different parts of the world in hundreds – even thousands – of different varieties. Incomparable eaten as they are, cheeses also have many uses as ingredients of other dishes because they are extremely versatile.

In general, cheeses are good sources of vitamins and calcium, and most also provide useful amounts of protein. However, for those wanting to eat adventurously and stay in trim, the problem with most cheeses is fat. Nearly all the "hard" cheeses are high in fat and calories although most "soft" cheeses are slightly lower. For instance, Stilton contains 130 Calories per ounce, while Camembert has 85, and there are cheeses, such as Ricotta and Austrian smoked cheese, which are even lower in calories. (See the charts on pages 201–6 for details of the various types.)

A good way to cut down on fat and calories from cheese is to experiment with some of the low-fat varieties, such as curd cheese, cottage cheese, *framage blanc* and quark. Don't expect the same results as achieved with Cheddar or Gruyère for instance, but low-fat cheeses are worth trying. Having said that, there's no point in rejecting our finest cheeses simply because they are high in fat. It's far better to have a choice and to enjoy the pleasure of eating good cheese as part of a balanced diet.

EGGS

Like cheese, eggs are highly nutritious. They are compact little packages of vitamins, protein and minerals, but they are also the most concentrated source of cholesterol in our diet. Most nutritionists now agree that we should eat between three to five eggs each week if we want to stay healthy. Fresh eggs from free-range rather than battery hens are worth seeking out, because they do taste better and are more nutritious.

Eggs are wonderfully versatile: you can boil them, poach them, fry them, scramble them, turn them into omelets, coat them in sauces – the possibilities are almost endless. And they appear in countless dishes to provide body, colour, binding, not to mention all the specific qualities of yolk and white separated, which are well known to pâtissiers and pastry cooks.

HOT QUICHE OF LEEKS AND ROQUEFORT
with celery coulis

A delicate quiche which is baked in individual cases and served hot with a smooth celery sauce.

INGREDIENTS

1 lb (½ kg) quiche pastry
4 eggs
10 fl oz (300 ml) milk
10 fl oz (300 ml) double
  cream
salt and pepper
2 medium leeks
4 oz (120 g) Roquefort
  cheese

COULIS

1 small head celery
1 medium onion
knob of butter*
15 fl oz (450 ml) chicken
  stock

SERVES 4

METHOD

Line four individual quiche cases with pastry and leave to cool in the refrigerator for 4 hours.

To make the filling, whisk the eggs and beat in the milk and cream. Season with salt and pepper and leave to rest for 30 minutes. Dice the leeks and blanch in hot water for a couple of minutes, then refresh under cold water.

Prepare the coulis as follows. Cook the chopped celery and diced onion in butter for 5 minutes, then add the chicken stock and boil for 20 minutes. Liquidize and pass through a fine sieve.

Cook the quiches by baking blind for 5-7 minutes. Put a good portion of diced leeks into each case with some small knobs of crumbled Roquefort cheese. Add the milk and cream mixture and bake for about 25 minutes in a moderate oven at 350°F (180°C), Gas Mark 4 until set.

Pour a ribbon of hot celery coulis on to each plate before turning the quiche out of its case.

Robert Jones, Ston Easton Park

Calories per serving: 860
Food value: Fibre, vitamins and minerals.
Moderate fat.
Note: The proportions of cream and milk can be adjusted if you want a slightly less rich quiche.

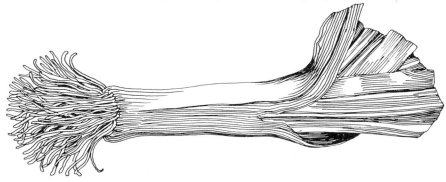

SAVOURY CAMEMBERT PROFITEROLES

An unexpected savoury version of the familiar sweet dessert. It is important that the profiteroles are made on the day on which they are required.

INGREDIENTS

CHOUX PASTRY
5 fl oz (150 ml) water
2 oz (60 g) butter*
3 oz (90 g) 85%
  wholemeal flour
2 eggs

FILLING
1 clove garlic
12 oz (360 g) Camembert
6 oz (180 g) cream cheese
1 hard-boiled egg
1 tsp tomato purée
2 oz (60 g) tofu
  (bean curd)
1 tsp chopped parsley
salt and black pepper

TOPPING
6 tbs mayonnaise
grated zest of ½ lemon
1 small clove garlic
½ tsp chopped parsley
½ tsp medium curry paste

GARNISH
fresh watercress

SERVES 4

METHOD

Put the water and butter in a saucepan and bring to the boil. Immediately add the flour and beat with a wooden spoon over a low heat until the mixture leaves the sides of the pan and forms a smooth ball. Allow to cool slightly.

Beat the eggs together lightly and add to the dough a little at a time, whisking well. Put the mixture into a piping bag with a plain nozzle and pipe out 12 small balls on to a well greased baking tray. Bake at 425°F (220°C), Gas Mark 7 for 10 minutes, then turn down to 375°F (190°C), Gas Mark 5 for about 15 minutes until golden brown and crisp. Pierce the side of each profiterole with a knife and place on a wire rack to cool.

To make the filling, chop the garlic finely in a food processor. Remove the rind from the Camembert and cut into small cubes. Put into a liquidizer together with all the other ingredients and blend until smooth. Season with salt and black pepper to taste.

Divide the mayonnaise into three bowls. To one add grated lemon zest; to the second add very finely chopped garlic and parsley; to the third add curry paste. Thoroughly blend the ingredients in each bowl.

Put the cheese filling into a piping bag with a medium-size plain nozzle, and pipe into the pierced side of each profiterole. Lay three profiteroles on each plate and top each one with a teaspoon of different mayonnaise. Garnish with fresh watercress.

Robert Jackson, Herbs Restaurant

Calories per serving: 660 + 115 for the mayonnaise.
Food value: Protein, fibre, vitamins and minerals.
Moderate fat.
Note: As an alternative to mayonnaise you might try low-fat yogurt for the toppings.

LITTLE CHEESE SOUFFLÉ

The great advantage of this soufflé is that it can be prepared in advance and reheated when required. It is ideally served with Raymond Blanc's Mushroom and Bean Salad.

INGREDIENTS

4 fl oz (125 ml) water
⅓ oz (10 g) dried skimmed milk
½ onion
pinch of grated nutmeg
8 turns of pepper mill
⅓ oz (10 g) arrowroot
2 tbs water
1 egg, separated
3 oz (90 g) Edam cheese
juice of ¼ lemon
4 oz (120 g) dry wholemeal breadcrumbs

SERVES 6-8

METHOD

Prepare individual ramekin dishes: brush with melted butter, sprinkle the insides with flour and shake out any excess. Place a circle of buttered greaseproof paper on the bottom of each ramekin.

Whisk together the water and skimmed milk, bring to the boil and add the finely chopped onion, nutmeg and black pepper. Simmer for 5 minutes so that the onion imparts its flavour to the milk.

In a separate bowl mix the arrowroot with 2 tbs of water. Then stir into the milk and bring to the boil, whisking all the time so that you obtain a smooth sauce. Force through a conical strainer into a round bowl. Cool for 5 minutes then mix in the egg yolk and the grated cheese.

Put the egg white into another bowl and whisk until peaks begin to form. Then add the lemon juice (this helps to coagulate the egg white) and continue to whisk. Take a quarter of this and mix into the cheese sauce using a spatula; then fold in the remainder. Fill the ramekins almost to the top then place in a *bain-marie*. Bake for 8 minutes in a pre-heated oven at 450°F (230°C), Gas Mark 8. Remove and cool for 5 minutes.

Loosen the sides of the soufflés with a knife, turn out and roll in breadcrumbs. Finish by placing on a lightly oiled roasting tray and cook in a pre-heated oven at 450°F (230°C), Gas Mark 8 for 5 minutes. When puffed up they can be served surrounded by salad (see recipe on page 170).
Raymond Blanc, Le Manoir aux Quat' Saisons

Calories per serving: 90
Food value: Protein, fibre, vitamins and minerals.
Low fat.
Note: This is a specially devised low-fat soufflé that is cheap and simple to prepare. It makes a stunning dish for any dinner party and you can be confident of success at your first attempt.

MUSHROOM AND CHICKEN OMELET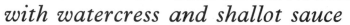
with watercress and shallot sauce

An attractive and delicate omelet that can be served as a starter and makes a pleasant change from soups and salads.

INGREDIENTS

8 eggs
1½ oz (45 g) butter*

FILLING
2 oz (60 g) morels
2 oz (60 g) ceps
2 oz (60 g) girolles
2 oz (60 g) butter*
4 oz (120 g) cooked
  chicken
salt and pepper

SAUCE
2 oz (60 g) shallots
2 bunches watercress
16 fl oz (480 ml) chicken
  stock
8 fl oz (240 ml) cream
2 oz (60 g) butter*
salt and pepper

GARNISH
sprig of thyme
slice of truffle

SERVES 4

METHOD

Prepare the filling by sautéeing the cleaned mushrooms in butter with the chicken cut into strips. Season to taste.

To make the sauce, sweat the finely chopped shallots and the stalks of the watercress (strip off and reserve the leaves). Add the chicken stock and reduce by two-thirds. Then stir in the cream and reduce again until the sauce is well amalgamated. Liquidize and pass through a sieve. Blanch the watercress leaves, add to the sauce and liquidize again. Finally bring to the boil and whisk in the butter a little at a time. Adjust the seasoning.

Lightly whisk the eggs (two per person) and season. Heat the butter in an omelet pan until it begins to brown. Pour in the beaten eggs, shaking the pan and stirring briskly with a wooden spoon so that it cooks evenly. Fold and roll into shape and put on a plate.

Make a slit down the centre of the omelet, slightly opening it. Place a spoonful of the filling inside. Pour a little of the sauce around the omelet and garnish with a sprig of thyme and a slice of truffle.

Andrew Mitchell, Greywalls

Calories per serving: 290
Food value: Protein, fibre, vitamins and minerals. Moderate fat.

HARLEQUIN OMELET

An attractive and colourful dish layered with tomato, Gruyère cheese and spinach leaves, originally made famous by that most flamboyant of modern French chefs, Roger Vergé.

INGREDIENTS

12 oz (360 g) ripe
   tomatoes
5 tbs olive oil
pinch of thyme leaves
18 oz (540 g) spinach
   leaves
2 cloves garlic
9 large eggs
pinch of grated nutmeg
salt and pepper
8 tbs double cream
2½ oz (75 g) Gruyère
   cheese

GARNISH
sprigs of fresh thyme

SERVES 6-8

METHOD

Skin and de-pip the ripe tomatoes and cook in 2 tbs of hot olive oil with a pinch of thyme until the moisture has evaporated.

Thoroughly clean the spinach and remove the central stalks. Cook with the whole cloves of garlic and a pinch of salt in 3 tbs hot olive oil, again until the moisture has evaporated. Remove the garlic and roughly chop the spinach.

Take three bowls and break three eggs into each one. To the first bowl add the spinach plus a little grated nutmeg, salt and pepper and 3 tbs cream. To the second bowl add the tomatoes, salt and pepper and 2 tbs cream. To the third bowl add the grated Gruyère cheese, salt and pepper and 3 tbs cream. Mix each one well.

Oil a terrine thoroughly and pour in the tomato mixture. Place in a *bain-marie* and cook in an oven pre-heated to 275°F (150°C), Gas Mark 1 for 25 minutes. Allow a crust to form on top, then pour in the Gruyère mixture and return to the oven for a further 25 minutes. Once again allow a crust to form before pouring in the spinach mixture and finally returning to the oven for 25 minutes.

Allow the omelet to rest for 20 minutes in a warm place, then turn out and serve in slices. If serving cold, trickle a little olive oil over the surface and decorate each slice with a sprig of thyme.
Christopher Bradley, Mr Underhill's Restaurant

Calories per serving: 310
Food value: Protein, vitamins and minerals.
Moderate fat.

"A recipe is not intended to be followed exactly – it is a canvas on which you can embroider. Improvise and invent."
Roger Vergé

OMELET AU RATATOUILLE

Ratatouille is best made up in reasonable quantity, so it makes sense either to produce this dish for several people, or to freeze any left-over ratatouille.

INGREDIENTS

2 large eggs
1 tbs cold water
½ oz (15 g) butter*
2 oz (60 g) cooked
 ratatouille (see below)
2 fl oz (60 ml) double
 cream
2 oz (60 g) Gruyère
 cheese

RATATOUILLE
 (for 4 omelets)
2 aubergines
2 courgettes
1 medium onion
2 large red peppers
2 large tomatoes
1 clove garlic
2 fl oz (60 ml) olive oil
salt and pepper

SERVES 1

METHOD

First prepare the ratatouille. Slice the aubergines and courgettes, sprinkle with salt and leave in a bowl for an hour or so to remove excess moisture. Peel and slice the onion, de-seed and cut the peppers into strips, skin the tomatoes and chop the garlic.

Warm the olive oil in a heavy shallow pan and cook the onions gently until soft. Then add the aubergines, peppers, courgettes and garlic. Cover and cook for about 20 minutes. Add the chopped tomatoes and season to taste. Cook for another 20 minutes or so, until the vegetables are soft, but not mushy. Keep warm.

Break the eggs into a small basin and add the cold water. Whisk lightly with a fork; do not over-beat – the eggs should be just broken down.

Heat an omelet pan and add the butter. When it begins to turn brown, pour in the eggs and immediately whisk with a fork for a few seconds until just beginning to set. Spoon a little of the ratatouille along the centre of the omelet and fold over.

Turn out on to a plate, pour over the double cream, cover with grated cheese and glaze under a very hot grill. Serve at once.
Allan Holland, Mallory Court

Calories per serving: 820
Food value: Protein, vitamins and minerals.
Moderate fat.

SCRAMBLED EGGS IN PASTRY
with rhubarb and sorrel

An extraordinary dish which contrasts the sharp acidity of rhubarb and sorrel with the creaminess of scrambled eggs.

INGREDIENTS

10 sorrel leaves
3 sticks of rhubarb
salt and pepper
juice of 10 oranges
5 fl oz (150 ml) double
  cream
12 oz (360 g) puff pastry
8 large eggs
1 tbs clarified butter*

GARNISH
4 sorrel leaves
4 tomato roses

SERVES 4

METHOD

Wash and coarsely chop the sorrel leaves and dice the rhubarb. Season and marinade in orange juice and cream for a couple of hours. Leave in the refrigerator.

Roll out the puff pastry and cut out four pastry boxes. Egg wash them and lay them carefully on a baking tray using a palette knife. Bake in a pre-heated oven at 450°F (230°C), Gas Mark 8 for 10-12 minutes until the pastry is golden brown and well risen. Allow to cool on a wire rack. Then cut off the tops of the boxes and cut out the inside of each one.

Spread some of the rhubarb and sorrel mixture evenly on four plates and keep warm in the oven. Also keep the pastry boxes warm on a separate tray.

Whisk the eggs in a bowl with 4 tbs double cream and season. Melt the butter in a heavy-bottomed saucepan, add the egg mixture and beat until scrambled.

To serve, remove the plates from the oven and put a pastry box on each portion of rhubarb and sorrel. Fill the boxes evenly with scrambled egg and garnish with a fresh leaf of sorrel and a tomato rose.

Barbara Deane and Jonathon Hayes, The Perfumed Conservatory

Calories per serving: 720
Food value: Protein, fibre, vitamins and minerals.
Moderate fat.

FISH
Introduction

An enormous choice of fish and seafood of all kinds is available nowadays, and yet we are still conservative about which varieties we choose to eat and how we cook them. Every country has its favourite local and seasonal fish, and thanks to speedy transport and refrigeration, it is now possible to eat good fish from almost any part of the world.

FISH COOKERY
Always buy fresh fish if you can, or fish that has been chilled on ice. Frozen fish has its place, but cannot match fresh fish for flavour, texture and quality.

Fish cookery is perhaps the most refined and delicate type of cookery. It needs extremely accurate timing because overcooking is one of the easiest ways to ruin a fine piece of fish. It also needs careful handling, subtle seasoning and a particular eye for balance in garnishes and sauces. It is important not to overwhelm fish with copious quantities of a sauce that simply drowns its natural flavour.

Steaming, grilling and poaching are all appropriate methods of cooking fish; frying can occasionally be useful, although most fish tends to absorb fat, which not only impairs its quality, but increases its calorie count.

THE FOOD VALUE OF FISH
Fish is highly nutritious and an excellent source of protein, vitamins and minerals. It compares very favourably with the best lean meat, but has the advantage that its fat is largely unsaturated, and generally it contains a smaller proportion of fat in comparison to protein. Even the "oily" varieties, such as salmon and mackerel, are high in protein and quite low in fat, which is good news for anyone who wants to eat healthily.

GENERAL GUIDELINES
Be adventurous when buying fish and try out new varieties when you see them. Make good use of seasonal specialities and always try to buy locally. Keep the heads and bones for making stock, and remember that freshness is the key to getting the best from all kinds of fish.

RAGOÛT DE LOTTE
et moules au safran

Serve this straight from the pot or decoratively presented on the plate.

INGREDIENTS

1 lb (½ kg) monkfish
2 pts mussels
½ onion
1½ fl oz (45 ml) olive oil
3 fl oz (90 ml) white wine
4 sprigs of thyme
1 stick of celery
4 large potatoes
2 tomatoes
1 red pepper
1 yellow pepper
4 small courgettes
4 leeks
1 clove garlic
2 sachets powdered saffron
½ bay leaf
4 star anise
3 fl oz (90 ml) water
12 turns of the pepper mill

SERVES 4

METHOD

Cut the monkfish into strips and keep in the refrigerator. Wash and clean the mussels well, remove their beards and discard any that are damaged or open. Sweat the finely chopped onion in 1 tbs olive oil, add the wine and bring to the boil. Toss in a sprig of thyme and some chopped celery, then add the mussels, cover the pan and cook for 2–3 minutes until the shells are just open. Filter the cooking liquid, remove the mussels from their shells (reserve these for decoration) and put back into the liquid.

Prepare the vegetables as follows. Peel and slice the potatoes and keep under water to prevent discoloration. Blanch the tomatoes, remove the skin and pips and cut the flesh into diamond shapes. Peel and de-seed the peppers and cut into strips; blanch for 1 minute then refresh under cold water. Cut the courgettes into sticks, and thinly slice the leeks.

Sweat the chopped garlic and saffron in a large deep pan with the rest of the olive oil over a low heat. Drain the potatoes and add to the pan. When they have turned yellow, add all the mussel liquor, plus three sprigs of thyme, half a bay leaf and the star anise. Top up with 3 fl oz (90 ml) water. Then put in the courgettes, leeks and peppers and lay the monkfish on top. Season with pepper, cover, bring to the boil and put the pan in a pre-heated oven at 450°F (230°C), Gas Mark 8 for 10 minutes. Finally add the mussels and tomato segments and cook for a further 3 minutes.

The dish can be served as it is or arranged decoratively on the plate, with the peppers, leeks, courgettes and tomatoes around the outside and an overlapping circle of potato slices in the centre. Top this with the monkfish and mussels. Pour the juice over and garnish with a few mussels put back in their shells.
Raymond Blanc, Le Manoir aux Quat' Saisons

Calories per serving: 240
Food value: Protein, fibre, vitamins and minerals.
Low fat.

FILLET OF MONKFISH
in lime sauce

INGREDIENTS

8 oz (240 g) monkfish
salt and pepper
juice and finely grated zest
  of 1 lime

GARNISH
sprigs of parsley
½ lime, sliced

SERVES 1

METHOD

Ask your fishmonger to prepare a meaty fillet from the tail end of the fish. Score the fillet, season it lightly with salt and pepper, wrap it loosely in foil and bake in the oven at 425°F (220°C), Gas Mark 7, for 8 minutes until "medium rare". Remove from the oven.

Drain off the juices and mix with the lime juice and grated lime zest. Reduce slightly over a low heat until the sauce is well amalgamated.

Arrange the fish on a plate, pour over the sauce and decorate with a garnish of parsley and julienned twists of lime. Serve with a selection of crisp, colourful vegetables such as mange-tout and florets of steamed broccoli.

Somerset Moore, Flitwick Manor

Calories per serving: 170
Food value: Protein and vitamins. No added fat.

STEAMED SALMON
over seaweed

INGRÈDIENTS

4 oz (120 g) salmon
dried seaweed (wakame)
salt and pepper
1 tbs dry white wine

SERVES 1

METHOD

Prepare and trim a meaty fillet of salmon, removing all bones. Soften the seaweed by soaking it in cold water.

Spread some seaweed on a large piece of foil, set the fish on it and cover with more seaweed. Season with salt and pepper, and add the dry white wine to moisten the fish. Seal carefully, making sure that the foil is loose and does not touch the fish. Cook in the oven at 375°F (190°C), Gas Mark 5 for 6 minutes.

When ready, carefully remove the fish from the foil, arrange some seaweed on a plate and lay the fish on top of it. Pour over a little of the juice and serve with new potatoes and a selection of crisp steamed vegetables.
Somerset Moore, Flitwick Manor

Calories per serving: 210
Food value: Protein, vitamins and minerals. No added fat.

POACHED SALMON
with dill sauce

Delicate and fragrant, the combination of salmon and dill appears in numerous contemporary recipes.

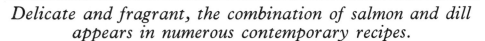

INGREDIENTS

4 fresh salmon steaks
1 slice of lemon (or lemon
  rind)
2–3 black peppercorns
1 bay leaf
parsley stalks
salt and pepper
knob of butter*
¼ onion
2 sprigs of fresh dill
2 tbs cream

GARNISH
sprigs of fresh dill

SERVES 4

METHOD

Prepare the salmon steaks, leaving the bones in and the skin on. Keep in a damp cloth until ready to cook.

Make a stock using the trimmings from the fish (plus any additional fish bones from your fishmonger). Put into a large pan with the lemon, peppercorns, bay leaf and parsley stalks. Cover with water and simmer for about 1 hour. Strain and reduce the stock by half. Adjust the seasoning if necessary.

Grease a large sauté pan with butter, add the salmon steaks (seasoned with salt and pepper) and dot with a knob of butter. Bring the stock to the boil and pour in enough to cover the fish. Allow the liquid to come to simmering point, by which time the fish should be just cooked. Lift out, remove skin and bones and keep warm.

Sauté the chopped onion and freshly chopped dill in butter. Liquidize with the remaining stock and blend with the liquor in the pan. Stir in the cream and adjust the seasoning.

Spread a little of the sauce over each plate, lay the salmon on top and garnish with a small sprig of dill.
Bronwen Nixon and Jane Binns, Rothay Manor

Calories per serving: 325
Food value: Protein and vitamins. Low fat.

SALMON IN PASTRY
with ginger and currants

Use half a side of good fresh salmon for this dish and serve it with a delicate cucumber or chive and lime sauce.

INGREDIENTS

2 lb (1 kg) fresh salmon
1 onion
knob of butter*
1 lb (½ kg) puff pastry
salt and pepper
1 tbs chopped parsley
sprinkling of powdered
  ginger
a few currants
1 egg

SERVES 4–6

METHOD

Prepare the salmon in one piece, remove the skin and make sure that there are no bones remaining. Sauté the chopped onion in a little butter, drain and leave to cool.

Take one third of the puff pastry and roll out thinly, so that it is slightly larger than the piece of salmon. Lay the fish in the centre, season with salt and a little black pepper and sprinkle with chopped parsley. Arrange the cooked onion along the centre of the fish, sprinkle with powdered ginger and add a few currants.

Roll out the rest of the pastry slightly larger than before. Wet the edges of the pastry with the salmon on it, then place the larger piece on top and press with the thumb to make sure the edges are well sealed.

Egg-wash and decorate the top with any pastry that is left over. Bake in a fairly hot oven at 375°F (190°C), Gas Mark 5 for 30–40 minutes until the pastry is golden brown and the salmon just cooked.

Serve with an accompanying sauce and either a green salad or a dish of garden peas.
Francis Coulson, Sharrow Bay Hotel

Calories per serving: 580
Food value: Protein and vitamins. Low fat.

PAPILLOTE DE TURBOT ET SAUMON
au beurre de caviar

These little parcels of turbot and salmon are wrapped in cabbage leaves and then steamed to preserve their flavour.

INGREDIENTS

8 Savoy cabbage leaves
2 pts (1 litre) salted water
1 lb (½ kg) turbot fillet
8 oz (240 g) salmon fillet
juice of ½ lemon
salt and pepper
4 sprigs of dill
5 fl oz (150 ml) cream
3 oz (90 g) butter*
1 tbs caviar

STEAMING LIQUOR

¼ onion
1 carrot
¼ stick of celery
½ leek
2 sprigs of fresh dill
1 star anise
½ clove garlic
pinch of salt
4 turns of pepper mill
3 fl oz (90 ml) white wine
14 fl oz (420 ml) water

SERVES 4

METHOD

Prepare a steaming liquor by putting the finely diced vegetables (onion, carrot, celery and leek) into a large casserole with the herbs, spices and wine. Add the water, bring to the boil, skim off the impurities and simmer for 20 minutes. Strain through a fine sieve and put to one side.

Carefully remove eight leaves from a Savoy cabbage and boil in the salted water for 2 minutes. Refresh under cold water, pat dry with a cloth and cut away the thick core of each leaf. Brush with melted butter and put to one side.

Cut the turbot fillet into eight squares and the salmon into four squares of equal size. Brush with melted butter and lemon juice (with salt and pepper added). Sandwich a square of salmon between two squares of turbot.

Put one fish parcel on a cabbage leaf, place a sprig of dill on top, then cover with a second cabbage leaf. Wrap up neatly and secure with string. Steam over the prepared vegetable liquor for 5 minutes so that the fish is just cooked through. Remove the cabbage leaves and keep the fish warm in a low oven.

Strain the liquor into a pan, stir in the cream then whisk in the butter. Remove from the heat, and when the sauce is barely warm, gently stir in the caviar.

To serve, slice the fish parcels through the middle, open up and arrange on the plate surrounded by the caviar butter sauce.

Raymond Blanc, Le Manoir aux Quat' Saisons

Calories per serving: 360
Food value: Protein, vitamins and minerals. Low fat.
Note: If you are unable to obtain caviar, Raymond Blanc recommends that you add more dill to the steaming liquor. The result is less spectacular, but just as acceptable.

POACHED SALMON TROUT
with cider and basil

In this recipe the fish is lightly poached in its own stock to which Normandy cider has been added.

INGREDIENTS

1 salmon trout, about
  2½–3 lb (1¼–1½ kg)
1 stick of celery
1 carrot
1 small onion
6 black peppercorns
bouquet garni
5 fl oz (150 ml) white
  wine
10 fl oz (300 ml) water
1 pt (600 ml) sparkling
  Normandy cider
4 tomatoes
salt and pepper
2 tbs fresh basil

SERVES 4

METHOD

Fillet the salmon trout, skin the two fillets and cut each one into two pieces.

Put the bones into a large saucepan with the chopped celery, carrot and onion, add the peppercorns and bouquet garni and top up with white wine and water. Simmer until a concentrated stock is formed. Strain, then reduce until about 5 fl oz (150 ml) remains.

In a separate pan reduce the cider to about 10 fl oz (300 ml) then mix with the stock. Add the skinned and chopped tomatoes and simmer gently for 5 minutes. Liquidize and check the seasoning.

Put the sauce in a shallow pan, add the pieces of fish and scatter freshly chopped basil on top. Cover and simmer gently until the fish is just cooked.

Serve the fish with the sauce and a crisp green salad with a light vinaigrette dressing.

Paul and Muriel Wadsworth, Pebbles Restaurant

Calories per serving: 290
Food value: Protein, vitamins and minerals. No added fat.
Note: This delicate sauce needs no thickening or added ingredients, although 2 oz (60 g) butter could be whisked in to produce a richer dish.

POACHED TROUT
with pears and red wine

Pears and red wine are commonly used in venison recipes; with trout the combination is quite unexpected, yet very successful.

INGREDIENTS

2 trout
10 fl oz (300 ml) red wine
5 fl oz (150 ml) fish stock
10 fl oz (300 ml) double
  cream
salt and pepper
2 pears, poached in red
  wine

SERVES 4

METHOD

Prepare and fillet the trout, using the skin and bones to make stock. Put the fillets into a pan, cover with red wine and stock and poach very slowly until the fish is just cooked. Remove the fillets and keep warm.

Reduce the red wine and stock by half, stir in the cream, then reduce again until the sauce coats the back of a spoon. Season to taste.

Arrange the fillets on individual plates. Cut the poached pears into slices and arrange on top of the fish. Coat with the sauce and serve.

Robert Jones, Ston Easton Park

Calories per serving: 330
Food value: Protein, fibre, vitamins and minerals. Moderate fat.

TROUT IN WHITE WINE JELLY

Serve garnished with sliced cucumber, carrot or fresh tarragon.

INGREDIENTS

2 onions
4 oz (120 g) carrots
2 sticks of celery
1 bottle dry white wine
10 fl oz (300 ml) water
24 black peppercorns
bunch of parsley
salt
6 trout, cleaned and
  trimmed
1 egg white
¼ oz (7 g) gelatine

SERVES 6

METHOD

Slice the onions and carrots and chop the celery. Bring the wine, water, vegetables, peppercorns, parsley and salt to the boil, then simmer for 20 minutes.

To make the jelly, strain the cooking liquid, bring to the boil and reduce to just under 1 pt (600 ml). Clarify it with the egg white, melt the gelatine in a little boiling water and stir it in. Let the liquid cool, and when it is syrupy but not set, glaze the trout with it. Keep chilled, and when the rest of the jelly has set, chop it and place around the trout. Garnish with sliced cucumber, carrot or fresh tarragon.

Calories per serving: 230
Food value: Protein, vitamins and minerals. No added fat.

COULIBIAC OF TROUT

Koulibiaka is a traditional Russian fish pie, often made with salmon and cooked buckwheat. This is a variation in the French style.

INGREDIENTS

1 large pink-fleshed trout about 3–4 lb (1½–2 kg)
8 oz (240 g) brioche pastry
8 oz (240 g) puff pastry
6 oz (180 g) sliced mushrooms
juice of 1 lemon
1 tbs chopped herbs (tarragon, chives, parsley, chervil)
4 oz (120 g) cooked wild rice
salt and pepper
6 quail eggs, hard-boiled

MOUSSE
4 oz (120 g) white fish
1 egg white
4 fl oz (120 ml) double cream

GARNISH
sprigs of watercress

SERVES 4

METHOD

Skin and fillet the fish. Roll together the brioche and puff pastry, then roll out into a rectangle slightly larger than that of the fillets. Liquidize the ingredients for the mousse and pass through a fine sieve.

Spread the centre of the pastry with a thin layer of mousse and on top of this lay half the mushrooms (lightly cooked in lemon juice), half the mixed herbs, then half the cooked wild rice. On top of this put one fillet of trout, seasoned with salt and pepper.

Continue with another layer of mousse topped with halved quail's eggs. Spread with mousse again and lay another seasoned fillet on top. Finish with more mousse, another layer of mushrooms, herbs and rice, and a final covering of mousse.

Neatly wrap up the pastry and decorate with any trimmings. Bake in a moderate oven at 350°F (180°C), Gas Mark 4 for 30–40 minutes until golden brown.

Serve in thick slices, garnished with sprigs of watercress and accompanied by a sauce (for example, a lemon butter sauce or a rich crab and lobster sauce).
Michael Croft, The Royal Crescent Hotel

Calories per serving: 800
Food value: Protein, fibre, vitamins and minerals. Moderate fat.

FILLET OF TROUT
with cucumber sauce

A stylish recipe in which the trout fillets are rolled around fish mousseline and spinach leaves.

INGREDIENTS

2 x 6 oz (180 g) trout
  fillets
salt and pepper
mousseline of sole and
  mussels (see page 38)
2 oz (60 g) spinach leaves
½ cucumber
10 fl oz (300 ml) fish stock
5 fl oz (150 ml) white
  wine
knob of butter*

SERVES 2

METHOD

Clean and skin the trout fillets and lay skin-side up on a board. Lightly season. Spread a thin layer of fish mousseline on top.

Wash the spinach leaves thoroughly, then blanch in boiling water. Lay on top of the mousseline. Then spread another thin layer of mousseline on top of the spinach. Roll up the fillets from tail to head-end and wrap carefully in cling film.

Skin and de-pip the cucumber, blanch the flesh in boiling water, then drain and purée in a liquidizer. Poach the trout fillets in a mixture of stock and white wine. When cooked, remove and allow the stock to reduce to a syrup. Add the cucumber purée and whisk in a knob of butter. Adjust the seasoning.

Remove the trout fillets from the cling film and carve into five slices each. Pour a little of the cucumber sauce on each plate and arrange the fish on top.
Russell Allen, The English Garden

Calories per serving: 340
Food value: Protein, vitamins and minerals. Low fat.
Note: The fish mousseline should be prepared using the directions given on page 38.

PIKE QUENELLES

Alternative kinds of fish that can be used in this recipe include whiting, halibut, turbot, hake, John Dory and eel. Serve the dish with a velouté or a vouvrillonne sauce.

INGREDIENTS

12 oz (360 g) pike
3 slices of day-old white
  bread, crusts removed
4 tbs cream
5 oz (150 g) butter*
2 eggs
1 egg white
salt and freshly ground
  white pepper
pinch of nutmeg
10 fl oz (300 ml) velouté
sauce or vouvrillonne
  sauce

SERVES 4

METHOD

Skin and bone the fish and cut into small cubes. Soak the bread in the cream, drain it and squeeze out most of the liquid. Crumble it into a small saucepan, add a knob of butter and stir over a low heat until it forms a smooth mixture which leaves the sides of the pan. Remove from the heat and cool.

Put the fish, eggs and the bread mixture (*panade*) into a liquidizer and reduce to a smooth purée, or alternatively mince the ingredients and pound them together using a pestle and mortar. Melt the remaining butter and, if you are using a liquidizer, pour it on to the other ingredients in a thin stream, letting the machine run slowly until you have a soft, fine, white purée. If you are using a pestle and mortar, pound the butter into the fish mixture a little at a time. Season with salt, pepper and a pinch of nutmeg.

Chill the mixture in the refrigerator for at least 1 hour, then, using two spoons, mould it into little torpedo shapes. Place these on a very lightly floured plate and chill thoroughly, or freeze briefly to firm them up.

Pre-heat the oven to 375 F (190 C), Gas Mark 5, or if you are in a hurry, heat the grill. Meanwhile, bring a wide, shallow pan of salted water to the boil. Turn down the heat until the water is gently simmering and poach the quenelles for 6 minutes, turning them over after 3 minutes.

Remove the quenelles carefully with a slotted spoon and place in a heated gratin dish, cover with sauce and bake in the oven until lightly glazed, or glaze to a golden brown under the grill.

Calories per serving: 590
Food value: Protein, vitamins and minerals.
Moderate fat.

BAKED WHITING
with grapes

Whiting can be a dull fish unless it is very fresh, but this simple recipe is a good way of enhancing its natural flavour.

INGREDIENTS

4 whiting, about 8 oz
 (240 g) each
2 fl oz (60 ml) olive oil
1 sprig of thyme
1 bay leaf
3 tbs dry cider
salt and pepper
12 seedless white grapes

GARNISH
slices of lemon

SERVES 4

METHOD

Clean and gut the fish, but keep them whole. Arrange in a shallow fireproof dish. Pour over the olive oil and add the sprig of thyme and bay leaf. Finally add the cider and season with salt and pepper.

Bake uncovered in a moderate oven at 350 F (180 C), Gas Mark 4 for 15 minutes. Wash the grapes and add them to the dish. Cook for a further 5 minutes.

To serve, decorate each fish with slices of lemon and bring to the table. Spoon some of the cooking juices over each whiting on the plate.

Calories per serving: 240
Food value: Protein, vitamins and minerals. Low fat.

SPICED HALIBUT IN MANGO JUICE

This Indian recipe can be adapted for all kinds of white fish.

INGREDIENTS

4 halibut steaks
1 tbs butter*
1 tbs coriander seeds
1 piece fresh root ginger
4 dried chillies
1 tbs coconut
6 cloves garlic
1 large onion
1 tbs flour
1 cup water
5 fl oz (150 ml) mango
 juice
salt

GARNISH
fresh coriander leaves

SERVES 4

METHOD

Clean and trim the halibut steaks. Heat the butter in a saucepan. Pound the coriander seeds, ginger, chillies, coconut and garlic to a paste with a little water and add to the butter. Stir in the finely sliced onion and fry until brown.

Blend the flour with a cup of water. Add to the onions and stir well. Add the fresh mango juice and bring to boiling point, stirring frequently. Lower the heat and add the fish. Season with salt and simmer until the fish is just cooked.

Serve hot, garnished with fresh coriander leaves and accompanied by rice.

Calories per serving: 230
Food value: Protein, fibre, vitamins and minerals. Low fat.

ESCABECHE

A particular method of pickling fish, which originated in Spain and came to England in the 18th century, probably by way of the West Indies.

INGREDIENTS

1 lb (½ kg) white fish
dusting of flour
2 tbs vegetable oil

PICKLE

1 carrot
1 onion
2 cloves garlic
5 fl oz (150 ml) olive oil
2 bay leaves
1 sprig of thyme
2 dried chillies
10 fl oz (300 ml) wine
   vinegar

SERVES 4

METHOD

Clean and prepare the fish; small fish, like sprats, should be gutted but left whole, larger fish should be filleted. Roll them in flour so that they are lightly coated and shake off any excess. Fry briskly in vegetable oil, allowing about 3 minutes for each side. Lift them out, drain well on absorbent paper and lay in a shallow earthenware dish.

Meanwhile, make up the pickling liquid. Peel the carrot, onion and garlic and chop into pieces. Fry lightly in a little olive oil until nicely browned. Then add the herbs, chillies, vinegar and the remainder of the oil and cook for a further 15 minutes until the carrots are soft.

Pour the hot pickle over the fish, leave it to cool and then put in the refrigerator. This dish needs to be left for at least 24 hours before it is eaten, during which time the liquid will become slightly jellied.

Escabeche can be served as a light meal with crusty bread, or as a starter.

Calories per serving: 250
Food value: Protein, vitamins and minerals. Low fat.
Note: Any kind of fish can be used for this dish. Small, whole sprats or sardines are particularly effective, but you can also use fillets of mackerel, haddock or whiting, or even chunks of cod and halibut.

SOUTH AFRICAN PICKLED FISH

An interesting method of preserving fish which combines Eastern and Western traditions. It is related to escabeche but is flavoured with Indian curry spices.

INGREDIENTS

1 lb (½ kg) white fish
salt and black pepper
dusting of flour
2 tbs vegetable oil

PICKLE
2 large onions
10 fl oz (300 ml) malt
  vinegar
1 tbs sugar
1 tsp turmeric
½ tsp ground cumin
½ tsp ground ginger
1 tsp ground coriander
cayenne pepper (to taste)
2 bay leaves
1 stick cinnamon

SERVES 4

METHOD

Cut the fish into large pieces, removing any skin and bones. Rub with salt and black pepper and leave for 1 hour. Then coat lightly in flour and fry briskly in vegetable oil until browned. Lift out the fish, drain well on absorbent paper and put into a large shallow dish.

Meanwhile, slice the onions and put into a pan with the vinegar and sugar. Mix together the curry spices (use as much or as little cayenne pepper as suits your taste) and blend to a paste with a little water. Add to the vinegar, together with the bay leaves and cinnamon stick. Bring to the boil, stirring well, then allow to simmer for about 10 minutes.

Pour the hot pickle over the fish, making sure that the pieces are completely covered. Put a lid or a piece of foil over the dish and leave in a cool place for 24 hours. Eat cold with plenty of bread.

Calories per serving: 170
Food value: Protein, vitamins and minerals. Low fat.
Note: Any type of white fish from cod to grey mullet can be used for this dish, provided it is quite meaty. More delicate fish, such as sole, is not suitable, as its flavour would be swamped by the strong pickle.

This dish is not dissimilar to a cold curry, and the sauce is an essential feature.

LEMON SOLE WITH ORANGES

An interesting combination of flavours which was popular in the 18th century and is well worth trying out today. This recipe works equally well with fillets of John Dory.

INGREDIENTS

4 fillets lemon sole
salt and pepper
2 oranges
1 lemon
3 oz (90 g) butter*
1 shallot
dash of cayenne pepper
5 fl oz (150 ml) Madeira

SERVES 4

METHOD

Clean and prepare the fillets, making sure there are no bones. Season lightly with salt and pepper. Remove the peel from the oranges and lemon and cut into thin strips; squeeze out the juice. Blanch the peel for a couple of minutes in boiling water, then drain.

Melt 2 oz (60 g) butter in a large pan, add the chopped shallot and the fillets of sole. Pour in a little water to cover the bottom of the pan. Add the orange and lemon juice and a dash of cayenne pepper, then cover the pieces of fish with strips of peel. Cover the pan and poach gently until the fillets are just cooked.

Remove the fish and keep warm. Bring the liquor in the pan to the boil and reduce. Add the Madeira and reduce again until you have a concentrated liquid. If you want to enrich the sauce, whisk in a knob of butter at the last moment.

Serve the fish on individual plates with a little of the sauce poured around.

Calories per serving: 285
Food value: Protein, vitamins and minerals. Low fat.
Note: Some versions of this dish incorporate egg yolks and cream, obviously producing a richer result. The above recipe is for those who want something a little lighter and with fewer calories.

"When it comes to cooking, a minute for a piece of fish is a lifetime."
Somerset Moore

FILLET OF LEMON SOLE
with smoked salmon

A very neat and straightforward dish that needs few ingredients and little preparation.

INGREDIENTS

3 fillets lemon sole
2 oz (60 g) smoked salmon
2 tbs double cream
salt and pepper

GARNISH
smoked salmon pieces
fresh parsley

SERVES 2

METHOD

Skin and fillet the fish, allowing 1½ fillets per person. (Use fish that has been refrigerated for 2–3 days to allow its full flavour to develop.) Cut the smoked salmon into matchstick-size pieces.

Grease an ovenproof dish and lay the half fillets on the bottom. Cover each one with some of the smoked salmon, then lay a whole fillet of sole on top, tucking in the edges. Pour on the cream, cover and bake in the oven at 425°F (220°C), Gas Mark 7 for 8 minutes. Remove and decorate with pieces of smoked salmon and a rosette of parsley.

Somerset Moore, Flitwick Manor

Calories per serving: 200
Food value: Protein, and vitamins. Low fat.

SOLE WITH BASIL AND TOMATO

Use large, fresh Dover sole for this recipe.

INGREDIENTS

3 Dover sole, weighing at least 1 lb (½ kg) each
4 tomatoes
10 fl oz (300 ml) fish stock
2 fl oz (60 ml) dry white wine
1 dsp freshly chopped basil
1 knob of unsalted butter*
2 tbs double cream
salt and pepper

SERVES 4

METHOD

Skin and fillet the sole and put into a large, flat dish. Make stock from the skin and bones.

Blanch the tomatoes for 30 seconds in boiling water, peel off the skins and cut in half. Remove the seeds and cut each half into four pieces.

Cover the fish with the stock and wine, adding half the tomatoes and half the basil. Cook briskly for a few minutes until the fish is milky white. Do not overcook. Remove the fillets. Return the pan to the stove and reduce the cooking liquid by half. Add the rest of the basil and tomato, then whisk in the butter and cream. Bring to the boil, season to taste and pour over the fish.

Richard Sandford, Milton Sandford Restaurant

Calories per serving: 260
Food value: Protein and vitamins. Low fat.

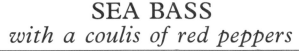

SEA BASS
with a coulis of red peppers

A beautiful dish to look at, with a marvellous display of colour from the sauce and peppers.

INGREDIENTS

1 red pepper
1 oz (30 g) each of red, green and yellow peppers
a few broccoli florets
6 oz (180 g) sea bass steak
1 tbs olive oil
1 clove garlic
2 fl oz (60 ml) raspberry vinegar
5 fl oz (150 ml) strong vegetable stock
2 fl oz (60 ml) cream
salt and pepper
knob of butter*

GARNISH
chervil leaves

SERVES 1

METHOD

Wrap the red pepper in foil and put into a fireproof dish with a little water. Cook in the oven for 15 minutes. When ready, peel off the skin, liquidize the flesh and pass through a sieve.

Peel the assortment of different coloured peppers and cut into strips. Blanch in boiling water, drain and cool on ice. Blanch the broccoli florets and treat in a similar fashion.

Pan-fry the sea bass in olive oil with a chopped clove of garlic. Remove when just cooked and keep warm.

Skim off any excess oil from the pan, and deglaze with raspberry vinegar. Reduce, then add the vegetable stock and reduce again. Stir in half the red pepper purée, whisk well, and add the cream. Adjust the seasoning and finally whisk in a knob of butter.

To serve, put the fish in the centre of a hot plate and surround with a ribbon of red pepper sauce. Decorate the top with strips of pepper and broccoli florets (lightly tossed in olive oil). Garnish with a few chervil leaves.

René Gaté, Les Semailles

Calories per serving: 420
Food value: Protein, fibre, vitamins and minerals. Moderate fat.
Note: René Gaté suggests halibut as an alternative to sea bass.

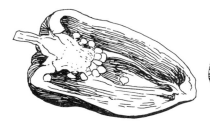

PLAITED FILLET OF SEA BASS
with fennel and pernod

A very appealing dish, where the sea bass is delicately plaited and garnished with a fleuron of puff pastry.

INGREDIENTS

7 oz (210 g) fillet of sea
bass
1 pt (600 ml) fish stock
1 tbs Pernod (or Ricard)
1 slice cooked fennel
1 fl oz (30 ml) double
cream
1½ oz (45 g) unsalted
butter*

GARNISH
puff pastry fleuron

SERVES 1

METHOD

Clean the sea bass fillet and make sure that it is free from all bones. Then plait it by making a cut down the centre of the fillet along its length, leaving one end intact. Overlap each side alternately until the plait is complete.

Put the fillet in a pan, cover with fish stock and add the Pernod. Poach until the fish is almost cooked. Remove from the pan and lay it on top of a piece of warm, freshly cooked fennel. Keep warm.

Reduce the liquid in the pan by half, stir in the cream and reduce again slightly. Finally add the butter carefully, whisking vigorously until the sauce is well amalgamated.

To serve, arrange the sea bass on a hot plate, coat with the sauce and garnish with a fleuron of puff pastry.
Russell Allen, The English Garden

Calories per serving: 660
Food value: Protein, fibre, vitamins and minerals. Moderate fat.
Note: The fish and butter both contribute to the calories in this dish, although one is protein and the other fat.

POACHED SEA BASS
with courgettes and saffron

Ask your fishmonger to fillet the fish for you, but keep the bones to use as a base for the stock.

INGREDIENTS

2 x 1½ lb (¾ kg) sea bass
2 small onions
2–3 sticks of celery
2–3 bay leaves
5 fl oz (150 ml) white
  wine
10 fl oz (300 ml) water
2 medium courgettes
3 sachets of saffron
10 fl oz (300 ml) whipping
  cream
salt and pepper

GARNISH
4 tomato roses

SERVES 4

METHOD

Put the trimmings and bones (but not the skin) from the fish into a pan with one chopped onion, the celery, bay leaves, white wine and water. Bring to the boil and simmer for 15 minutes. Pass through a muslin cloth and leave to cool for at least 4 hours.

Slice the courgettes thinly and put into boiling water. Bring back to the boil, then refresh under cold water and leave to drain.

Put the sea bass fillets into a large pan and cover with some of the fish stock. Add the sachets of saffron and the other diced onion. Cover with butter paper and bring to the boil. Simmer for 5 minutes, remove the fish and reduce the stock until 10 fl oz (300 ml) is left. Slowly stir in the whipping cream and reduce until the sauce coats the back of a spoon. Return the fillets to the pan.

Warm the courgettes by dipping in hot water and arrange on individual plates, beside the fillets. Pass the sauce through a fine sieve, adjust the seasoning and add a little more stock if the sauce has become too thick.

Coat each fillet with a little of the sauce, decorate with tomato roses and serve the remainder of the sauce in a sauce boat.
Robert Jones, Ston Easton Park

Calories per serving: 250
Food value: Protein, vitamins and minerals.
Moderate fat.
Note: Although the sauce for this dish contains a good deal of cream, the quantities actually eaten are quite small. It is also worth remembering that the fish is cooked without any fat, which helps to compensate.

This recipe can be adapted to suit other kinds of top-quality white fish, such as halibut, turbot, monkfish or sole.

SEA BASS
with saffron, tomato and parsley mousse

INGREDIENTS

4 fillets sea bass
4 tomatoes
juice of 1 lemon

MOUSSE
6 oz (180 g) parsley
1 egg and 1 egg yolk
salt, pepper and nutmeg

SAUCE
pinch of saffron threads
5 fl oz (150 ml) white wine
10 fl oz (300 ml) fish stock
½ Spanish onion
5 fl oz (150 ml) double
  cream
salt and pepper

SERVES 4

METHOD

Clean and prepare the fish. Peel, de-seed and dice the tomatoes.

Blanch the parsley leaves in boiling water, then refresh. Drain and liquidize, adding a little water if necessary. Pass through a fine sieve. Blend the eggs, mix with the purée, season and add the grated nutmeg. Put into four buttered moulds and bake in a *bain-marie* at 325°F (170°C), Gas Mark 3 for 30 minutes. Turn out when ready.

Soak the saffron in hot water for 10 minutes. Reduce the wine and stock with the chopped onion. Add the cream, sieve, blend in the saffron, and season.

Put the fish into a large pan, sprinkle with salt and lemon juice, cover and cook for 10 minutes. Arrange on the plate as above.

Stephen Bull, Lichfield's

Calories per serving: 390
Food value: Protein, vitamins and minerals. Low fat.

SKATE BRAISED IN DRY CIDER
with apples, tomatoes and cream sauce

INGREDIENTS

4 skate wings
1 shallot
2 medium tomatoes
1 cooking apple
1 small bunch tarragon
salt and pepper
5 fl oz (150 ml) dry cider
2½ fl oz (75 ml) white
  wine
8 fl oz (240 ml) fish stock
4 fl oz (120 ml) double
  cream
2 oz (60 g) butter*
1 tsp Dijon mustard
2 fl oz (60 ml) Calvados

SERVES 4

METHOD

Clean and prepare the skate wings. Finely chop the shallot. Blanch, peel and chop the tomatoes into small dice. Peel, core and cut the apple into similar sized pieces. Roughly chop the tarragon.

Put the shallot, tomatoes and apple into a buttered heatproof dish. Season the skate and place it on top. Add half the cider, the wine and stock. Cover with buttered greaseproof paper, bring to the boil and place in a moderate oven at 350°F (180°C), Gas Mark 4 for 10-15 minutes. Remove the fish and keep warm.

Strain the cooking liquor into a saucepan. Add the cream and reduce. Finally add the butter, mustard, remaining cider and Calvados; then adjust the seasoning. Spoon the sauce over the fish and sprinkle with chopped tarragon.

Paul Gaylor, Inigo Jones

Calories per serving: 400
Food value: Protein, vitamins and minerals. Low fat.

STEAMED RED MULLET
with vinaigrette sauce

Vinaigrette is normally served cold as a salad dressing, but in this dish it is warmed and served as a sauce.

INGREDIENTS

4 small fillets of red mullet
sea salt and white pepper
1 oz (30 g) onion
1 oz (30 g) carrot
1 pt (600 ml) fish stock
chopped parsley

SAUCE
1 tbs red wine vinegar
3 tbs olive oil
salt and black pepper

SERVES 1

METHOD

Scale and fillet the fish, remove the bones but leave the skin on, and season. Cut the onion into rings, blanch for 1 minute and refresh under cold water. Chop the carrot and blanch for 2 minutes.

Steam the fillets, carrot and onion over boiling fish stock for 2 minutes until just cooked. Make up the vinaigrette sauce, and warm gently. Arrange the fillets decoratively on a plate, pour over some of the warm vinaigrette and sprinkle with parsley.

Allan Holland, Mallory Court

Calories per serving: 310
Food value: Protein and vitamins. Moderate fat.

RED MULLET ON YOUNG VEGETABLES

A recipe that brings out the delicate flavour of red mullet.

INGREDIENTS

4 red mullet
1 bulb of fennel
1 young leek
1 young carrot
2 shallots
1 tsp black peppercorns
1 sprig of dill
1 bay leaf
1 tsp chopped chives
½ pt (300 ml) fish stock
¼ pt (150 ml) white wine

BEURRE BLANC
8 oz (240 g) butter*
juice of 2 lemons
1 shallot
2 fl oz (60 ml) white wine

SERVES 4

METHOD

Clean and prepare the fish, but leave them whole. Chop the vegetables into small cubes (*mirepoix*) and scatter over the bottom of a large shallow copper dish. Arrange the fish on top. Add the peppercorns and herbs, then the fish stock and wine. Bring to simmering point over heat, then bake in a hot oven at 375°F (190°C), Gas Mark 5 for 10 minutes.

To prepare the *beurre blanc* sauce, whisk together the butter and lemon juice over heat. Add the shallot, then the wine and season to taste. Continue whisking until the butter has melted and the sauce is well amalgamated. Decorate the fish with julienne of leek, carrot and fennel; serve the sauce separately.

Jean Brunner, Le Français

Calories per serving: 190 + 400 for the sauce.
Food value: Protein, vitamins and minerals. Moderate fat (sauce only).

89

PETIT PAILLETTES OF TURBOT
with mange-tout and mussels

*For the best results cook this dish in a wok which conducts heat
evenly and efficiently.*

INGREDIENTS

1 pt (600 ml) mussels
3 fl oz (90 ml) white wine
1 oz (30 g) shallots
1 pinch saffron
*1–1½ lb (½–¾ kg) fillet of
turbot*
2 oz (60 g) butter*
8 spring onions
6 oz (180 g) mange-tout
*4 fl oz (120 ml) double
cream*

SERVES 4

METHOD

Sort through the mussels and throw out any that are
damaged or open. Scrub them well and remove their
beards. Heat a large saucepan and put in the mussels,
white wine and chopped shallots. Steam with the
lid on until all the mussels are just open. Strain the
liquor and reduce by half with the saffron added.
Meanwhile shell the mussels, and set aside.

Trim the fillet of turbot and cut into thin slivers of
equal size. Melt a knob of butter in a wok (or a large
frying pan) and when sizzling, add the seasoned
fish. Toss quickly, then add the trimmed spring onions
and blanched mange-tout. Cook briskly for 2–3
minutes, then add the mussels, reduced mussel liquor
and cream. Reduce rapidly for 1 minute, toss in
the remaining butter and serve immediately in soup
plates.
Michael Croft, The Royal Crescent Hotel

Calories per serving: 350
Food value: Protein, fibre, vitamins and minerals.
Moderate fat.
Note: As a variation, you can try cooking this dish
Chinese style, by using a little vegetable oil instead of
butter and omitting the cream. This will change its
rating from 2 to 1.

To make the dish even more attractive, cut the
mange-tout into diamond shapes and fan the ends of
the spring onions.

KAI LUNG STEAMED FISH
interleaved with ham and broccoli

Fillets of white flatfish such as sole or plaice are recommended for this colourful dish.

INGREDIENTS

1 lb (½ kg) filleted white
  fish
2 tsp salt and pepper
1½ tbs cornflour
1½ tbs vegetable oil
1 egg white
1 tbs light soya sauce
2 tbs good stock
¼ tsp taste powder
  (optional)
8 oz (240 g) smoked ham
8 oz (240 g) broccoli

SERVES 4–6

METHOD

Cut the fish into small pieces. Rub with salt, pepper, cornflour, ½ tbs oil and egg white. Mix the remaining oil with soya sauce, stock and taste powder (optional).

Cut the ham and broccoli into similar size pieces as the fish. Wet and soak them for a few minutes in the oil, soya sauce and stock mixture.

Arrange the fish, ham and broccoli interleaved in a heatproof dish in an interesting pattern. Place the dish in a steamer and steam vigorously for 8–10 minutes. Remove the dish and serve with rice.

Kenneth Lo and Kam-Po But, Ken Lo's Memories of China

Calories per serving: 290
Food value: Protein, fibre, vitamins and minerals.
Low fat.

STUFFED CABBAGE ROLLS

This dish should be served with soya and chilli sauce as dips.

INGREDIENTS

6–8 large Chinese cabbage
  leaves
8 oz (240 g) filleted white
  fish, coarsely chopped
2 slices ginger, finely
  chopped
1½ tsp salt
1 egg white
pepper (to taste)
1 tsp sesame oil
8 oz (240 g) crabmeat

SERVES 6–8

METHOD

Blanch the cabbage leaves in boiling water for 1 minute to soften. Drain and dry. Put the fish, ginger, salt, egg white, pepper, sesame oil and crabmeat into a basin and mix together with a fork.

Open two cabbage leaves on a board, and put a third to a quarter of the fish and crabmeat into the centre of the leaves and form the stuffing into an elongated strip. Roll the leaves over carefully and firmly into a roll. Trim off the edges, and place in a heatproof dish. Repeat until all the stuffing has been used.

Place the heatproof dish in a steamer and steam vigorously for 12–13 minutes. Remove the dish, cut each roll into four or five sections and serve.

Kenneth Lo and Kam-Po But, Ken Lo's Memories of China

Calories per serving: 90
Food value: Protein, vitamins and minerals. Low fat.

MATELOTE NORMANDE

This rich stew can also be made with a mixture of either sea fish or freshwater fish, or with a single variety, such as turbot, monkfish or eel.

INGREDIENTS

2 lb (1 kg) brill
2 pts (1 litre) mussels
3 tbs water
3 onions
3 oz (90 g) butter*
10 fl oz (300 ml) dry
  white wine or dry cider
1 oz (30 g) flour
2 tbs chopped parsley
a few shelled shrimps
juice of ½ lemon (optional)
salt and freshly ground
  pepper

SERVES 4

METHOD

Skin the brill and cut it in large slices. Wash and scrub the mussels, remove their beards and throw out any that are damaged or open. Put them into a large saucepan with the water, cover the pan and shake it over a fierce heat until all the mussels have opened. Strain the liquid into a bowl and allow the mussels to cool, then shell them.

Chop the onions finely and soften them gently in 1 oz (30 g) of the butter in a large saucepan until they are tender and translucent, but not brown. Add the liquid from the mussels, the wine and the slices of fish, which should be just covered by the liquid (add water if necessary). Simmer gently for 5–8 minutes until the fish is just cooked.

Work the flour into the remaining butter and add it to the simmering liquid, letting it dissolve and thicken the liquid. Add the parsley, shrimps, shelled mussels and, if you think it necessary, the lemon juice and salt and pepper to taste. Simmer for a few more seconds, just long enough for the shellfish to be piping hot, but not overcooked or they will be tough.

Serve in a large tureen with plenty of bread or with croutons fried in butter.

Calories per serving: 430
Food value: Protein, vitamins and minerals. Low fat.

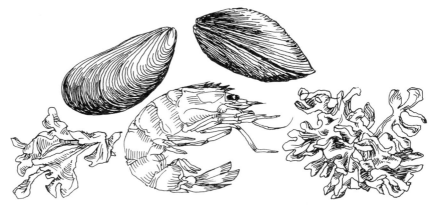

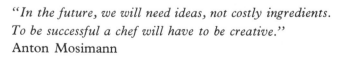

MILLE-FEUILLE OF MUSSELS
with lemon sauce

A delicate dish, rather like a feuilleté, which can be served as a starter or as a light main course.

INGREDIENTS

2 pts (1 litre) mussels
1 clove garlic
5 fl oz (150 ml) white wine
5 fl oz (150 ml) water
4 courgettes
4 small puff pastry rectangles

SAUCE
zest and juice of 3 lemons
2 onions
10 fl oz (300 ml) mussel stock
10 fl oz (300 ml) double cream
1 oz (30 g) unsalted butter*
salt and pepper

GARNISH
coriander leaves

SERVES 4

METHOD

Wash and clean the mussels, remove their beards and discard any that are damaged or open. Put into a large pan with the chopped garlic, wine and water and cook briskly with the lid on until the shells are just open. Strain off and reserve the stock. Remove the mussels from their shells.

Cut and turn the courgettes into small barrel shapes, blanch in boiling water, then refresh under cold water.

Split the rectangles of cooked puff pastry through the middle to give a "top" and a "bottom".

To prepare the sauce, cook the lemon zest with the finely chopped onions in mussel stock. Reduce by two-thirds, then add the lemon juice and cream. Simmer for 5 minutes, strain, whisk in the butter and season to taste.

To serve, sauté the courgettes, add the mussels and a little of the sauce and allow to warm together. Spread a large plate with some of the sauce, place a pastry "bottom" on this and cover it with a spoonful or two of the courgettes and mussels. Top with a pastry lid, and garnish with a few coriander leaves placed around the edge of the plate.

Anthony Rudge, Salisbury House

Calories per serving: 380
Food value: Protein, vitamins and minerals.
Moderate fat.

"In the future, we will need ideas, not costly ingredients. To be successful a chef will have to be creative."
Anton Mosimann

SAUTÉED SCALLOPS
with chive sauce

Quark, an essential ingredient in this dish, is a low-fat cheese similar in character to cottage cheese and fromage blanc.

INGREDIENTS

1 lb ($\frac{1}{2}$ kg) fresh scallops
salt and pepper
10 fl oz (300 ml) fish stock
9 oz (270 g) plain quark
2 dsp fresh chives, chopped
1$\frac{1}{2}$ lb ($\frac{3}{4}$ kg) fresh spinach
knob of butter*
pinch of nutmeg

SERVES 4

METHOD

Wash and clean the scallops carefully, slice in half and lightly season. Heat a non-stick frying pan and place the scallops in it so that each one is touching the bottom (you may need to cook them in two batches). Cook for about 1 minute on each side.

Heat up the fish stock in a saucepan and reduce by half. Then whisk in the quark and the chopped chives. Make sure that the sauce doesn't boil for any length of time after the quark has been added.

Sort out the spinach, strip from the stalks and wash well. Cook, without any added water, for about 2 minutes. Refresh in cold water and drain very thoroughly. Just before serving, melt a knob of butter in a pan, add a pinch of grated nutmeg and toss the spinach lightly.

To serve, arrange the spinach on a plate, lay the scallops on top and pour over the sauce.
Allan Garth and Bernard Rendler, Gravetye Manor

Calories per serving: 210
Food value: Protein, vitamins and minerals. Low fat.
Note: In most versions of this dish, the scallops are sautéed in butter and the sauce is enriched with cream, but here the sautéeing is done "dry", without any fat, and quark replaces cream: hence the low rating.

COQUILLES ST JACQUES
au gingembre

Steaming the scallops with fresh ginger on a covered plate produces a wonderfully fragrant dish.

INGREDIENTS

20 large scallops
knob of butter*
salt and pepper
3 oz (90 g) French beans,
  cooked
½ oz (15 g) fresh ginger
3 medium tomatoes

SAUCE
3 shallots
6 fl oz (180 ml) white
  wine
1 tbs wine vinegar
pinch of ground pepper
3 fl oz (90 ml) double
  cream
10 oz (300 g) unsalted
  butter*
salt and pepper

SERVES 4

METHOD

Remove the scallops from their shells, clean and trim well. Take four medium-sized plates and spread a little butter over the centre of each one.

Cut each scallop into three horizontal slices and arrange them evenly on the plates so that they do not overlap one another. Season with salt and pepper. Cut the French beans and the fresh ginger into strips, and chop the peeled tomatoes. Arrange on top of the scallops. Cover each plate with foil and put into the refrigerator.

To make the sauce, finely chop the shallots and cook with the white wine, vinegar and pepper until reduced to one soup-spoonful. Stir in the cream, bring to the boil, then reduce the heat and whisk in the butter a little at a time. Season to taste and keep warm in a sauce boat.

Pre-heat the oven to 425 F (220 C), Gas Mark 7 and put in the covered plates containing the scallops. Cook for about 10 minutes, then remove the foil and drain off any excess juice. Serve immediately with the sauce.
Pierre Chevillard, Chewton Glen Hotel

Calories per serving: 230 + 220 for the sauce.
Food value: Protein, fibre, vitamins and minerals.
Moderate fat (sauce only).

LANGOUSTINES GRILLÉES
à la moutarde verte

Whole Dublin Bay prawns are needed for this dish, although only the tails are eaten.

INGREDIENTS

1 lb (½ kg) spinach
1 oz (30 g) butter*
salt and pepper
3 medium tomatoes
3 fl oz (90 ml) olive oil
24 Dublin Bay prawns (in
their shells)

SAUCE
2 shallots
7 fl oz (210 ml) dry white
wine
10 fl oz (300 ml) fish stock
1 dsp green herb mustard
10 fl oz (300 ml) double
cream
salt and pepper

SERVES 4

METHOD

First prepare a spinach purée. Remove the stalks and wash the spinach leaves well in cold water. Drain, then boil for 3–4 minutes. Strain off all the liquid, then liquidize with the butter. Season to taste and keep hot.

Blanch the tomatoes in boiling water for 15 seconds, then peel off the skins. Cut in half, remove the pips and chop the flesh into small squares. Place in a dish and mix with the olive oil. Season to taste and warm gently on top of the stove.

To make the sauce, finely chop the shallots and cook with the wine and fish stock until reduced by three-quarters. Stir in the mustard and cream and reduce again until the sauce is thick and smooth. Season to taste and keep hot.

Remove the shell from the tails of the Dublin Bay prawns but leave the rest intact. Heat a large pan with a little olive oil and when it is very hot add the prawns. Cook under the grill for 3–4 minutes.

To serve, pour some of the sauce over four hot plates and arrange six prawns in a semi-circle on each, with squares of tomato between each one. Finally put a quenelle of spinach purée (made by shaping between two dessert spoons) in the space on each plate.
Pierre Chevillard, Chewton Glen Hotel

Calories per serving: 400
Food value: Protein, vitamins and minerals.
Moderate fat.

MEDITERRANEAN PRAWNS
with saffron rice

Whole, cooked Mediterranean prawns are usually served cold with salad or mayonnaise, but in this dish they are eaten hot.

INGREDIENTS

36 large Mediterranean
  prawns (whole, boiled)
chopped parsley

SAUCE
2 large shallots
2 oz (60 g) butter*
2 tbs flour
2 tsp Dijon mustard
1 oz (30 g) Gruyère
  cheese
10 fl oz (300 ml) fish stock
2 fl oz (60 ml) dry white
  wine
1 tbs Madeira
2 egg yolks
2 tbs cream
salt and pepper

RICE
2 large cups chicken stock
1 large cup Patna rice
1 good pinch of saffron
1 oz (30 g) red and green
  peppers
1 oz (30 g) onion
1 oz (30 g) peas
salt and pepper

SERVES 4

METHOD

First prepare the rice. Bring the chicken stock to the boil and add the washed rice with the saffron, finely chopped peppers and onion, peas and seasoning. Transfer to a large casserole dish, cover and cook in the oven at 425°F (220°C), Gas Mark 7 for about 20 minutes or until all the liquid has been absorbed. Keep hot.

Meanwhile make the sauce. Sauté the chopped shallots lightly in butter, then stir in the flour, mustard and grated cheese. Whisk in the fish stock, wine and Madeira over a low heat and simmer until the sauce coats the back of a spoon. Carefully blend in the egg yolks and cream, making sure that the sauce does not boil. Season to taste.

To serve, shell all except four of the prawns and keep warm. Arrange the rice on a dish, put the shelled prawns in the centre, then pour over the sauce. Sprinkle with chopped parsley and place the whole prawns as a garnish around the dish.

Martin Hoefkens, Tarn End Hotel

Calories per serving: 580
Food value: Protein, fibre and vitamins. Low fat.

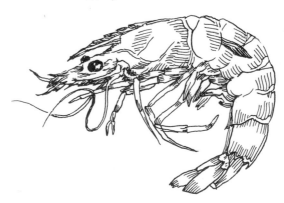

SCAMPI WITH LEMON AND HONEY

A sweet and sour dish that enhances the flavour of scampi. Garnish it with lemon and orange zest, toasted almonds and chopped parsley, and serve with Basmati rice.

INGREDIENTS

salt and pepper
2 lb (1 kg) jumbo scampi
flour for dusting
2 oz (60 g) butter*
7 fl oz (210 ml) dry white
  wine
3 fl oz (90 ml) honey
1 fl oz (30 ml) lemon juice

GARNISH
lemon and orange zest
toasted almonds
freshly chopped parsley

SERVES 4

METHOD

Season and lightly dust the scampi with flour, shaking off any excess. Shallow fry in a knob of butter till lightly browned on each side, then drain and put to one side in the frying pan.

In a separate pan, reduce the white wine, honey, lemon juice and butter to a syrupy consistency. Add to the scampi and cook for 3–4 minutes until the fish has a shiny glaze.

Serve the scampi with a dish of baked Basmati rice and garnish with shredded zest of lemon and orange, a few toasted almonds and some freshly chopped parsley.

Robert Thornton, The Moss Nook Restaurant

Calories per serving: 440
Food value: Protein, vitamins and minerals. Low fat.

MEAT
Introduction

Meat has been a mainstay of our cooking for centuries, and we have tended to give it pride of place on the table in our restaurants and our own homes. But attitudes are changing and we are now starting to buy and eat less meat.

MEAT IN THE SHOP AND THE KITCHEN
Four kinds of meat dominate our butchers' shops: beef, lamb (and occasionally mutton), pork (including bacon and hams) and veal, as well as a wide range of offal (liver, kidneys, sweetbreads, etc.). Unfortunately quantity and choice isn't always matched by quality. The vast proportion of the meat we buy has been intensively reared, and is often short on flavour, despite being lean and tender.

Meat is an excellent source of protein, but it is also high in saturated animal fat, even when it is lean. So it makes sense to control the amount we eat for health reasons alone.

COOKING MEAT
There are several points worth remembering when you are planning to cook meat. Buy the leanest cuts, if possible, and trim off any excess visible fat before cooking. Try to cook without fat, for example by grilling rather than frying. Also reduce the quantity of meat in particular dishes and aim for a better balance between meat and other ingredients, which is something that cooks in the East have understood for hundreds of years.

The real message is to eat more fish and game in place of meat, so that you obtain the valuable protein without the large amounts of saturated fat as well.

GETTING THE BEST FROM MEAT
While meat remains a part of our diet, try to get the best from it. Find a good reliable butcher, who buys his meat with care and who is prepared to hang it properly (particularly beef). Meat can only develop its full flavour if it is allowed to hang for a reasonable time before being sold. Keep an eye open for butchers selling organically produced meat, reared without hormones or growth promoters and fed naturally.

STEAMED BEST END OF LAMB
with rosemary

This dish requires considerable preparation, but as a result it highlights the natural flavour of the meat.

INGREDIENTS

1 pair best ends of lamb
½ *clove garlic*
1 sprig of thyme
1 sprig of rosemary
½ *onion*
1 carrot

SERVES 4

METHOD

Remove the meat from the bone and trim off all the sinew and fat. Then pare off the fat and chop into small pieces. Place the bones and fat with all the other ingredients (crushed garlic, herbs, chopped onion and sliced carrot) in a large pan. Cover with cold water, bring to the boil and simmer for about 45 minutes. Remove any scum.

Strain off the stock, leave to cool and skim off all the fat as it rises to the surface. Bring to the boil and reduce until there is about 1 pt (600 ml) of liquid left. This is the liquid used for steaming the lamb.

Put the meat on a steaming rack and steam for about 10 minutes. Serve sliced on a bed of root vegetables and pour over the juices and liquor used for the steaming. Rosemary jelly complements this dish well.
Allan Garth and Bernard Rendler, Gravetye Manor

Calories per serving: 280
Food value: Protein, vitamins and minerals. No added fat.
Note: The initial preparation of the meat, the use of fat-free stock and the technique of steaming all help to keep down the calorie count of this dish.

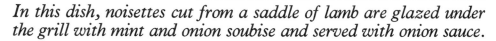

NOISETTES OF LAMB
with mint and onion soubise

In this dish, noisettes cut from a saddle of lamb are glazed under the grill with mint and onion soubise and served with onion sauce.

INGREDIENTS

1 oz (30 g) butter*
½ onion
5 fl oz (150 ml) cream
small bunch of mint
salt and pepper
1 saddle of lamb

SAUCE
1 oz (30 g) butter*
2 tbs flour
10 fl oz (300 ml) milk
½ onion
salt and pepper

GARNISH
12 spring onions

SERVES 4

METHOD

To make the soubise, put the butter in a saucepan with the diced onion and sauté until soft. Add the cream and reduce by half, stirring in a little of the chopped mint at the same time. Liquidize and pass through a fine sieve. Put into a clean bowl, add the rest of the chopped mint and season to taste. Leave to cool.

For the sauce, make a light roux by melting the butter in a thick-bottomed pan, then stirring in the flour with a wooden spoon until well blended. Gradually add the warmed milk a little at a time, stirring until the sauce coats the back of the spoon. Add the chopped onion, season with salt and pepper and cook gently for about 30 minutes. Keep warm in a *bain-marie* or reheat in another saucepan when needed.

Cut the boned and rolled saddle of lamb into 12 pieces, season with salt and pepper and lightly fry for 2-3 minutes on each side. Remove from the pan, cut off the string and place the slices on a tray, topping each one with a spoonful of mint and onion soubise. Glaze under the grill until the topping is light brown.

Spoon some of the warmed onion sauce over four plates and arrange three noisettes on each one in the form of a triangle. Garnish with lightly poached spring onions tucked between each noisette.

Peter Hollins, The Marquee Restaurant

Calories per serving: 300
Food value: Protein, vitamins and minerals. Low fat.

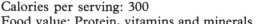

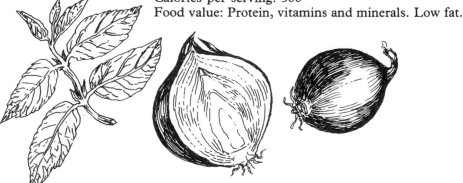

LAMB CHARLOTTE

A savoury version of the familiar fruit charlotte, this recipe, consisting of aubergine, lamb mousseline and lamb ragout layers, is loosely based on Michel Guérard's original recipe.

INGREDIENTS

2 large aubergines
salt
olive oil for frying
2 lb (1 kg) leg of lamb
1 oz (30 g) fresh
  breadcrumbs
2 tbs milk
7 fl oz (210 ml)
  double cream
salt and pepper
pinch of grated nutmeg
1 crushed allspice berry
2 oz (60 g) butter*
2 fl oz (60 ml) brandy
5 fl oz (150 ml)
  chicken stock
6 tomatoes
6 cloves garlic
1 tbs finely chopped
  parsley and thyme
1 bay leaf

SAUCE
1 onion
1 clove garlic
1 tbs olive oil
1 lb (½ kg) tomatoes
1 dsp each of chopped
  thyme, basil and parsley
5 fl oz (150 ml) white
  wine

SERVES 6

METHOD

Peel the aubergines, slice and sprinkle with salt. Leave for 30 minutes, then pat dry. Fry in olive oil until golden brown, drain and put to one side.

Purée 4 oz (120 g) of the leanest meat in a liquidizer, and add the breadcrumbs soaked in milk. When well blended add the cream slowly as the machine turns. Transfer to a bowl, season with salt, pepper, nutmeg and allspice and refrigerate.

Cut the rest of the lamb into cubes. Season and sauté in butter. Transfer the meat to a casserole and flame with brandy. Deglaze the frying pan with chicken stock and add to the casserole. Add the chopped tomatoes, crushed garlic, herbs and seasoning. Bring to the boil, cover and cook in the oven at 325°F (170°C), Gas Mark 3 for 1 hour. Then cool.

Line six greased ramekin dishes with aubergine slices and smear some of the lamb mousseline over them. Fill the centre with lamb ragout (which should not be too wet). Top with another layer of mousseline and buttered greaseproof paper. Put the dishes in a *bain-marie* and bake at 400°F (200°C), Gas Mark 6 for 20-30 minutes. Meanwhile make the tomato sauce, finely chop the onion and garlic and cook gently in olive oil. Add the roughly chopped tomatoes, mixed herbs, wine and salt and pepper to taste. Stew for 15-20 minutes over a low heat. Pass through a medium sieve and serve with the lamb charlotte.

Tim Cumming, The Hole in the Wall

Calories per serving: 670
Food value: Protein, fibre, vitamins and minerals.
Moderate fat.

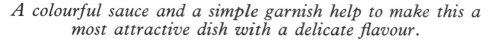

LOIN OF VEAL
with saffron sauce

A colourful sauce and a simple garnish help to make this a most attractive dish with a delicate flavour.

INGREDIENTS

salt and pepper
4 slices loin of veal
flour for dusting
1 oz (30 g) butter*

SAUCE
1 onion
1 clove garlic
2 tbs butter*
2 tbs vegetable oil
sprigs of tarragon and sage
2 bay leaves
4 tomatoes
pinch of saffron
5 fl oz (150 ml) dry white
 wine
5 fl oz (150 ml) chicken
 or veal stock
5 fl oz (150 ml) cream

GARNISH
sprigs of tarragon

SERVES 4

METHOD

First make the sauce. Soften the finely chopped onion and garlic in the butter and oil. Then add the herbs and the tomatoes (chopped and pulped), together with a good pinch of saffron. Cook for a further 5 minutes, stirring well.

Pour on the white wine, bring to the boil and reduce. Then add the stock and reduce again. Pass the sauce through a sieve, then whisk in the cream and keep warm.

Season the slices of veal and lightly dust with flour. Pan-fry in butter until just golden on both sides. Allow to rest in a warm oven for a few minutes.

To serve, spoon some of the sauce on to four plates and arrange the meat on top. Decorate with a sprig of fresh tarragon and serve with rice.

Melanie de Blank, Shipdham Place

Calories per serving: 310
Food value: Protein, vitamins and minerals.
Moderate fat.
Note: Melanie de Blank suggests thin, creamy yogurt as an alternative to cream in this recipe.

TOURNEDOS OF VEAL
with mushroom mousseline

The delicate mushroom mousseline is used like pâté in this recipe to add a final flourish to the meat.

INGREDIENTS

2 fillets of veal
6 rashers of bacon
1 oz (30 g) butter*
4 fl oz (120 ml)
  Noilly Prat
4 fl oz (120 ml) veal stock
salt and pepper

MOUSSELINE
6 oz (180 g) mushrooms
1 oz (30 g) butter*
salt and pepper
3 egg whites
2 fl oz (60 ml) cream
pinch of nutmeg

GARNISH
fleurons of puff pastry

SERVES 6

METHOD

To prepare the mousseline, sauté the mushrooms in butter with seasoning until lightly browned. Allow to cool. Place in a liquidizer with the egg whites and blend until smooth. Stir in the cream, then pour into individual circular moulds (the same diameter as the tournedos). Cover with foil and cook in the oven at 350°F (180°C), Gas Mark 4 for about 15 minutes or until set.

Trim the veal fillets of all fat and sinew, and cut into six thick steaks. Wrap each one in bacon and secure with a wooden toothpick. Sauté in butter over a very low heat for about 5 minutes each side, then remove from the pan and keep warm. Add the Noilly Prat and veal stock to the pan juices and reduce over a high heat until the sauce is syrupy. Adjust the seasoning.

To serve, place the tournedos in the centre of the plates, coat with some of the sauce and top with a little of the mousseline. Garnish with a fleuron of puff pastry.

Baba Hine, Corse Lawn House Hotel

Calories per serving: 330
Food value: Protein, fibre, vitamins and minerals.
Low fat.

ESCALOPE OF VEAL
with mustard sauce

INGREDIENTS

4 veal escalopes
1 oz (30 g) butter*
5 fl oz (150 ml) dry
  white wine
10 fl oz (300 ml) light
  chicken or veal stock
5 fl oz (150 ml) cream
2 tsp coarse-grain mustard
salt and pepper

GARNISH
chives
1 tomato, deseeded and
  diced

SERVES 4

METHOD

Trim and flatten the veal escalopes and pan-fry in
butter for a few minutes, turning once. When cooked,
remove from the pan and keep warm.

Deglaze the pan with white wine, then add the stock
and reduce. Whisk in the cream and reduce again until
a smooth consistency is achieved. Sieve, then finally
blend in the mustard and season to taste.

To serve, pour the sauce on to a large serving dish,
and arrange the escalopes on top. Chop the tomato
flesh into small dice and use to decorate the sauce.
Finally lay a few chives over the meat.

Calories per serving: 280
Food value: Protein, vitamins and minerals. Low fat.

FEUILLETÉS DES FOIE DE VEAU
au cassis

INGREDIENTS

1 lb (½ kg) calf's liver
12 oz (360 g) puff pastry
10 fl oz (300 ml) veal
  stock
2 tbs cassis
1 tbs raspberry vinegar
2 fl oz (60 ml) red wine
2 fl oz (60 ml) port
1 oz (30 g) butter*

GARNISH

4 rashers bacon
a selection of seasonal
  vegetables

SERVES 4

METHOD

Carefully cut the calf's liver into four thin escalopes and grill lightly. Roll out the puff pastry, cut it into four rectangles, glaze with egg-wash and score with a criss-cross pattern. Bake in a hot oven at 425°F (220°C), Gas Mark 7 for 10-15 minutes.

To make the sauce, reduce the veal stock, add the cassis, raspberry vinegar, wine and port, then at the last minute whisk in the butter to thicken it.

Place an escalope topped with puff pastry on each plate. Surround with sauce and garnish with strips of grilled bacon and a few colourful cooked vegetables.
Nico Ladenis, Chez Nico

Calories per serving: 490
Food value: Protein, vitamins and minerals.
Moderate fat.

STEAK, KIDNEY AND OYSTER PIE

An interesting and unusual feature of this dish is the pastry crust, which is made by mixing a quantity of boiled and sieved potato with flour.

INGREDIENTS

1 lb (½ kg) rump steak
seasoned flour
knob of beef dripping
8 lamb's kidneys
2 onions
4 oz (120 g) mushrooms
handful of mixed herbs
 (sage, thyme, parsley)
1 pt (600 ml) beef stock
8 smoked oysters (tinned)

CRUST

8 oz (240 g) self-raising
 flour
4 oz (120 g) boiled and
 sieved potatoes
½ tsp salt
2 oz (60 g) lard
2 oz (60 g) beef dripping
beaten egg

SERVES 4

METHOD

Cut the steak into chunks and toss in seasoned flour. Sauté in dripping until sealed. Halve and core the kidneys, chop the onions into large pieces and wipe the mushrooms with a damp cloth (halve if very large). Add to the meat, sprinkle with herbs and pour on the beef stock. Blend well, then transfer to a casserole dish and cook in the oven slowly until the meat is tender.

Meanwhile make the pastry crust. Mix the flour with the sieved potato and salt. Rub in the fat and add a little water until you have a stiff dough. Roll out thickly.

Transfer the casseroled meat to a large pie dish, add the smoked oysters and cover with the pastry. Brush with beaten egg and bake in the oven at 325°F (170°C), Gas Mark 3 for 20-30 minutes until golden brown.

Bronwen Nixon and Jane Binns, Rothay Manor

Calories per serving: 570
Food value: Protein, fibre, vitamins and minerals. Moderate fat.
Note: You can use polyunsaturated margarine as a low-fat substitute for lard and dripping in this recipe.

Traditionally fresh oysters are used as an ingredient in this dish, but smoked oysters make an interesting alternative with a more pronounced flavour.

FEUILLETÉ OF BEEF FILLET
with mustard and chervil sauce

It is important to use the best fillet of beef – either from the head or tail end – for this recipe, because of its tenderness.

INGREDIENTS

1½ lb (¾ kg) beef fillet
1 lb (½ kg) puff pastry
salt and pepper
1 oz (30 g) butter*

SAUCE
½ Spanish onion
chervil stalks
4 fl oz (120 ml) dry white
  wine
10 fl oz (300 ml) strong
  beef, chicken or veal
  stock
salt
2 tbs Dijon mustard
5 fl oz (150 ml) double
  cream
1 bunch chervil

SERVES 4

METHOD

Trim the meat and cut into cubes. Put to one side. Roll out the puff pastry thinly and cut into eight equal squares. Cut the centre out of four of these pieces. Place the "frames" over the four intact squares, moisten the rims with water and press together. Glaze the tops with egg-wash. Lightly score a criss-cross pattern on the cut-out centres of the frames (these form the lids). Bake the pastry in a hot oven at 425°F (220°C), Gas Mark 7 for 10-15 minutes, allowing slightly less for the lids.

To make the sauce, boil together the finely chopped onion, chervil stalks, wine and stock until reduced by three-quarters. Salt lightly to test the strength of the flavour and reduce further if necessary. Add the mustard and cream and adjust the seasoning. Pass through a sieve and add the finely chopped chervil leaves.

Season the beef fillet with salt and pepper, and sauté very quickly in hot butter, shaking the pan and turning the meat. After about 1 minute remove and use to fill the four pastry cases. Finally pour round the sauce and serve.

Stephen Bull, Lichfield's

Calories per serving: 950
Food value: Protein, fibre, vitamins and minerals.
Moderate fat.

CASSEROLED BEEF
with orange juice and ale

This casserole is greatly improved if made a day in advance so that the flavours of the orange and ale can penetrate the meat.

INGREDIENTS

2 lb (1 kg) rump steak
seasoned flour
2 oz (60 g) butter*
1 large onion
2 large carrots
2 sticks celery
2 cloves garlic
10 fl oz (300 ml)
  strong ale
½ tsp ground allspice
½ tsp grated nutmeg
juice of 2 oranges
salt and black pepper

GARNISH
chopped parsley

SERVES 4-6

METHOD

Cut the rump steak into large cubes and coat in seasoned flour. Melt the butter in a large pan and sauté the meat until browned all over. Transfer to a casserole dish.

Finely chop the onion, carrots, celery and garlic and add to the pan. Sauté in the butter and meat juices for 2-3 minutes. Pour in the ale, mixing well so that all the pan juices are blended. Add the allspice and grated nutmeg, then pour the liquid over the meat in the casserole dish. Cover and cook slowly in the oven at 250°F (130°C), Gas Mark 1 for about 3 hours.

Add the orange juice and adjust the seasoning. Dust the casserole with freshly chopped parsley and serve.
Betty and Peter Saville, The Weavers Shed Restaurant

Calories per serving: 480
Food value: Protein, vitamins and minerals. Low fat.
Note: The Savilles use a strong ale brewed locally called Old Peculier for this dish, but any equivalent dark bottled beer or stout can be used.

GRILLED SIRLOIN STEAK
with caper and watercress butter

If you like to eat steak, it pays dividends to deal with a reputable butcher and insist on well-hung meat.

INGREDIENTS

6-8 oz (180-240 g) sirloin
  steak (per person)

BUTTER
1 tbs capers
10 sprigs of watercress
6 oz (180 g) butter*
black pepper

GARNISH
sprigs of watercress

SERVES 1

METHOD

The caper and watercress butter can be made in advance. Finely chop the capers and the washed watercress, cream the butter and mix well. Mould into a roll, wrap in greaseproof paper and chill until firm.

Heat the grill until red hot. Brush a little oil over the steaks, season with black pepper and cook as required. Serve topped with a pat of caper and watercress butter and some extra sprigs of watercress. Eat with baked potatoes and braised chicory cooked with lemon juice.

Victoria Stephenson, Bradfield House Restaurant

Calories per serving: 490
Food value: Protein, vitamins and minerals. Low fat.

CALF'S LIVER
with lemon and honey

The sweet, yet sharp sauce provides a contrast to the soft texture and delicate flavour of the liver.

INGREDIENTS

3 lemons
3 tbs clear honey
1 dsp sugar
3-4 tbs water
1 oz (30 g) butter*
1 tbs olive oil
salt and pepper
4 × 6 oz (180 g) calf's
  liver
flour

GARNISH
lemon peel and segments

SERVES 4

METHOD

Mix the juice of two lemons with the warm honey in a saucepan. Zest the third lemon and slice the pieces of zest thinly. Blanch, refresh in cold water and drain. Add sugar and 3-4 tbs of water and slowly reduce over a low heat until the zest begins to crystallize.

Melt the butter and oil in a large pan, season the liver, dip in flour and cook briefly over a high heat (30-60 seconds per side).

Remove the liver, add the lemon and honey to the pan and bubble for 1 minute. Adjust the seasoning and strain over the liver. Garnish with lemon peel and segments.

Tim Cumming, The Hole in the Wall

Calories per serving: 430
Food value: Protein, vitamins and minerals. Low fat.

CALF'S LIVER
with shallots and beetroot mousse

An elaborate dish in four parts, including shallot purée, beetroot mousse and beetroot sauce as well as sautéed liver.

INGREDIENTS

1 lb (½ kg) calf's liver
flour
knob of butter*

MOUSSE
8 oz (240 g) cooked
  beetroot
1 carrot
1 small onion
10 fl oz (300 ml)
  chicken stock
4 sheets gelatine
5 fl oz (150 ml) cream
salt and pepper

PURÉE
8 oz (240 g) shallots
1 oz (30 g) butter*
5 fl oz (150 ml) stock
2 fl oz (60 ml) cream
small bunch of parsley

SAUCE
1 small cooked beetroot
2 tsp raspberry vinegar
2 tbs white wine
5 fl oz (150 ml) cream
salt and pepper

SERVES 4

METHOD

First prepare the beetroot mousse. Slice the beetroot, peel and dice the carrot and onion and cook in stock until the vegetables are soft. Liquidize, then pass through a sieve to remove any excess lumps.

Soak the gelatine sheets in a little warm water until soft. Then stir in the vegetables and mix well. Finally add the cream, season with salt and pepper and put in the refrigerator to set.

To make the purée, peel and dice the shallots and cook gently in butter until soft and transparent. Stir in the stock and cream, then reduce by half. Liquidize and pass through a sieve to obtain a smooth texture. Stir in finely chopped parsley and allow to cool.

Prepare the sauce by finely dicing the small beetroot and cooking in a pan with the raspberry vinegar, white wine and cream. Simmer and reduce by half until the sauce has a good texture, then adjust the seasoning.

Cut the liver into thin strips and lightly dust with flour. Sauté in butter for about 1 minute. Remove from the pan and arrange like a fan on a warm plate. Put a spoonful of purée at the base of the "fan" and warm under the grill. Pour some of the warmed sauce around the top of the fanned meat and decorate with two quenelles of beetroot mousse.
Peter Hollins, The Marquee Restaurant

Calories per serving: 380
Food value: Protein, fibre, vitamins and minerals. Moderate fat.
Note: Although there is some fat (in the form of butter and cream) in every part of this dish, the overall effect is not at all rich because the quantities of mousse, purée and sauce are quite small in each serving.

CASSEROLED OX TONGUE
with black grapes and red wine

Salted ox tongues are readily available from many butcher's shops, particularly around Christmas time.

INGREDIENTS

1 salted ox tongue
1 large onion
2 tomatoes
4 pieces orange peel
3 cloves garlic
handful of mixed herbs
1 bottle red wine
2 lb (1 kg) black grapes
1 tsp cornflour
salt and pepper

GARNISH
sprigs of fresh chervil

SERVES 6-8

METHOD

Put the salted tongue into a large pan of water, bring to the boil and simmer for 15 minutes. Meanwhile, put the sliced onion, chopped tomatoes, orange peel, chopped garlic and herbs into a deep casserole dish. Drain the ox tongue when ready and lay it on top of the vegetables. Pour over a bottle of red wine and add the grapes.

Cover the dish and cook in the oven at 350°F (180°C), Gas Mark 4 for 3½ hours. Remove the tongue, peel off the skin and cut the meat into thin slices. Keep warm.

Sieve all the vegetables and grapes into a saucepan. Stir in the cornflour (blended with a little water), season to taste, bring to the boil and pour hot over the sliced tongue. Decorate with sprigs of fresh chervil, and serve with boiled potatoes and a crisp salad.

Victoria Stephenson, Bradfield House Restaurant

Calories per serving: 350
Food value: Protein, vitamins and minerals. No added fat.

SOYA-BRAISED KNUCKLE OF PORK

An interesting way of preparing a relatively inexpensive cut of pork. It should be served with plain boiled rice and a selection of quick-fried green vegetables.

INGREDIENTS

1 knuckle of pork, about
  3-4 lb (1½-2 kg)
5½ tbs dark soya sauce
oil for frying
1½ pts (900 ml)
  chicken stock
2-3 slices root ginger
1 large onion
3-4 heads star anise
1 tbs sugar
1½ tsp salt

SAUCE
4-5 dried Chinese
  mushrooms
2-3 oz (60-90 g) bamboo
  shoots
½ chicken stock cube
2-3 tbs dry sherry
1½ heaped tbs cornflour
3-4 tbs water

SERVES 5-6

METHOD

Clean the knuckle of pork and put it in a pan of boiling water to simmer for 20 minutes. Drain and rub the knuckle with 2 tbs soya sauce. Leave to season for ½ hour.

Deep-fry the knuckle (or shallow-fry by turning it in a smaller amount of oil) for 8-10 minutes until it is quite brown.

Soak the dried mushrooms in warm water for 20 minutes, then remove the stems. Cut the bamboo shoots into small slices.

Heat the chicken stock in a deep frying pan or casserole. When hot, add the knuckle, together with the ginger, sliced onion, anise, sugar, soya sauce and salt. Cover the casserole and leave to cook gently at 325°F (170°C), Gas Mark 3, for 2 hours in a pre-heated oven. Turn the knuckle over every ½-¾ hour.

Remove the knuckle and place it in a deep-sided dish. Place the casserole on top of the cooker. Add the dried mushrooms, bamboo shoots and crushed chicken stock cube. Reduce the sauce over a high heat to about half. Add the sherry and cornflour (blended in 3-4 tbs water) and stir for 2-3 minutes for the gravy to thicken. Pour the sauce over the knuckle and serve, surrounded by quick-fried green vegetables, such as mange-tout, French beans or spinach.
Kenneth Lo and Kam-Po But, Ken Lo's Memories of China

Calories per serving: 390
Food value: Protein, vitamins and minerals. Low fat.

BAKED LOIN OF PORK
garnished with melon and limes

In this recipe the meat is seasoned with lemon, garlic, rosemary and black pepper before it is cooked.

INGREDIENTS

3-4 lb (1½-2 kg) loin of
  pork
grated rind of 1 lime
2 cloves garlic
2 tsp rosemary
black pepper
1 onion
1 carrot
1 stick celery
5 fl oz (150 ml) medium
  sherry
5 fl oz (150 ml) water
1 tbs butter*

GARNISH
½ melon, sliced
1 lime, sliced

SERVES 4

METHOD

Bone the loin of pork (or ask your butcher to do it for you), remove the rind from the meat and put to one side. Take off all the fat until well trimmed. Rub the meat with a mixture of grated lime rind, crushed garlic, rosemary and plenty of black pepper. Roll up the joint and tie it tight.

Chop the onion, carrot and celery and spread over the bottom of a large baking dish. Set the pork on top and secure the rind over the meat. Pour in the sherry and water mixed together. Cover the meat with greaseproof paper, seal with foil and cook in a moderate oven at 350°F (180°C), Gas Mark 4, allowing 30 minutes to the pound.

When cooked, strain the juices and liquor into a saucepan and boil until reduced by one-third. While the liquid is reducing, slice the meat on to a large hot plate and decorate with a garnish of sliced melon and sliced lime.

Finally add the butter to the reduced sauce, whisk well and pour over the meat.

Ann Long, The Count House Restaurant

Calories per serving: 375
Food value: Protein, vitamins and minerals. Low fat.
Note: Although the pork is quite high in calories, it is cooked without added fat and the sauce contains only a very small amount of fat in the form of butter. So the dish, as a whole, is well balanced.

STUFFED PORK TENDERLOIN
on a bed of vegetables

In this dish, the pork tenderloin is split and arranged in layers with a mixture of smoked ham and Lancashire cheese.

INGREDIENTS

3 pork fillets
8 oz (240 g) smoked ham
8 oz (240 g) Lancashire cheese
2 oz (60 g) carrots
2 oz (60 g) celery
10 fl oz (300 ml) medium sherry

SERVES 4-6

METHOD

Trim and prepare the pork fillets, removing all traces of fat and sinew. Cut each fillet lengthways, but leave one side intact; open out like the pages of a book and flatten.

Thinly slice the smoked ham and Lancashire cheese. Place half over the first pork fillet and lay the second fillet on top. Cover with the remaining ham and cheese and finally top with the last pork fillet. Tie the fillets together with string at regular intervals.

Chop the carrots and celery and scatter over the bottom of a baking tray. Place the tenderloin on top and pour over the sherry. Cover the dish with lightly buttered greaseproof paper and seal with foil. Cook in the oven at 375°F (190°C), Gas Mark 5 for 45 minutes or until the meat is tender.

To serve, remove the meat, take off the string and cut into slices. Strain the cooking juices and pour over the meat.

Ann Long, The Count House Restaurant

Calories per serving: 360
Food value: Protein, fibre, vitamins and minerals. Low fat.
Note: Lancashire cheese is recommended for this dish, but you can use any light coloured cheese that melts well.

ENGLISH HOUSE "KEBOBS"

"Kebobs" is the old English word for pieces of meat marinated and grilled on skewers. The herbs in the marinade impart a delicate, aromatic flavour to the meat.

INGREDIENTS

8 oz (240 g) beef fillet
8 oz (240 g) veal fillet
8 oz (240 g) pork fillet
2 lamb fillets (or "eyes"
 from 8 cutlets)

MARINADE
10 fl oz (300 ml) olive oil
juice of 2 lemons
1 green pepper, cut into
 8 pieces
1 onion, cut into 16 chunks
3-4 sprigs of thyme
1 heaped tsp chopped fresh
 marjoram
4 bay leaves
salt and black pepper

SERVES 4

METHOD

Chop the different meats so that you have eight cubes of each. Mix together the ingredients for the marinade and allow the meat to steep in it overnight.

Lightly oil four skewers and thread as follows: beef, onion, veal, green pepper, lamb, onion, pork, bay leaf, pork, onion, lamb, green pepper, veal, onion, beef. Push close together and grill over a medium heat for 8-10 minutes, turning two or three times. Baste with the marinade, using sprigs of thyme as a brush. Serve on a rice pilau with spicy tomato sauce or lemon wedges.

Liam Barr, The English House

Calories per serving: 465
Food value: Protein, vitamins and minerals. Low fat.

POULTRY AND GAME
Introduction

We use the term "poultry" for all kinds of birds that are bred commercially for the table, for example chickens, ducks and turkeys. "Game" generally refers to any animal that is hunted both for sport and food, such as *wild* duck, pheasant, partridge, hare and venison. There are also a few birds and animals that are farmed, but still count as game, such as rabbits and quail.

THE VIRTUES OF POULTRY AND GAME
Both poultry and game are high in protein and relatively low in fat, which makes them nutritious and attractive to anyone wishing to reduce their fat intake. They also make very good eating, which is why more and more people are buying poultry and game instead of red meat (which can be short on flavour and high in fat and protein).

POULTRY
There was a time when chicken was a luxury food, but now it's one of our most common sources of protein. When buying chicken, try to seek out fresh, free-range birds, because their flavour is infinitely superior to that of battery-reared chickens.

Poultry can be cooked in any number of ways – poached, grilled, roast, etc. – and is extremely versatile. It's worth remembering that most of the fat resides under the skin, which can be removed before cooking, or pricked to allow the fat to drain out. This is particularly important with fatty birds such as duck and goose.

GAME
Wild game is full of natural flavour and offers a vast range of possibilities for the adventurous cook. Many types are only available for a few months each year because of restrictions on hunting and shooting, so make full use of them when they appear in the shops.

The main problem with game is that it tends to be rather dry unless cooked very carefully. In general young game is best grilled or roasted, while other slower methods of cooking suit older game. All game benefits from hanging, which brings out its true flavour and makes it more tender.

STEAMED CHICKEN AND AVOCADO
with tarragon and vermouth sauce

Steaming helps to bring out the natural flavour of the chicken and avocado, while the sauce provides richness and fragrance.

INGREDIENTS

1 ripe avocado
juice of ½ lemon
4 chicken breasts, about
  8 oz (240 g) each
1 tsp chopped shallots
1 tsp chopped fresh
  tarragon
4 oz (120 g) butter*
8 fl oz (240 ml) vermouth
16 fl oz (480 ml) stock
8 fl oz (240 ml) cream
salt and pepper

GARNISH
4 tomato roses
4 sprigs of sweet marjoram

SERVES 4

METHOD

Quarter and peel the avocado and cut each piece lengthways into three slices. Brush with lemon juice to avoid discoloration.

Skin and bone the chicken breasts. Make three diagonal cuts in each one and insert the slices of avocado. Place in a steamer and cook gently for 9 minutes. Remove and keep warm.

Sweat the shallots and chopped tarragon in 2 oz (60 g) butter. Stir in the vermouth and reduce to a glaze. Add the stock and reduce by two-thirds. Finally incorporate the cream and reduce until the sauce coats the back of a spoon. Blend in the remainder of the butter, a little at a time, and season to taste.

Coat four plates with some of the sauce, place each breast to the right of centre and garnish with a tomato rose and sprig of sweet marjoram.

Andrew Mitchell, Greywalls

Calories per serving: 850
Food value: Protein, vitamins and minerals.
Moderate fat.
Note: Both the avocado and the vermouth contribute a large number of calories to this dish, in addition to the chicken, butter and cream.

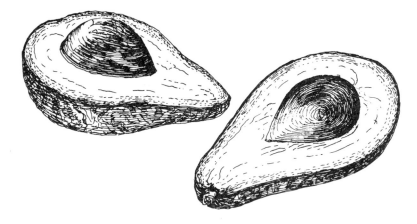

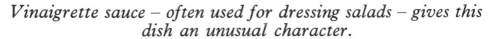

POACHED CHICKEN BREAST
with vegetables and vinaigrette sauce

Vinaigrette sauce – often used for dressing salads – gives this dish an unusual character.

INGREDIENTS

4 pieces asparagus
4 new baby turnips
4 new baby carrots
4 chicken breasts
2 pts (1 litre) chicken stock

SAUCE
3 fl oz (90 ml) wine vinegar
salt and pepper
2 tbs chopped shallots
5 fl oz (150 ml) hazelnut oil
5 fl oz (150 ml) olive oil
⅓ oz (10 g) fresh chives
⅓ oz (10 g) fresh chervil

GARNISH
⅔ oz (20 g) truffle (optional)

SERVES 4

METHOD

Peel and clean the vegetables and cook each briefly in boiling salted water until tender but still firm. Immediately refresh under cold running water for 1 minute. Drain and keep cool until needed.

Trim the chicken breasts, removing all fat, skin and bone. Heat the stock, bring to the boil and add the meat. Reduce the heat and poach gently for 10 minutes, making sure the stock does not boil. Remove the chicken breasts and keep hot.

Meanwhile prepare the vinaigrette sauce. Mix the vinegar and salt and pepper together, add the finely chopped shallots, then blend in the two types of oil. Mix well and check the taste.

To serve, reheat the vegetables quickly in the stock and cut the chicken into very thin slices. Arrange the chicken on each plate in the shape of a fan. Decorate the rest of the plate with the vegetables. Add the chopped herbs to the vinaigrette sauce and use it to coat the chicken. Garnish each with a slice of truffle.
Pierre Chevillard, Chewton Glen Hotel

Calories per serving: 360
Food value: Protein, fibre, vitamins and minerals. Low fat.
Note: The only fat in this dish comes from the oils used in the vinaigrette sauce, so the result is light and delicate.

ROAST POUSSIN
on raspberry butter sauce

A very simple, yet sophisticated dish with a sauce made from raspberry vinegar, butter and chicken stock.

INGREDIENTS

4 × 14 oz (420 g) poussin
 (baby chicken)

SAUCE
6 oz (180 g) raspberries
2 dsp white wine vinegar
10 fl oz (300 ml)
 chicken stock
6 oz (180 g) unsalted
 butter*
salt and pepper

SERVES 4

METHOD

Steep the raspberries in vinegar overnight. Put the soaked raspberries and vinegar into a thick-bottomed pan with the stock, and reduce. Whisk in the butter slowly. Pass through a fine sieve to remove all the raspberry pips and season to taste.

Roast the poussin in a hot oven for 30 minutes until golden brown. To serve, separate the legs and breasts of each bird, and arrange on the plate with the sauce. Alternatively serve whole.

Richard Sandford, Milton Sandford Restaurant

Calories per serving: 400
Food value: Protein, fibre, vitamins and minerals. Low fat.

INVOLTINI DI POLLO

In this dish boned chicken legs are rolled around a stuffing.

INGREDIENTS

2 oz (60 g) butter*
4 cloves garlic, crushed
4 oz (120 g) ham, cooked
 and diced
2 tbs chopped parsley
8 oz (240 g) breadcrumbs
12 oz (360 g) tomatoes,
 fresh or tinned
1 tsp dried oregano
salt and pepper
2 eggs
6 chicken legs

GARNISH
freshly chopped parsley

SERVES 6

METHOD

Melt the butter in a pan, add the garlic and cook slowly. Mix in the ham, parsley and breadcrumbs. Remove from the heat and cool. Sieve the tomatoes, add the oregano and season to taste. Warm through.

Add the beaten eggs to the stuffing, divide into six portions and shape each into a sausage. Lay the chicken legs on a board and make a horizontal cut into the thick side. Insert the stuffing and roll up. Arrange (with the open side underneath) in a casserole and pour over the tomato sauce.

Cover and cook in the oven at 300°F (160°C), Gas Mark 3 for 1½-2 hours. Serve sprinkled with parsley.

Vincenzo Iannone, La Fiorentina

Calories per serving: 470
Food value: Protein, fibre, vitamins and minerals. Low fat.

CHICKEN BREAST
with spinach and pine kernel stuffing

Use large, complete chicken breasts for this dish so that they can be neatly stuffed with the spinach and pine kernels.

INGREDIENTS

6 *chicken breasts*
8 *oz (240 g) spinach*
1 *oz (30 g) butter**
2 *oz (60 g) pine kernels*
salt and pepper
5 *fl oz (150 ml)*
 white wine
5 *fl oz (150 ml) cream*

SERVES 6

METHOD

Trim the chicken breasts, removing skin, bone and all traces of fat. There will be a pocket between the fillets; deepen this slightly to contain the stuffing, but do not cut right through the meat.

Strip the spinach leaves from the stalks and wash in three changes of water to remove all grit. Drain well. Melt the butter in a pan, add the spinach and cook until all the liquid has evaporated. Chop if the leaves are very large. Add the pine kernels and season to taste.

Pack some of the filling into each of the pockets in the chicken breasts. Fasten with toothpicks and tuck in the ends to produce a tight, rounded package. Brush with melted butter and sprinkle with a little salt. Bake in a hot oven at 400°F (200°C), Gas Mark 6 for 20 minutes.

Pour the pan juices into a saucepan and blend with the white wine and cream. Reduce until the sauce is smooth and syrupy. (Any left-over filling can be puréed and added to the sauce, giving it an attractive green colour.) Serve the chicken and sauce together.
Judy Knock, The Gentle Gardener

Calories per serving: 470
Food value: Protein, vitamins and minerals.
Moderate fat.

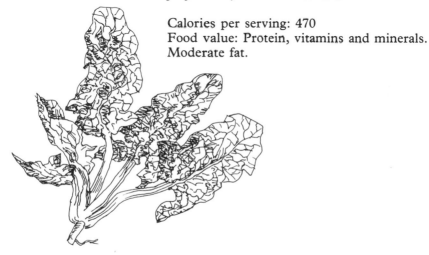

BREAST OF CHICKEN
with pigeon mousse stuffing

Stuffing one bird with the meat from another provides a good contrast in both colour and texture, as well as flavour.

INGREDIENTS

4 chicken breasts
2 oz (60 g) butter*
salt and pepper
3 fl oz (90 ml) Madeira
5 fl oz (150 ml)
  chicken stock
3 fl oz (90 ml)
  double cream

MOUSSE
3 pigeon breasts
1 egg yolk
3 fl oz (90 ml) cream
1 tsp chopped mixed herbs,
  e.g. tarragon, chives,
  parsley, chervil

GARNISH
4 tomato roses
4 sprigs of watercress

SERVES 4

METHOD

First prepare the mousse. Blend the pigeon breasts and egg yolk in a food processor, add the cream and pass the mixture through a fine sieve. Mix in the freshly chopped herbs. Put the mousse into a piping bag with a small plain nozzle.

Make a small incision in the top of each chicken breast with a long thin knife and carefully cut out a pocket leaving as small an entry hole as possible. Pipe in the mousse until the breast is plump and well shaped.

Melt a knob of butter in a sauté pan and when sizzling add the seasoned chicken breasts. Turn quickly to seal and leave plump side up. Add the Madeira and chicken stock, cover and cook slowly for 25 minutes. Remove the chicken and keep warm. Reduce the stock by half with the cream, whisk in the remainder of the butter and transfer to a clean saucepan.

Pour some of the sauce on to each plate. Thinly slice the chicken lengthways to show the dark pigeon mousse in the centre. Arrange on the sauce and garnish with a tomato rose and a sprig of watercress.
Michael Croft, The Royal Crescent Hotel

Calories per serving: 480
Food value: Protein, vitamins and minerals.
Moderate fat.

SESAME CHICKEN
with sweet and sour sauce

INGREDIENTS

3 lb (1½ kg) chicken,
  jointed
3 tbs plum sauce
1 tbs vinegar
2 cups chicken stock
⅓ cup dry sherry
1 tbs chopped green ginger
1 onion, quartered
5 oz (150 g) straw
  mushrooms
2 sticks of celery, sliced
7 oz (210 g) water
  chestnuts
7 oz (210 g) bamboo
  shoots, sliced
2 tbs cornflour
1 tbs sesame seeds

SERVES 6

METHOD

Pre-heat a moderate oven to 350°F (180°C), Gas Mark 4. Place the chicken in an ovenproof dish. Combine the plum sauce, vinegar, stock, sherry and finely chopped ginger and pour over the chicken. Cover and bake for 40 minutes.

Add the vegetables, return the dish to the oven and cook for a further 15 minutes. Remove the chicken and vegetables to a heated serving dish.

Thicken the remaining liquid with cornflour blended with a little water. Bring to the boil and simmer for 2 minutes; then pour over the chicken.

Sprinkle the chicken and vegetables with sesame seeds and serve hot with Chinese rice.

Calories per serving: 420
Food value: Protein and vitamins. Moderate fat.

AIGUILLETTES OF GUINEA FOWL
with whole garlic

INGREDIENTS

2 guinea fowl
2 dsp breadcrumbs
2 shallots
24 cloves garlic
1 oz (30 g) butter*
chopped parsley and
  thyme
salt and pepper
1 beaten egg
2 pts (1 litre) stock
1 onion
10 fl oz (300 ml) dry
  white wine
5 fl oz (150 ml) double
  cream
bouquet garni

SERVES 4

METHOD

Skin and remove the guinea fowl breasts, cut off the legs, bone them and open out flat. Put them on four sheets of greased foil. Make stock from the bones.

Chop up the scraps of meat from the carcasses with the breadcrumbs, finely chopped shallots and one clove of garlic, and soften in butter. Add the herbs, seasoning and egg. Spread the stuffing on each leg and roll up to form a sausage. Poach in seasoned stock for 45 minutes, then cool. Make sauce from the stock, onion, wine and 12 garlic cloves. Reduce, sieve and add the cream.

Brown the breasts in butter, cover and cook gently for 8 minutes. Simmer 11 garlic cloves in olive oil and stock with a bouquet garni. Serve as above.
Stephen Bull, Lichfield's

Calories per serving: 490
Food value: Protein, vitamins and minerals. Low fat.

SUPRÊME DE VOLAILLE
au pamplemousse

In this recipe the chicken breasts are marinated lightly in spirits before being cooked in white wine.

INGREDIENTS

4 chicken breasts
1 tbs arrowroot
1 fl oz (30 ml) gin
1 tsp Pontac sauce
  (see Note)
3 pink grapefruit
4 spring onions
3 tbs groundnut oil
4 fl oz (120 ml)
  white wine
1 clove garlic
1 tsp tomato purée
salt and pepper

SERVES 4

METHOD

Skin the chicken breasts and remove any excess fat. Mix the arrowroot with the gin and Pontac sauce and marinade the meat for up to 12 hours, turning frequently.

Carefully peel the grapefruit and remove 12 segments intact. Squeeze the remainder and collect the juice.

Finely chop the spring onions and sauté gently in oil for 5 minutes. Add the chicken (reserve the marinade) and cook for a further 5 minutes, turning once. Stir in the white wine, cover and simmer for 10 minutes, making sure that the mixture does not dry out. Remove the chicken and keep warm, also warm the grapefruit segments.

Add the marinade, chopped garlic and tomato purée to the pan and season to taste. Stir in the remaining grapefruit juice, bring to the boil and simmer until thickened.

Arrange the chicken on the plate, cover with a little of the sauce and decorate with three grapefruit segments. This dish goes well with *gratin dauphinoise* and stuffed tomatoes.

Paul and Muriel Wadsworth, Pebbles Restaurant

Calories per serving: 320
Food value: Protein, vitamins and minerals. Low fat.
Note: Pontac sauce is an old-fashioned ketchup made from elderberries. It has to be made at home. Sherry can be used as a substitute.

POACHED CHICKEN BREAST
with apple and clove sauce

In this recipe the breasts are stuffed with minced chicken and herbs or mushrooms before being poached in stock.

INGREDIENTS

6 chicken breasts
1 egg
2 tbs double cream
2 tsp mixed herbs, or 2 oz
  (60 g) mushrooms
salt and pepper
1 pt (600 ml)
  chicken stock

SAUCE

1 lb (½ kg) cooking apples
1 tsp sugar
6 cloves
knob of butter*
pinch of powdered clove

SERVES 4

METHOD

Skin and bone four of the chicken breasts, put each between a sheet of cling film and flatten slightly with a rolling pin.

Mince or blend the two remaining breasts (also skinned and boned), beat in the egg and the cream, then add the mixed herbs (or chopped mushrooms) and seasoning.

Put a quarter of the stuffing on the edge of each breast and roll up in cling film, twisting the ends tightly and tucking them underneath so that meat and stuffing are protected during cooking.

Lay the breasts in a roasting tin, cover with chicken stock and seal with foil. Bring to the boil then turn down the heat and simmer for 30 minutes, or oven-poach at 375°F (190°C), Gas Mark 5 for 45-50 minutes.

Meanwhile, stew the chopped cooking apples with sugar, a minimal amount of water and the cloves until really soft. Press through a sieve to obtain a smooth purée and stir in a knob of butter. Taste and add a little powdered clove to accent the spicy flavour if necessary, without making it overpowering.

Remove the chicken from the stock, unwrap and serve with the sauce.

Jean Butterworth, White Moss House

Calories per serving: 380
Food value: Protein, fibre and vitamins. Low fat.

CHICKEN SATAY
with peanut sauce

Satay – strips of meat marinated and grilled on skewers – is a classic Malaysian speciality, well-known in the West.

INGREDIENTS

4 chicken breasts

MARINADE
2 tbs light soya sauce
2 cloves garlic, chopped
2 tbs sunflower oil
1 tsp brown sugar
1 tsp lemon juice
pinch of ground ginger
$\frac{1}{4}$ tsp salt

SAUCE
4 cloves garlic
4-5 spring onions
4 tbs sunflower oil
8 oz (225 g) peanut
  butter, crunchy
3 dsp light soya sauce
3 dsp brown sugar
1 tbs lemon juice
2 oz (60 g) creamed
  coconut
sweet chilli sauce

TO SERVE
yogurt
cucumber
spring onions

SERVES 4

METHOD

Mix together the ingredients for the marinade, making sure that the sugar is completely dissolved.

Soak 12 thin bamboo skewers in water to prevent charring while cooking. Bone and skin the chicken breasts, cut each into six thin strips and thread two on to each skewer. Put into a large dish, pour over the marinade and allow to stand for 30 minutes at room temperature (or 4 hours in the refrigerator).

To make the sauce, lightly brown the chopped garlic and spring onions in oil. Add the peanut butter, light soya sauce, brown sugar and lemon juice and mix well.

Dilute the creamed coconut until it is the consistency of milk. Mix together two parts coconut to one part peanut mixture and add chilli sauce to taste. (The sauce thickens very quickly, so if you need to keep it warm, it may be necessary to dilute it with water before serving.)

Grill the chicken under a high heat, turning frequently, for about 8 minutes until crisp and brown on the outside, but soft and succulent inside. Serve with a bowl of peanut sauce for dipping, some yogurt with finely diced cucumber and spring onions.

Christopher Bradley, Mr Underhill's Restaurant

Calories per serving: 270
Food value: Protein, fibre, vitamins and minerals.
Low fat.

Note: The quantities listed above will be sufficient for a main course, particularly if the dish is served with rice, noodles or a salad. If you want to serve it as a starter, simply halve the quantity of meat, but use the same amount of marinade and sauce.

Very lean beef, pork or lamb can be substituted for chicken, although they are considerably higher in calories.

Traditionally satay is grilled over charcoal, but a simple domestic grill can be used, as in this recipe, if the meat has been marinated first.

127

ESCALOPES OF TURKEY
with prunes

A variation of the classic French provincial speciality which combines pork noisettes with prunes and Vouvray wine.

INGREDIENTS

1 lb (½ kg) large prunes
  (Californian)
½ bottle fruity white wine
salt and pepper
4 large slices turkey breast
1 tbs butter*
2 tbs redcurrant jelly
juice of ½ lemon
8 fl oz (240 ml) whipping
  cream

SERVES 4

METHOD

Soak the prunes for a few hours (or overnight) in the wine, then cover and cook very slowly in the oven for at least 1 hour until tender.

Season the slices of turkey breast (which should be cut thin) and fry in butter for 2-3 minutes each side, using a large, heavy-bottomed pan. When lightly browned remove the meat and keep warm.

Drain any excess fat from the pan, then pour in the juice from the prunes, let it reduce and bubble until you have about ¼ pt (150 ml) remaining. Stir in the redcurrant jelly and the lemon juice. Finally stir in the cream, a little at a time, letting it bubble and thicken. (You may not need to add all the specified amount of cream.) Judge when the sauce is starting to become thick and shiny, adjust the seasoning, then pour over the meat on a large dish.

Arrange the prunes around the turkey (don't cover them with sauce) and serve.

Colin White, White's Restaurant

Calories per serving: 400
Food value: Protein, fibre, vitamins and minerals. Moderate fat.
Note: Although this is a rich dish with a rating of 3, you can control the amount of cream you add quite precisely.

ROAST DUCK WITH COINTREAU
and ribbons of vegetables

The stock and sauce for this dish can be prepared 24 hours in advance and stored in the refrigerator until needed.

INGREDIENTS

2 oven-ready duckling,
  about 3½ lb (1¾ kg) each

SAUCE
4 oz (120 g) carrots
4 oz (120 g) onions
4 fl oz (120 ml) white
  wine
bouquet garni
2 fl oz (60 ml) Cointreau
2 fl oz (60 ml) fresh
  orange juice
2 oz (60 g) butter*

VEGETABLES
6 oz (180 g) carrots
4 oz (120 g) leeks
2 oz (60 g) sweet red
  pepper (optional)
2 oz (60 g) butter*
salt and pepper

SERVES 4

METHOD

Remove the breasts and legs from the ducks and put aside. Chop up the carcasses and brown in the oven at 400°F (200°C), Gas Mark 6. Remove, put into a large pan with the chopped carrots and onions and cook gently without browning. Pour off the excess fat.

Deglaze the pan with the white wine, blend well with the meat juices and reduce by two-thirds. Cover the bones and vegetables with water, add the bouquet garni and simmer for 1½ hours, skimming well. Strain the stock through a fine sieve and reduce to a syrupy consistency so that you end up with about 4 fl oz (120 ml) of stock. Add the Cointreau and orange juice, mix well and put aside.

Peel strips from the trimmed carrots until you reach the woody core, which should be discarded. Cut the leeks into similar strips and the red pepper into very fine ribbons. Melt the butter in a large pan, add the leeks and cook lightly for a few minutes. Then add the red pepper and finally the carrots. Season and put to one side.

Pre-heat the oven to 475°F (240°C), Gas Mark 9 and cook the duck on a rack over a roasting tin. The breasts will need 10-15 minutes, so that they are still slightly pink, while the legs should be cooked for 25 minutes. Allow the meat to "rest" between two hot plates for 10 minutes before carving.

Reheat the vegetables in the sauce and, at the last moment, stir in the butter, blending well.

Separate the thighs from the drumsticks and carve the breasts diagonally into four slices. Arrange the breast meat in a semi-circle on a hot plate with a drumstick and thigh at either end. Spoon the vegetables into the centre and coat the meat with a little sauce.

Christopher Bradley, Mr Underhill's Restaurant

Calories per serving: 580
Food value: Protein, fibre, vitamins and minerals.
Low fat.

129

ROAST MALLARD
with kumquats

The combination of wild duck and kumquats – tiny "gold oranges" from the Orient – is a new variation on a familiar theme.

INGREDIENTS

2 lb (1 kg) kumquats
2 onions
1 tsp chopped tarragon
2 bay leaves
salt and pepper
2 oz (60 g) butter*
6 young mallard
streaky bacon
4 fl oz (120 ml) stock,
  preferably mallard
2 fl oz (60 ml) Grand
  Marnier
1 tsp sugar (optional)

GARNISH
6 kumquats
sprigs of watercress

SERVES 6

METHOD

Wash the kumquats well, put aside six for the garnish and roughly chop the remainder (the whole fruit including the peel). Divide into two equal quantities.

Make a stuffing for the mallard. Mix one portion of chopped kumquats with the peeled and chopped onion, the chopped tarragon and bay leaves. Season with salt and pepper and toss lightly in melted butter. Clean and prepare the mallard and fill each one with some of the stuffing.

Cover the birds with some rashers of streaky bacon to prevent drying out during cooking, then roast in a hot oven at 400°F (200°C), Gas Mark 6, for 45 minutes until cooked through but still pink. Remove from the roasting tin and keep warm.

Add the remaining portion of chopped kumquats to the juices in the pan and simmer for 10 minutes. Then add the stock and Grand Marnier and reduce. Pass through a sieve and add a teaspoon of sugar if the sauce tastes rather too sharp.

Carve the breasts of the mallard and arrange on individual plates (use the legs and carcasses for casseroles and future stock). Pour over a little of the sauce and garnish each plate with a single kumquat and a sprig of watercress.
Baba Hine, Corse Lawn House Hotel

Calories per serving: 500
Food value: Protein, vitamins and minerals. Low fat.
Note: Mallard is the most common species of wild duck in Britain and Northern Europe and makes very good eating. However, other birds such as teal and widgeon can also be used for this recipe, and in the United States, the highly prized canvas back might be the best choice.

Kumquats are now quite common and widely available in the West.

ROAST DUCK BREAST
with blackberry sauce

Prepare the duck stock in advance from carcasses, vegetables, mushrooms, herbs and red wine, and remove all traces of fat.

INGREDIENTS

4 large duck breasts
3 oz (90 g) caster sugar
1 pt (600 ml) duck stock
12 oz (360 g) blackberries
10 fl oz (300 ml) water
2 tbs brandy (or port)
1 tbs honey
salt and pepper

GARNISH
fresh figs

SERVES 4

METHOD

Trim each duck breast, removing all excess fat, and score the skin so that any fat can run out. Sprinkle the meat liberally with caster sugar and seal each breast in a hot pan for a few seconds. Make sure that the sugar does not caramelize or burn.

Reduce the duck stock in a separate pan until it has a syrupy consistency. Meanwhile cook the blackberries in a stainless steel pan with the water and a little sugar. Simmer for 20 minutes and then strain through muslin. Reduce to a syrup.

Combine both the stock and the blackberry syrup in a separate pan. Flame the brandy and mix with the sauce.

Pre-heat the oven to 450°F (230°C), Gas Mark 8. Brush the duck breasts with honey, then cook for about 10 minutes so that the meat is cooked but still pink.

Slice the duck breasts, arrange on plates with the sauce and a garnish of fresh figs presented in the form of a flower.

Barbara Deane and Jonathon Hayes, The Perfumed Conservatory

Calories per serving: 480
Food value: Protein, fibre, vitamins and minerals. No added fat.
Note: There is very little fat in this dish, although it is quite sweet and fruity.

131

ROAST DUCK BREAST
with mange-tout and mild mustard sauce

A simple, refined dish that contrasts the rich succulence of duck with the light crispness of mange-tout.

INGREDIENTS

4 duck breasts
1 tsp chopped shallots
4 oz (120 g) butter*
16 fl oz (480 ml) game stock
8 fl oz (240 ml) cream
3 oz (90 g) Moutarde de Meaux
salt and pepper
6 oz (180 g) mange-tout

GARNISH
black or green grapes

SERVES 4

METHOD

Pre-heat the oven to 500°F (250°C), Gas Mark 10. Prick the skin of the duck before cooking so that the fat can run out. Roast for 5 minutes on each side, making sure that the meat remains slightly pink. Set aside and keep warm.

Sweat the finely chopped shallots in 2 oz (60 g) butter, add the stock and reduce by two-thirds. Stir in the cream and the mustard. Reduce again until the sauce is smooth and coats the back of a spoon. Incorporate the remainder of the butter a little at a time. Season to taste.

Top and tail the mange-tout and cook swiftly in a little boiling salted water so that they retain their crispness and flavour.

To serve, arrange the mange-tout in the shape of a fan on each plate. Thinly slice the duck breasts, fan out and lay on top of the mange-tout (one breast per person). Pour some of the sauce over half the plate and garnish with a few grapes placed around the duck.
Andrew Mitchell, Greywalls

Calories per serving: 570
Food value: Protein, fibre, vitamins and minerals. Moderate fat.

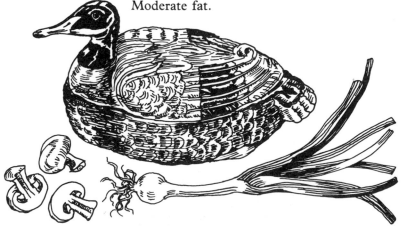

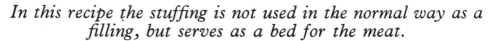

GRILLED DUCK BREAST
with chestnut stuffing and ginger

In this recipe the stuffing is not used in the normal way as a filling, but serves as a bed for the meat.

INGREDIENTS

4 duck breasts (with winglets)

SAUCE
10 fl oz (300 ml) ginger wine
5 fl oz (150 ml) red wine
5 fl oz (150 ml) white wine
2 tbs brandy
6 oz (180 g) chestnuts (tinned)
6 oz (180 g) chestnut purée (tinned)
5 fl oz (150 ml) stem ginger syrup
4 tsp ground ginger
2 tsp ground mixed spice
1½ pts (900 ml) duck stock
salt and pepper

STUFFING
2 onions
1 oz (30 g) butter*
6 oz (180 g) chestnut purée (tinned)
2 oz (60 g) chestnuts (tinned)
1 oz (30 g) stem ginger
1 tsp ground ginger
1 tsp ground mixed spice
fresh breadcrumbs
1 egg

SERVES 4

METHOD

Remove the winglets from the duck breasts and roast in a hot oven to remove excess fat. Put into a saucepan with all the other ingredients for the sauce and cook for 2-3 hours until it acquires a good flavour. Strain through a fine sieve and skim off any excess fat. Adjust the seasoning and put to one side.

To make the stuffing, chop the onions and cook slowly in butter with the chestnut purée and whole chestnuts. Add the stem ginger and spices, then cook slowly for 10-15 minutes, mixing well. Remove from the heat and add enough fresh breadcrumbs to make a firm stuffing, then bind with a beaten egg.

Charcoal grill the duck breasts and finish off in a hot oven until cooked as required. Spread some of the warmed stuffing on to each plate and slice each duck breast on top. Pour over a little of the sauce and serve accompanied by a cucumber and tomato salad.
Robert Jones, Ston Easton Park

Calories per serving: 530
Food value: Protein, fibre, vitamins and minerals. Low fat.
Note: Both the sauce and the stuffing can be made in advance, and will keep well in a refrigerator for about one week.

"Experience, intuition and continuous adjustment during cooking are crucially important."
John Kenward

PARCELS OF BRAISED DUCKLING

Duck legs are used for this dish, stuffed with a traditional mincemeat made from beef, fruit and nuts, and topped with an apricot and ginger sauce.

INGREDIENTS

4 duck legs

STUFFING
4 oz (120 g) lean topside
2 oz (60 g) dried apricots
1 oz (30 g) flaked almonds
1 oz (30 g) sultanas
1 oz (30 g) stem ginger
2 fl oz (60 ml) rum
1 egg
salt and black pepper

SAUCE
2 oz (60 g) butter*
1 small onion
1 small carrot
1 celery stalk
1 small piece fresh root
ginger
2 tsp tomato purée
2 oz (60 g) flour
5 fl oz (150 ml) ginger
wine
1 pt (600 ml) chicken
stock
bay leaf
salt and black pepper
4 oz (120 g) dried apricots

GARNISH
sprig of parsley

SERVES 4

METHOD

Remove the bones and sinews from the duck legs (a good butcher will do this for you if you are not sure how to).

To make the stuffing, mince the topside and the dried apricots and mix with all the other ingredients. Stuff the mixture into the duck legs and sew up, using a trussing needle and strong butcher's string (leave a generous overhang of string on each leg so that it can be removed easily after cooking).

To make the sauce, melt the butter in a large saucepan and add the chopped vegetables and ginger. Cook for 6-7 minutes. Stir in the tomato purée and the flour, making sure that no lumps form. Then pour in the ginger wine very gradually along with the chicken stock. Season with the bay leaf and a little milled black pepper and leave to cook for 1 hour over a low heat.

Liquidize the sauce, adjust the seasoning and fold in the minced apricots. (If the sauce is a little too thick, dilute with ginger wine.)

Cook the duck parcels for 40-50 minutes at 400°F (200°C), Gas Mark 6, until they are a deep golden brown. Set the meat on a rack or trivet above the pan so that the fat can drain away during cooking.

Allow the parcels to rest in a warm place for 5-6 minutes, then remove the string and slice the meat on to warmed plates. Spoon over the apricot and ginger sauce and garnish with a sprig of parsley or a bouquet of herbs.

Liam Barr, The English House

Calories per serving: 700
Food value: Protein, fibre, vitamins and minerals.
Low fat.
Note: Duck is quite fatty and the meat contributes more than half the calories for this dish. The stuffing represents approximately 230 calories per serving.

PIGEON WITH BLACKCURRANTS

The preparation of a good pigeon stock, enriched with a pig's trotter, is an essential feature of this dish, which is light, gamey and fruity.

INGREDIENTS

4 pigeons
1 lb (½ kg) onions
2 oz (60 g) blackcurrants
1 pig's trotter
salt and pepper
½ oz (15 g) butter*

GARNISH
a few blackcurrants
sprigs of fresh parsley

SERVES 4

METHOD

Have the pigeons plucked and dressed. Carefully slice off the breasts and put to one side. Chop up the carcasses and put into a large saucepan with the chopped onions, a few blackcurrants and the split pig's trotter (which provides plenty of gelatine). Season and cover with water. Bring to the boil and simmer for about 1 hour until a good stock is obtained. Then sieve and reduce until the stock is well concentrated.

Skin the pigeon breasts and season with salt and pepper. Melt the butter in a pan, and when it is hot add the breasts together with a few blackcurrants. Turn several times and after a few minutes the breasts will be cooked, but still slightly soft to the touch. Remove from the pan and keep warm.

Mix the pan juices with some stock and a little butter, adjusting the volume and consistency of the sauce until it is smooth and thick.

Coat the plates with some of the sauce, thinly slice the meat and arrange on top. Finally toss together a few more blackcurrants and some freshly chopped parsley in the pan and use as a garnish.

John Kenward, Kenwards Restaurant

Calories per serving: 110
Food value: Protein, fibre, vitamins and minerals.
Low fat.

SAUTÉED PIGEON BREAST
with plum and mustard sauce

Use only the breasts of the pigeons for this dish, and turn the carcasses into stock or soup. Don't waste anything.

INGREDIENTS

4 pigeons
5 fl oz (150 ml) red port
2 tbs olive oil
8 rashers rindless bacon,
  long-back
1 tbs butter*

SAUCE
1 lb (½ kg) plums
5 fl oz (150 ml) red wine
3 tbs redcurrant jelly
1 tbs orange juice
1 tbs coarse-grain mustard
1 tsp ground cinnamon
2 cloves
pinch of powdered ginger
pinch of grated nutmeg

SERVES 4

METHOD

Clean and prepare the pigeons, remove the breasts and carefully take off all the skin and any fat. Mix together the port and olive oil and marinate the meat for a couple of hours.

Take out the breasts, wipe them and wrap each one in a rasher of rindless bacon. Tie with string and lightly sauté in a little butter until the meat is cooked but still slightly pink.

Prepare the sauce as follows. Wash the plums, slit them open and simmer gently in red wine until soft. Remove from the heat and stir in the redcurrant jelly, orange juice and mustard. Finally blend in the spices. Continue to simmer until the sauce is well amalgamated. Pass through a sieve.

To serve, coat four hot plates with a little of the sauce. Remove the string from the meat and slice on to the plates, allowing two breasts for each person.

Ann Long, The Count House Restaurant

Calories per serving: 160
Food value: Protein, vitamins and minerals. Low fat.
Note: Use fresh plums if possible, although in this recipe tinned plums make an acceptable alternative.

PHEASANT BREAST ON CHICORY
with redcurrant and marsala sauce

A useful dish for those who prefer to eat pheasant "off the bone". Try to use young hen birds if possible.

INGREDIENTS

4 pheasant breasts
8 oz (240 g) butter*
10 fl oz (300 ml) Marsala
8 oz (240 g) redcurrants
2 oz (60 g) sugar
12 fl oz (360 ml) game
  stock
salt and pepper
4 heads Belgian chicory
1 pt (600 ml) water
juice of 1 lemon

GARNISH
a few redcurrants

SERVES 4

METHOD

Trim the pheasant breasts and sauté lightly in 4 oz (120 g) butter until golden. Then cook for a further 5 minutes each side in the oven at 450°F (230°C), Gas Mark 8, making sure they are still pink in the middle. Keep warm.

Deglaze the roasting pan with Marsala and add the redcurrants. Cook over a high heat and reduce by two-thirds. Pass the sauce through a sieve. Add the sugar and game stock and reduce again until the liquid becomes syrupy. Incorporate the remaining butter a little at a time and sieve again if necessary. Season to taste.

Clean, wash and drain the chicory. Place in an oven-proof dish, add the water, lemon juice and a knob of butter. Cover with buttered paper and a lid. Bring to the boil and cook on the side of the stove or in the oven for 30-35 minutes.

To serve, fan out the braised chicory on the plates. Thinly slice the pheasant and arrange on top of the chicory. Finally pour the sauce over half of the pheasant and garnish with a few redcurrants.
Andrew Mitchell, Greywalls

Calories per serving: 300
Food value: Protein, vitamins and minerals.
Moderate fat.
Note: Although this dish contains a quantity of butter, the sauce contains no other fat.

SAUTÉED BREAST OF PHEASANT
with light orange sauce

*In this recipe, the sweetness of the light orange sauce provides
a vivid contrast to the rich, gamey pheasant.*

INGREDIENTS

4 pheasant breasts
juice of 1 large orange
½ oz (15 g) butter*

SAUCE

1 tbs caster sugar
2 tbs white wine vinegar
1 tbs orange marmalade
juice and zest of 1 orange
5 fl oz (150 ml) pheasant
  stock
salt and pepper

GARNISH

orange segments
sprigs of watercress

SERVES 4

METHOD

Skin the pheasant breasts, remove any fat and
marinate in orange juice for at least 4 hours in a cool
place (or overnight in the refrigerator).

Mix the sugar and wine vinegar in a small pan until
they begin to caramelize, then stir in the orange
marmalade and the juice and zest of the orange.

Drain and dry the pheasant breasts, then sauté in
butter for 3-4 minutes each side. Stir in a little of the
orange sauce, together with the pheasant stock, and
simmer until the meat is just cooked. Remove the
breasts and keep warm. Reduce the sauce in the pan
until it is thick and smooth.

Serve the pheasant coated with a little of the sauce
and garnished with orange segments and sprigs of
watercress.

Betty and Peter Saville, The Weavers Shed Restaurant

Calories per serving: 170
Food value: Protein, vitamins and minerals. Low fat.

ROAST GUINEA FOWL
with limes

Although guinea fowl are now farmed and reared commercially,
they can take on the flavour of wild game if properly hung.

INGREDIENTS

2 *guinea fowl*
⅓ *oz (10 g) butter**
1 *oz (30 g) shallots*
2 *fl oz (60 ml) red wine*
  vinegar
3 *oz (90 g) mushrooms*
1 *sprig of thyme*
4 *fl oz (120 ml) white*
  wine
2 *fl oz (60 ml) port*
4 *fl oz (60 ml) Madeira*
1 *pt (600 ml) chicken*
  stock
juice of 1 lime

GARNISH
1 *lime*
20 *redcurrants*

SERVES 4

METHOD

Flambé the guinea fowl to remove all traces of feathers and cut out the wishbone. Brush a small sauté pan with butter and cook the birds on their sides for 5 minutes over a high heat. Put aside the cooking fat produced by the birds. Transfer to a roasting pan and roast in the oven pre-heated to 450°F (230°C), Gas Mark 8, allowing 8 minutes for each side. Baste well.

Remove the guinea fowl from the oven, put the roasting juices to one side, cut off the legs and thighs and divide at the joint. Put the legs into a small dish and return to the oven for 5 minutes. Carve off the breasts intact and keep warm.

Chop the carcasses into small pieces and sweat in the cooking fat. Add the shallots and wine vinegar, reduce until dry, then mix in the mushrooms, thyme and white wine. Reduce by half, add the port and bring to the boil. Finally pour in the Madeira and chicken stock, bring to the boil again and skim off any impurities. Simmer for 10 minutes, pass through a sieve and reduce until you have a light, well-scented juice. Add 4 tbs roasting juices and lime juice to taste.

Peel the zest from the lime, cut into fine strips, blanch in boiling water for 10 minutes, then refresh under cold water. Sort through the redcurrants and wash. Cut the lime into segments.

To serve, place a thigh, leg and breast of the bird on each plate and warm in the oven for 2-3 minutes. Pour a little of the sauce around the meat and garnish with redcurrants, lime segments and zest (previously warmed). Put the rest of the sauce in a sauceboat.
Raymond Blanc, Le Manoir aux Quat' Saisons

Calories per serving: 220
Food value: Protein, vitamins and minerals. Low fat.

GUINEA FOWL
with spring onions and sweet herbs

*Use plenty of fresh herbs for this simple but effective dish,
and allow half a bird for each person.*

INGREDIENTS

2 guinea fowl
salt and pepper
bunch of "sweet" herbs,
 e.g. thyme, marjoram,
 parsley, chervil, etc.
1 large onion
8 spring onions
½ oz (15 g) butter*
juice of ½ lemon

SERVES 4

METHOD

First divide up the guinea fowl. Fillet the breasts from the birds, cut off the wings and remove the legs and thighs, which can be divided at the joint. Use the remainder of the carcass to make stock.

Cut a slit in the inside of the legs, rub with salt and pepper and insert some chopped herbs. Put the legs, thighs and wings into a well buttered oven-proof dish and cook at 400°F (200°C), Gas Mark 6 for about 25 minutes.

Line a separate dish with chopped onion and herbs and lay the breasts on top. Season and cook in a cooler part of the oven for 10-15 minutes, basting the skin several times.

To make the sauce, reduce the stock in a pan and add some of the juices from the meat, adjust the seasoning and cook until the sauce is smooth and syrupy.

Put a little of the sauce on each plate and arrange the wing and leg pieces of the guinea fowl on it. Cut the spring onions diagonally and toss lightly in butter with some more chopped herbs and lemon juice. Spread some of this mixture on each plate and top with strips of breast meat sliced lengthways. Decorate with a few sprigs of fresh herbs.

John Kenward, Kenwards Restaurant

Calories per serving: 160
Food value: Protein, fibre, vitamins and minerals.
Low fat.

QUAIL WITH APPLES
and Madeira sauce

Farmed quail are now widely available and can be eaten without hanging. Allow two of these small birds for each person.

INGREDIENTS

2 tbs vegetable oil
4 oz (120 g) butter*
8 quail
3 fl oz (90 ml) Madeira
6 fl oz (180 ml) chicken or
  veal stock
4 apples
juice of ½ lemon
2 pinches of caster sugar
black pepper
8 slices white bread

SERVES 4

METHOD

Heat the vegetable oil and half the butter in a large pan and sauté the dressed quails for about 3 minutes, turning from time to time. Cover the pan and cook for a further 5 minutes. Take out the quail and keep hot.

Deglaze the pan with Madeira, add the stock and bring to the boil. Return the quails to the pan, cover and leave to simmer for 8-10 minutes or until the birds are fully cooked.

In a separate pan melt the rest of the butter. Slice the apples, rub with lemon juice to prevent discoloration, and sauté over a high heat. Add the sugar, season with black pepper and continue to cook until golden brown and slightly soft, but still firm enough to handle.

Fry the slices of bread in butter until crisp brown on both sides. Drain on absorbent paper. Place the quails on the slices of fried bread, coat with the strained Madeira sauce and arrange the apples around them. The dish can also be decorated with fruit such as cherries, apricots and grapes.
Martin Hoefkens, Tarn End Hotel

Calories per serving: 230 + 150 for the fried bread.
Food value: Protein, fibre, vitamins and minerals.
Moderate fat.
Note: The pieces of fried bread can be omitted if you want a slightly lighter dish with less fat and fewer calories.

BRAISED SADDLE OF HARE
with fresh noodles and mustard sauce

*Hare makes excellent eating, although the skinning and
dressing of the animal is best left to a skilled butcher.*

INGREDIENTS

1 saddle of hare
1 pt (600 ml) red wine
1 tbs chopped shallots
½ oz (15 g) butter*
2 tbs whole-grain mustard
2 fl oz (60 ml) white wine
6 fl oz (180 ml) double
  cream

NOODLES

7 oz (210 g) strong white
  flour, sieved
1 oz (30 g) semolina
1 tbs vegetable oil
2 eggs
2 oz (60 g) spinach purée
pinch of salt

SERVES 2

METHOD

Trim and skin the saddle of hare and marinate in red
wine for at least 6 hours.

Meanwhile prepare the noodles. Sieve the flour and
mix with the semolina, then add the oil, eggs, spinach
purée and a good pinch of salt. Blend thoroughly until
you have a workable paste. Allow to rest for 20
minutes, then roll out very thin and cut into
ribbon-shaped noodles. When ready, these can be
cooked in boiling salted water until soft, but still firm.

Finely chop the shallots and sweat in butter. Stir in
the mustard and moisten with white wine. Finally add
the cream and reduce to a smooth sauce.

Drain and dry the meat and cut the saddle across to
make two portions. Braise in a hot oven at 400°F
(200°C), Gas Mark 6 for about 45 minutes, basting
from time to time with melted butter. The meat should
not be overcooked.

Carve slices from the saddle and arrange on top of
the noodles, surrounding the meat with the mustard
sauce.

Russell Allen, The English Garden

Calories per serving: 380 + 500 for the noodles.
Food value: Protein, vitamins and minerals.
Moderate fat.
Note: It's worth trying your hand at making fresh
noodles, although bought ones can be substituted if
necessary.

NOISETTES OF VENISON
with pears and broccoli mousseline

The combination of venison and pears is a current favourite with chefs, but the addition of broccoli makes this dish special.

INGREDIENTS

3 chestnuts
3 fl oz (90 ml) chicken
  stock
2 tbs caster sugar
1 small stick of celery
3 oz (90 g) broccoli
3 fl oz (90 ml) olive oil
salt and pepper
1 pear
juice of ½ lemon
2 knobs of butter*
3 noisettes of venison,
  about 2 oz (60 g) each
2 fl oz (60 ml) port
2 fl oz (60 ml) venison
  glaze

SERVES 1

METHOD

Skin the chestnuts, then cook gently in chicken stock with the caster sugar and celery until glazed.

Cook the broccoli swiftly in a minimal amount of boiling salted water. Drain and liquidize with the olive oil while still hot until well emulsified. Season with salt and pepper.

Peel the pear and sprinkle with lemon juice to prevent discoloration. Cut into three segments, taking care to discard the core. Gently roast in clarified butter until golden.

Pan-fry the noisettes of venison in clarified butter for a few minutes, turning once. Set aside and keep warm. Deglaze the pan with port and add the venison glaze and mix with the juices from the meat. Adjust the seasoning and pass through a sieve.

Arrange the broccoli mousseline in the centre of the plate and put three spoonfuls of sauce in a triangle around it. Set the noisettes on the sauce with the chestnuts. Arrange the pear segments in the spaces between the venison. Serve with a turnip gratin.
René Gaté, Les Semailles

Calories per serving: 400 + 500 for the mousseline.
Food value: Protein, fibre, vitamins and minerals.
Moderate fat.

NOISETTES OF VENISON
with port and cranberries

For this luxurious dish it is important to use the very best "eye" of the saddle of venison, and to cook it lightly.

INGREDIENTS

1½ lb (¾ kg) venison
2 oz (60 g) butter*
salt and pepper
4 fl oz (120 ml) stock
4 fl oz (120 ml) port
2 oz (60 g) cranberries

GARNISH
heart-shaped croutons
sprigs of fresh parsley

SERVES 4

METHOD

Trim the venison of all fat and sinews, and cut into 12 2 oz (60 g) noisettes. Sauté the venison in melted butter for a few minutes, turning once. Season lightly with salt and pepper, remove from the heat and keep warm.

Add the stock to the pan and reduce until it forms a syrup. Pour in the port and reduce again.

Cook the cranberries swiftly in equal quantities of sugar and port until they reach "popping point". Then strain off the liquid and add them to the sauce. Warm through. Pour a little of the sauce on to four plates and arrange the noisettes of venison on it. Garnish with heart-shaped croutons and sprigs of fresh parsley. Serve with a selection of lightly cooked vegetables.

Baba Hine, Corse Lawn House Hotel

Calories per serving: 400
Food value: Protein, vitamins and minerals. Low fat.

VEGETARIAN DISHES
Introduction

In recent years vegetarian food has taken on a new lease of life. Gone are the days when it was simply a conglomeration of wholemeal flour, pulses and dried fruit. Today's chefs can make vegetarian food as interesting, adventurous and imaginative as any other kind of cooking, and this new element of sophistication has helped to win over many people who want to enjoy top quality food.

THE RANGE OF VEGETARIAN COOKING
There are many kinds of vegetarians, some much stricter and more dedicated than others. At one extreme there are vegans who will not eat meat, fish or dairy products (including cheese and eggs) of any kind, while at the other there are people who simply don't want to eat meat.

In fact you don't need to be a vegetarian at all to enjoy vegetarian food, and the recipes in this section are meant to be as broadly based and appealing as possible to meat eaters and non-meat eaters alike.

Vegetarian dishes are becoming a standard feature of more and more restaurant menus, both as starters and main courses. Some are salads or unusual, but very simple dishes combining vegetables, fruit, nuts and herbs; others might be based on cheese or eggs. So readers should look through other sections of this book to find additional vegetarian recipes.

GOOD, HEALTHY VEGETARIAN FOOD
Now that chefs have shown the way to a more inventive approach to vegetarian food, it is likely that more people will favour this style of cooking. Although it would probably be an impossible task to convert hardened carnivores, vegetarian food has plenty of virtues: it is interesting, provides a new range of flavours and textures, is by and large based on fresh, natural ingredients, and can be highly nutritious. So it should appeal to anyone who is fond of good food.

RICOTTA AND DILL FLAN

Ricotta cheese contains less fat and fewer calories than many other cheeses, such as Cheddar, Double Gloucester and Stilton, which are commonly used in quiches and flans.

INGREDIENTS

PASTRY
2 oz (60 g) wholewheat
  flour
2 oz (60 g) self-raising
  flour
1 oz (30 g) cooking fat
1 oz (30 g) butter*

FILLING
8 oz (240 g) ricotta cheese
2 medium eggs
5 fl oz (150 ml) whipping
  cream
1 tbs freshly chopped dill
sea salt and black pepper

GARNISH
sprig of dill

SERVES 4

METHOD

First make the pastry. Mix the two types of flour together in a bowl, and rub in the fat and butter until you have fine crumbs. Stir in a little cold water and gently bind into a soft dough. Then leave in the refrigerator for at least 30 minutes.

Meanwhile, mix together the ricotta cheese, beaten eggs and whipping cream. Add the freshly chopped dill and season with salt and pepper.

Roll out the pastry and line four small loose-bottomed flan tins. Cover each with foil, so that the sides are protected, fill with dried beans and bake blind for 20 minutes at 350°F (180°C), Gas Mark 4.

The cases are then ready to be filled when needed. Pour the filling equally into the cases and bake at the top of the oven at 400°F (200°C), Gas Mark 6 for 20-30 minutes, until set and golden brown.

Remove from the flan tins, garnish with a sprig of fresh dill and serve with a crisp green salad.

Lin Scrannage, The Market Restaurant

Calories per serving: 455
Food value: Fibre, protein, vitamins and minerals. Moderate fat.

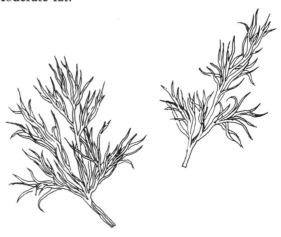

COURGETTES IN TOMATO SAUCE
with puff pastry cases

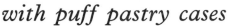

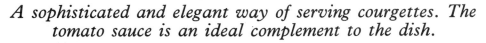

A sophisticated and elegant way of serving courgettes. The tomato sauce is an ideal complement to the dish.

INGREDIENTS

5 oz (150 g) puff pastry
2 lb (1 kg) very ripe
 tomatoes
1 oz (30 g) butter*
4 oz (120 g) coarsely
 chopped onion
3 cloves garlic
2-3 sprigs of parsley
14 basil leaves
1 sprig of fennel leaves or
 dill weed
1 bay leaf
pinch of powdered
 coriander
salt and freshly ground
 pepper
4 tbs white wine
1 lb (½ kg) small tender
 courgettes
1 egg yolk
1 tbs sesame seeds

SERVES 4

METHOD

Roll out the pastry and cut out four diamond shapes. Put on a baking tray rinsed in cold water and place in the refrigerator.

Dip the tomatoes quickly in boiling water and peel them. Cut them in half and remove the seeds. Reserve two halves and chop the rest roughly. Cook the tomatoes in ½ oz (15 g) butter with the coarsely chopped onion until the tomatoes fall apart (about 3 minutes). Add two garlic cloves, the parsley, six basil leaves, the fennel leaves and the bay leaf and continue to cook for about 15 minutes until the onion is soft. Strain the contents of the pan through a fine sieve. Season the resulting purée with the coriander, salt and pepper. Put in a small pan with the white wine and allow to thicken slowly over a gentle heat.

Cut the courgettes, unpeeled, into small strips. Cook them in the remaining butter, frying gently over a medium heat and turning constantly for about 3 minutes, until just cooked. Season with salt and pepper, four chopped basil leaves and the remaining clove of garlic, crushed. Put aside and keep warm.

Brush the puff pastry diamonds with the egg yolk and sprinkle with sesame seeds. Bake for 7-8 minutes in the oven at 475°F (240°C), Gas Mark 9 until golden brown. Allow to cool and then split in half.

Cut each reserved tomato half into four thin triangles. Pour the tomato sauce on to four plates and put the bottom half of each pastry case on top. Sprinkle the courgette batons over each pastry case and then cover with the top half of the case. Garnish each plate with two tomato triangles and one of the remaining basil leaves.

Anton Mosimann, The Dorchester

Calories per serving: 285
Food value: Vitamins and minerals. Low fat.

CARROT RING
with light tomato sauce

This delicate savoury tart highlights the affinity between carrots, oranges and tomatoes.

INGREDIENTS

8 medium carrots
1 clove garlic
juice of 1 orange
2 fl oz (60 ml) double
  cream
salt and pepper
2 sprigs of fresh coriander
12 oz (360 g) puff pastry
1 large orange, sliced
1 egg
1 tbs milk
1 oz (30 g) butter*

SAUCE
1 lb (½ kg) ripe tomatoes
½ oz (15 g) butter*
1 small onion
2 cloves garlic
2-3 sprigs of parsley
1 bay leaf
5 fl oz (150 ml) orange
  juice
2 fl oz (60 ml) white wine
bunch of fresh coriander

SERVES 4

METHOD

Peel and wash the carrots, cut into large chunks and steam until very soft. Add the finely chopped garlic and the orange juice, blend well and liquidize into a smooth purée. Simmer gently until nearly dry. Add the double cream and boil for 5 minutes. Season to taste, toss in some freshly chopped coriander and set aside to cool.

Roll out the pastry and cut into eight saucer-sized circles. Arrange thin slices of orange on to four of the circles, leaving a narrow border around the edge. Spoon over 2-3 tbs carrot purée and top with more thinly sliced orange.

Glaze the borders of the pastry circles with egg (beaten with 1 tbs milk), cover each tart with one of the remaining circles of pastry and seal. Glaze with the egg wash and leave for 10 minutes in a cool place. Cook at 425°F (220°C), Gas Mark 7 for 10 minutes.

To make the sauce, peel, de-seed and chop the tomatoes and cook in butter with the chopped onion until they fall apart. Add the crushed garlic, chopped parsley, bay leaf and orange juice and continue to cook for about 15 minutes until the onion is soft. Strain through a fine sieve, then add white wine to the sauce and thicken slowly over a gentle heat. At the last moment add the chopped coriander.

Serve the tarts brushed with a little melted clarified butter and accompanied by the sauce.

Paul and Muriel Wadsworth, Pebbles Restaurant

Calories per serving: 280
Food value: Fibre, vitamins and minerals. Low fat.

SORREL AND RED ONION TART

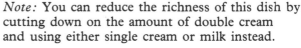

The combination of sharp, acidic sorrel and mellow cooked red onions is both colourful and unusual. This recipe can easily be adapted for individual tartlets.

INGREDIENTS

8 oz (240 g) shortcrust
  pastry
5 oz (150 g) butter*
2½ lb (1¼ kg) red onions
8 oz (240 g) sorrel leaves
salt and pepper
3 large eggs
15 fl oz (450 ml) double
  cream
pinch of grated nutmeg

SERVES 6-8

METHOD

Line a large deep flan ring with shortcrust pastry, prick the base and bake blind at 400°F (200°C), Gas Mark 6. After 20 minutes, remove and brush the base and sides of the flan with beaten egg. Return to the oven and bake for a further 6-7 minutes.

Melt 4 oz (120 g) butter in a pan with a tight fitting lid. Add the peeled and finely sliced red onions and cook slowly for 30-40 minutes stirring from time to time.

Remove the stalks from the sorrel leaves, wash well and cook in a separate pan with a knob of butter, stirring constantly with a wooden spoon. Press down, but do not allow the leaves to burn. Cook until you have a thick green purée.

Stir the sorrel into the onions and adjust the seasoning. Spread this mixture over the base of the cooked flan ring.

Make a custard by beating together the eggs and the cream, season with salt, pepper and nutmeg and pour over the onions. Bake at 325°F (170°C), Gas Mark 3 for 45-55 minutes until the custard has set. Brush the surface with melted butter and serve with a crisp green salad which includes fresh sorrel leaves.
Liam Barr, The English House

Calories per serving: 620
Food value: Protein, vitamins and minerals.
Moderate fat.
Note: You can reduce the richness of this dish by cutting down on the amount of double cream and using either single cream or milk instead.

149

FILO PASTRY "FRYING PANS"
with wild mushrooms and vegetables

In this recipe, delicate sheets of filo pastry are fashioned to form edible pans that contain the vegetables.

INGREDIENTS

10 sheets filo pastry
5 oz (150 g) unsalted
butter*, clarified
1 shallot
4 oz (120 g)
wild mushrooms, e.g.
1 oz (30 g) each of
chanterelles, oyster
mushrooms, wood
hedgehog mushrooms
and horns of plenty
assorted young vegetables,
e.g. carrots with foliage,
asparagus tips,
mange-tout, French
beans, broccoli,
courgettes, leeks,
cauliflower
salt and black pepper

GARNISH
1 oz (30 g) truffle
4 cherry tomatoes

SERVES 4

METHOD

Cut two of the pastry sheets in half horizontally and keep the rest intact. To make filo pastry "frying pans", brush one whole pastry sheet with melted butter and fold in two. Place it in a small iron frying pan, mould it to the shape of the pan, and trim off the excess. Butter a half sheet, roll it up to make a "handle" and lay it partly in the pan but with a few inches extending up the real pan handle.

To secure the "handle", cover the "pan" area with another sheet, folded. Trim this to shape and prick all over with a fork. Brush once more with butter. Bake, without removing from the real pan, in a hot oven for about 12 minutes, or until crisp and brown.

Detach the cooked "pan" gently from the real pan, and make three more "pans" in the same way. Five minutes before the last "pan" is finished, start cooking the vegetables. Add the finely chopped shallot to the remaining butter and cook in a large frying pan over gentle heat until softened. Increase the heat and add all the mushrooms (washed, dried and sliced). Cook for $1\frac{1}{2}$ minutes and then add the other vegetables (trimmed to similar sizes and blanched). Stir fry until heated through, then season.

Reheat the pastry "frying pans" in a warm oven for 3 minutes. Place them gently on plates. When the vegetables are ready, check the seasoning and arrange them in the pans. Top with truffle julienne and tomatoes.
Antony Worrall-Thompson, Ménage à Trois

Calories per serving: 200
Food value: Fibre, vitamins and minerals. Low fat.
Note: Antony Worrall-Thompson suggests that this dish be accompanied by wild mushroom sauce, served separately.

MUSHROOM AND CARROT GÂTEAU
with Gruyère cheese

If you cannot obtain wild mushrooms for this dish, use large cultivated ones.

INGREDIENTS

2 oz (60 g) celeriac
2 shallots
1 tbs olive oil
6 oz (180 g) mixed wild
 mushrooms
1 sprig of thyme
1 egg
8 oz (240 g) carrots
10 fl oz (300 ml)
 vegetable stock
juice of 1 lemon
1 oz (30 g) brown sugar
1 oz (30 g) butter*
salt and pepper
2 oz (60 g) Gruyère
 cheese
chopped chervil or parsley
1 egg

SERVES 4

METHOD

Peel the celeriac and cut into very small cubes. Finely chop the shallots. Fry both in hot olive oil for 1 minute. Clean and chop the mushrooms and cook separately with the thyme until all the moisture has evaporated. Allow to cool a little, then add the celeriac and shallots, plus one beaten egg. Blend well.

Slice the carrots and boil in vegetable stock with the lemon juice, brown sugar, butter and seasoning until the liquid is reduced to a syrup. Add the grated Gruyère cheese, finely chopped herbs, and one beaten egg. Blend well.

Butter four individual moulds and spoon the carrot mixture into each one until half full. Then top with the mushrooms. Put the moulds into a *bain-marie*, cover with foil and bake in the oven at 400°F (200°C), Gas Mark 6 for 20-25 minutes.

Turn out and serve on individual plates surrounded by a fresh tomato sauce flavoured with tarragon.

Robert Thornton, The Moss Nook Restaurant

Calories per serving: 245
Food value: Protein, fibre, vitamins and minerals.
Low fat.

STUFFED MUSHROOMS
with brown rice

Serve this wholesome vegetarian dish either as a starter or as a main course.

INGREDIENTS

1 lb (½ kg) large flat
mushrooms
1 tbs sunflower oil
4 oz (120 g) onions
1 carrot
2 cloves garlic
4 oz (120 g) long-grain
brown rice
1 pt (600 ml) vegetable
stock
salt and pepper
handful chopped herbs,
e.g. parsley, lemon balm
2 oz (60 g) hazelnuts
(or almonds)
1½ oz (45 g) fresh
breadcrumbs
½ oz (15 g) Parmesan
cheese
zest of ½ lemon

SERVES 4

METHOD

Wipe the mushrooms clean with a damp cloth, remove the stalks and put to one side. Heat the sunflower oil, add the finely chopped onions, grated carrot and sliced mushroom stalks and cook over a moderate heat until lightly browned. Add the chopped garlic, stir and remove from the heat.

Cook the brown rice in stock, with a little salt, until just tender. Wash and drain the rice well, then mix in the chopped herbs and nuts, together with the onion, carrot and mushroom stalks. Season well. Pile a little of this stuffing on to each flat mushroom, pressing carefully into shape with a spatula.

Mix the breadcrumbs with the grated Parmesan cheese and lemon zest and sprinkle over the mushrooms. Bake in a moderate oven at 350°F (180°C), Gas Mark 4 until brown and bubbling.
Colin White, White's Restaurant

Calories per serving: 260
Food value: Protein, fibre, vitamins and minerals. Low fat.
Note: This recipe will serve four people as a main course. A non-vegetarian version can be made by adding 3 oz (90 g) chopped bacon to the onion and mushroom stalks, and by using meat rather than vegetable stock.

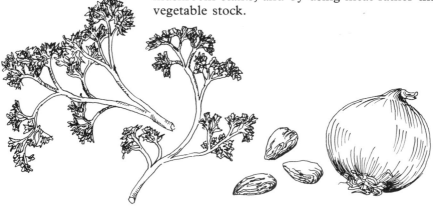

BUDDHIST'S DELIGHT

Sometimes known as "Monk's Mixed Vegetables", this splendid dish originally had great religious significance, with each ingredient chosen for its symbolic effect.

INGREDIENTS

1-2 oz (30-60 g) Chinese "hair seaweeds"
2-3 tiger lily stems ("golden needles")
1½ oz (45 g) wood ear fungi
2 oz (60 g) pea-starch noodles
2 cakes bean curd
vegetable oil for frying
4-8 oz (120-240 g) broccoli
2 young carrots
2-3 oz (60-90 g) bamboo shoots
4 oz (120 g) aubergine
4-8 oz (120-240 g) Chinese cabbage
4 oz (120 g) celery
2 tbs soya sauce
1½ tbs soya paste
1½ tbs oyster sauce
1 pt (600 ml) good stock
2 tbs dry sherry
2 tsp sesame oil

SERVES 6-8

METHOD

Soak the "seaweeds", tiger lily stems, wood ears and pea-starch noodles separately in water for 10 minutes and drain. Cut one bean curd into eight pieces, deep-fry for 4 minutes and drain. Cut the broccoli, carrots, bamboo shoots and aubergine into bite-size pieces, deep-fry for 3 minutes and drain. Cut the cabbage into small slices, and the celery into strips.

Heat 5 tbs oil in a large casserole. When hot add all the dried, soaked and drained vegetables, as well as the fresh vegetables. Turn them in the oil. Sprinkle with soya sauce, soya paste and oyster sauce. Continue to turn, and finally add the two cakes of bean curd, stock and transparent noodles. Stir, turn and mix all the ingredients together. When they come to the boil, reduce the heat to low and allow the contents to simmer gently for 25 minutes. Sprinkle the top with sherry and sesame oil.

Serve by bringing the casserole to the table, so that the diners can help themselves. The dish should be accompanied by large quantities of rice.

Kenneth Lo and Kam-Po But, Ken Lo's Memories of China

Calories per serving: 150
Food value: Protein, fibre, vitamins and minerals. Low fat.
Note: All the ingredients for this (and other Chinese recipes) are widely available in Oriental delicatessens.

PINE KERNEL AND PEPPER LOAF

An attractive, yet simple dish that is suitable for a vegetarian dinner party. It can be accompanied by a piquant or spicy tomato sauce.

INGREDIENTS

2 sticks celery
1 red pepper
1 green pepper
1 small onion
2 tbs vegetable oil
2 oz (60 g) wholemeal
  breadcrumbs
4 oz (120 g) pine kernels
2 oz (60 g) cashew nuts
2 oz (60 g) ground
  almonds
1 tsp dried marjoram
3 eggs
5 fl oz (150 ml) milk
1½ oz (45 g) butter*
salt and pepper

GARNISH
bunches of watercress

SERVES 4

METHOD

Finely chop the celery; de-seed and chop the peppers; peel and chop the onion. Heat the vegetable oil in a large pan and sauté the vegetables until they are quite soft. Strain and put into a large bowl.

Add the wholemeal breadcrumbs, pine kernels, chopped cashew nuts, ground almonds and dried marjoram. Mix well, then incorporate the beaten eggs and milk, together with the melted butter. Season with salt and pepper to taste.

Line a large loaf tin with lightly oiled silicone paper, spoon in the mixture and level off. Bake in a moderate oven at 375°F (190°C), Gas Mark 5 for 40-50 minutes until the loaf is golden brown and firm to the touch.

Allow to cool before turning out. When ready to serve, carve into thick slices and garnish with small bunches of fresh watercress.

Robert Jackson, Herbs Restaurant

Calories per serving: 530
Food value: Protein, fibre, vitamins and minerals. Low fat.
Note: This dish contains 2 oz (60 g) mixed nuts per serving, so it is rather high in calories; in fact over half the total calories come from the nuts.

A fresh tomato sauce, flavoured with herbs or spiced with chilli, is a good accompaniment to the loaf.

Serve as a main course or, in smaller portions, as a starter.

AUBERGINE AND PEPPER CASSEROLE
with garlic butter

This casserole can be served as a vegetarian speciality or as a vegetable side dish with a meat main course.

INGREDIENTS

3 aubergines
salt and pepper
flour
1 tbs olive oil
1 oz (30 g) butter*
1 pinch of caster sugar
6 peppers (2 each of red, green and yellow)
knob of garlic butter

SERVES 4

METHOD

Cut the aubergines into slices and divide into halves or quarters. Sprinkle with salt and leave them until the juices run. Drain, rinse thoroughly and pat dry with kitchen paper. Season and flour the slices lightly and fry briefly in olive oil and butter, stirring in the sugar at the same time.

De-seed the peppers, cut them lengthways into long strips, then halve.

Arrange the aubergines in layers in a shallow oven-proof dish and scatter the chopped peppers on top. Dot with garlic butter, cover the dish and bake for about 30 minutes at 350°F (180°C), Gas Mark 4.

Jean Butterworth, White Moss House

Calories per serving: 130
Food value: Vitamins and minerals. Low fat.
Note: To make the garlic butter, simply crush 2 cloves of garlic, blanch in boiling water for 5 minutes and drain. Then crush and blend with 1 oz (30 g) creamed butter. Season to taste and use when required.

As it stands, this is a very straightforward dish consisting largely of peppers and aubergines. It can of course be varied, provided that you keep the contrast in colour and texture.

If you are serving this casserole as a vegetarian speciality in its own right, then a bowl of low-fat natural yogurt – perhaps mixed with some strips of cucumber – might be a suitable accompaniment.

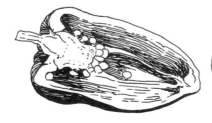

GALETTE D'AUBERGINES
with tomatoes and yogurt

Serve this light, refreshing dish as a starter or snack, or use it to accompany a main course such as roast lamb.

INGREDIENTS

1½ lb (¾ kg) aubergines
olive oil for frying
3 oz (90 g) onions
1½ lb (¾ kg) tomatoes
2 cloves garlic
salt and black pepper
1 tsp chopped parsley
1 tsp sugar
15 fl oz (450 ml) low-fat
 yogurt
2 tsp cornflour

SERVES 4

METHOD

Cut the aubergines into thin slices and fry in the oil so that they are brown on both sides. Drain well on kitchen paper.

Finely chop the onions and soften them in a little oil in a frying pan. Peel, de-seed and chop the tomatoes, and add the chopped flesh to the pan, together with the chopped garlic. Cook quickly.

Remove the tomatoes and onions and reduce the remaining liquid to almost nothing. Stir in the tomato mixture, together with salt and pepper, freshly chopped parsley and sugar to taste.

Stabilize the yogurt by mixing it with the cornflour and heating it very gently in a pan, stirring constantly. When it starts to boil, lower the heat to a minimum and allow to stand for 10 minutes.

Line one large dish (or four individual bowls) with a layer of aubergines, followed by tomato *concassé* and yogurt. Continue in layers, finishing with a layer of aubergines. Cover and bake in a moderate oven at 350°F (180°C), Gas Mark 4 for 15-30 minutes until thoroughly cooked. Turn out or serve direct from the dish.

Colin White, White's Restaurant

Calories per serving: 150
Food value: Vitamins and minerals. Low fat.

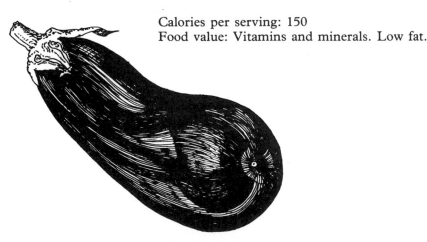

RATATOUILLE CHINOISE

An interesting variation on a classic European dish. In this recipe the addition of Chinese ingredients, such as hoisin sauce and black beans, produces an unusual result.

INGREDIENTS

2 medium onions
6 medium tomatoes
3 medium courgettes
3 small aubergines
1 each medium red and
  green peppers
2 small chilli peppers
2 spring onions
1½ tbs black beans
5-6 tbs vegetable oil
1 tsp salt
pepper (to taste)
½ tbs yellow bean sauce
1½ tbs hoisin sauce
1½ tbs soya sauce
3 tsp red bean curd cheese
5 fl oz (150 ml) good stock
4-6 tbs red wine
3 tsp sugar
3 tsp wine vinegar
2 tsp sesame oil

SERVES 6-7

METHOD

Cut the onions into thin slices, and the tomatoes into quarters. Cut the courgettes and aubergines into small wedge shaped pieces (including the skin), and the peppers into small strips. Chop the chilli peppers coarsely, and shred the spring onions into shavings. Soak the black beans in water for 10 minutes. Drain and chop coarsely.

Heat the oil in a frying pan. When hot, add the tomatoes, courgettes, aubergines, peppers, onions, chilli peppers and black beans. Turn them in the oil and sprinkle them with salt and pepper. Continue to stir fry for 3 minutes. Add all the sauces and the red bean curd cheese. Bring the contents to the boil, then reduce the heat to low and simmer gently for 9-10 minutes. Add the stock, together with the wine and sugar. Continue to cook, stirring gently for 10 minutes. Add the vinegar, sesame oil and spring onion shavings.

Serve with rice and either in small individual bowls or in a large serving bowl for the diners to help themselves.
Kenneth Lo and Kam-Po But, Ken Lo's Memories of China

Calories per serving: 150
Food value: Fibre, vitamins and minerals. Low fat.

MILLED NUTS IN SPINACH
with Roquefort sauce

In this recipe, the spinach acts as a wrapping for the mixture of roasted and milled nuts, cream and eggs.

INGREDIENTS

8 oz (240 g) spinach
2 oz (60 g) shelled
  hazelnuts
2 oz (60 g) shelled cashew
  nuts
2 oz (60 g) shelled walnuts
1 shallot
2 oz (60 g) butter*
3 fl oz (90 ml) vegetable
  stock
1 egg
1 egg yolk
5 fl oz (150 ml) cream
salt and pepper

SAUCE
2 shallots
2 oz (60 g) butter*
5 fl oz (150 ml) dry white
  wine
8 fl oz (240 ml) vegetable
  stock
4 fl oz (120 ml) double
  cream
3 oz (90 g) Roquefort
  cheese
salt and pepper

GARNISH
8 walnuts halved

SERVES 4

METHOD

Sort through the spinach leaves, wash well and blanch in boiling water for 1 minute. Refresh under cold water and spread out on tea towels. Generously butter four ramekin dishes. Remove the centre veins from the spinach, brush each leaf with melted butter and line the ramekins. Chill in the refrigerator.

Roast the hazelnuts and cashew nuts so that they are well browned. Roughly chop the walnuts. Put the hazelnuts and cashew nuts into a food processor and grind very finely.

Chop the shallot and sauté in butter until soft. Add the milled nuts and walnut pieces and mix well. Pour in the vegetable stock and cook until all the liquid has been absorbed. Beat the egg and egg yolk with the cream and mix thoroughly with the nuts. Season well.

Spoon the mixture into the lined moulds. Trim the spinach and loosely fold the edges over the top of the nut mixture. Place the moulds in a *bain-marie* and cover with dampened greaseproof paper. Cook in the middle of the oven at 350°F (180°C), Gas Mark 4 for 35 minutes.

To make the sauce, sauté the finely chopped shallots in butter until soft. Add the wine and stock and reduce by half. Strain the sauce through a sieve and return to the pan. Add the cream and bring to the boil. Whisk in the crumbled Roquefort cheese and season to taste.

Spread individual plates with the sauce, turn out a mould on to each one and garnish with halved walnuts.

Carol Trevor-Roper, Knights Farm

Calories per serving: 590
Food value: Protein, fibre, vitamins and minerals.
Moderate fat.

FRENCH BEANS WITH TARRAGON
and broad bean sauce

The combination of two kinds of beans – one whole, the other
puréed – gives this dish a special character.

INGREDIENTS

1 lb ($\frac{1}{2}$ kg) young broad
beans
1 potato
2 onions
$\frac{1}{2}$ oz (15 g) butter*
1 clove garlic
salt and pepper
1 tbs freshly chopped
tarragon
squeeze of lemon juice
8 oz (240 g) young French
beans

SERVES 4

METHOD

Chop the whole broad beans coarsely and cook gently
in water with the peeled and chopped potato and one
chopped onion. When the potato is soft, pass the
mixture through a sieve.

Chop the other onion and garlic, melt the butter in a
pan and lightly cook together. Stir in the broad
bean purée and adjust the consistency by adding water
and more butter if necessary. Season and toss in the
freshly chopped tarragon. Finish with a squeeze of
lemon juice and keep warm.

Cook the tailed French beans briefly in a little salted
water until just cooked but still crisp, then drain.

To serve, spread some of the sauce on to warm
plates and lay the French beans on top.

John Kenward, Kenwards Restaurant

Calories per serving: 100
Food value: Fibre, vitamins and minerals. Low fat.

CORAL CABBAGE

This is an extremely nutritious vegetable dish, which can be served as a side dish, but is most successful when made in quantity and served as a main course with rice.

INGREDIENTS

2½-3 lb (1¼-1½ kg)
  Chinese cabbage
2½ tbs red bean curd cheese
  (and sauce)
2½ tbs tomato purée
1 tbs light soya sauce
4 tbs vegetable oil
1-2 tbs winter pickle
  (optional)
salt and pepper
1-2 tbs butter*
1 cup good vegetable stock

SERVES 5-6

METHOD

Cut or tear the cabbage into pieces. Blend the cheese with the tomato purée and soya sauce.

Heat the oil in a large pan or wok. When hot add the pickle. Turn it in the oil a few times. Add all the cabbage, and sprinkle with salt and pepper. Turn the cabbage in the hot oil for a couple of minutes, until it is well coated with oil. Pour the cheese, tomato purée and soya mixture evenly over the cabbage. Turn the cabbage until it is well covered with the red sauce. Transfer the contents into a casserole. Top with the butter. Pour the stock over the contents. Put the casserole into a pre-heated oven at 350°F (175°C), Gas Mark 3 for 30-35 minutes. Serve in the casserole and with rice.

Kenneth Lo and Kam-Po But, Ken Lo's Memories of China

Calories per serving: 175
Food value: Fibre, vitamins and minerals. Low fat.

VEGETABLES AND SALADS
Introduction

Vegetables are a great source of pleasure and nourishment, but have suffered badly over the years from neglect and overcooking. The range now available, both home-grown and imported, is more extensive than ever before, so we should grasp every opportunity to try different types.

COOKING VEGETABLES
To bring out their flavour and retain as many nutrients as possible, vegetables should be very lightly cooked. Steaming is perhaps the best method, but boiling works well, provided you use very little water and don't cook the vegetables for too long. They should always remain colourful and crisp. Other methods that bring out the best in vegetables include stir-frying and lightly tossing in butter or oil. Baking and braising also have their uses, but deep-frying is best avoided (except for dishes such as Japanese tempura).

There has been a tendency in the past, not only to overcook vegetables, but also to use too much salt in their cooking. An excess of salt is not healthy and ruins the flavour of food, so use the salt cellar with care.

SERVING VEGETABLES
Many of the main courses in this book ought to be accompanied by a dish of vegetables, which, in most cases, is best prepared simply, but shouldn't be overshadowed by the centrepiece of the meal. In fact the traditional balance should be shifted so that more weight is given to vegetables. Serve a variety of different kinds in good quantities to provide nourishment and interest; providing wafer-thin courgettes and a solitary floret of broccoli is taking the refinement of *nouvelle cuisine* to extremes.

SALADS
Raw vegetables (and fruit) can be transformed into a variety of different salads, where the emphasis should be on colour, texture and lightness, with plenty of contrast. The possibilities and combinations are almost limitless: salads with vegetables, fruit, nuts, meat, offal, fish and so on, not to mention the variations in types of dressing and additional ingredients like herbs. Salads can be served at any point in the meal: as a starter, as an accompaniment to a main course, as a separate course in their own right (to refresh the palate) and even as a dessert.

YOUNG TURNIPS
with orange and parsley

A simple but imaginative dish which can be served as a starter or as an accompaniment to a main course.

INGREDIENTS

1 lb (½ kg) small young
  turnips
½ oz (15 g) butter*
1 small onion
juice of ½ orange
salt and pepper
freshly chopped parsley

SERVES 4

METHOD

Trim and clean the turnips, leaving a tuft or leaf stalk on each one. Slice them vertically into about five pieces. Melt the butter in a pan, add the finely chopped onion, sliced turnips and orange juice, plus a little water. Adjust the seasoning and cook briefly until the turnips are just beginning to turn soft and the sauce is slightly syrupy. Stir in plenty of freshly chopped parsley and serve at once.

John Kenward, Kenwards Restaurant

Calories per serving: 50
Food value: Fibre and vitamins. Low fat.

BAKED POTATOES SOUBISE

A nutritious and effective way of serving potatoes without too much fat. Useful as a snack or as a side dish.

INGREDIENTS

4 large potatoes
1 large onion
2 oz (60 g) butter*
6 leaves fresh basil
5 fl oz (150 ml) low-fat
  yogurt

SERVES 4

METHOD

Scrub the potatoes well and put them to bake in a moderate oven until cooked.

Meanwhile, chop the onion and sweat it in butter with the chopped fresh basil until almost transparent. Stir in the yogurt.

Slice the top off the baked potatoes and scoop out the middle. Put into a bowl, mash with a fork and mix with the onion and yogurt. Fill the potato skins and serve.

Allan Garth and Bernard Rendler, Gravetye Manor

Calories per serving: 235
Food value: Fibre, vitamins and minerals. Low fat.

"Food must look clean and attractive, and people should be able to see what they are eating. The decoration should not be too fussy."

162 Ann Long

POACHED ASPARAGUS
with orange sabayon sauce

Use tender plump asparagus for this dish, cut off the woody ends and peel each stick carefully from top to bottom.

INGREDIENTS

1 bunch asparagus, about
  1¼ lb (500 g) total weight
2-3 oranges
3 tbs white wine
1 shallot, chopped
4 green peppercorns,
  crushed
1 tbs double cream
3 oz (80 g) butter*
pinch of salt and cayenne
  pepper

SERVES 4

METHOD

Cook the peeled asparagus in salt water until soft, about 7-10 minutes.

Peel the skin of one orange very thinly with a potato peeler and cut the peel into small squares. Cook the pieces of peel in water for 3 minutes and then discard the water.

Squeeze the oranges into a saucepan and add the white wine, shallot and peppercorns. Boil for 8-10 minutes to reduce to 5 tbs of liquid. Strain the reduced liquid. Add the double cream and the butter. Then add the pieces of orange peel and season with salt and cayenne pepper.

Allow the asparagus to drain well, arrange on a plate and serve with the orange butter sauce.

Anton Mosimann, The Dorchester

Calories per serving: 275
Food value: Vitamins and minerals. Low fat.

PARSNIP PURÉE
with toasted pine kernels

A delicious purée that highlights the sweetness of parsnips without masking any of their natural flavour.

INGREDIENTS

1½ lb (¾ kg) parsnips
1 tsp salt
1 tbs double cream
1 tbs honey
pinch of mace
1 tbs butter*

GARNISH
sprinkling of pine kernels

SERVES 4

METHOD

Peel the parsnips, cut into chunks and cook in boiling salted water until soft, but not mushy. Purée in a liquidizer with the cream, honey, powdered mace and butter. Continue to liquidize until the purée is very smooth.

Toast the pine kernels by sprinkling on to a sheet of foil and putting under the grill for 2-3 minutes. Make sure they do not burn.

To serve, shape and purée into mounds using a tablespoon and sprinkle each portion with a few toasted pine kernels.

Peter Dixon, White Moss House

Calories per serving: 80
Food value: Fibre, vitamins and minerals. Low fat.

CELERIAC WITH GINGER

A subtle combination of flavours and textures, contrasting strips of celeriac and ginger.

INGREDIENTS

2 celeriac
1 oz (30 g) butter*
1 onion, chopped
1 clove garlic, crushed
1 oz (30 g) fresh ginger
pinch of mace
½ lemon, peeled and sliced
squeeze of lemon juice
salt and pepper

SERVES 4

METHOD

Peel and slice one celeriac and simmer in butter for 5-10 minutes with the onion, garlic, a few slices of ginger, the mace and lemon. Add water and boil until soft, then liquidize.

Peel and thinly slice the other celeriac and slice the rest of the ginger. Season and fry in butter with a squeeze of lemon juice until soft. Keep warm. Add water, butter and some of the purée to the pan, blending well to produce a thin sauce. Season to taste. Pour the sauce on to the plates and arrange slices of celeriac and ginger around it.

John Kenward, Kenwards Restaurant

Calories per serving: 180
Food value: Fibre and vitamins. Low fat.

CAULIFLOWER WITH SORREL SAUCE

A sharp sorrel sauce containing no flour makes an unusual and interesting alternative to the cheese sauce normally served with cauliflower.

INGREDIENTS

1 large cauliflower

SAUCE
6 sorrel leaves
knob of butter*
2 tbs dry white wine
8 fl oz (240 ml) cream
salt and pepper

SERVES 4

METHOD

Clean and prepare the cauliflower and break into neat florets. Steam until cooked but still firm.

Meanwhile make the sauce. De-stalk the sorrel leaves, chop finely and sweat in a little butter very briefly. Add the white wine and reduce. Stir in the cream, reduce again until the sauce is smooth and well blended, and season to taste. Do not boil or allow the sorrel and cream to stand for too long, otherwise the sauce may curdle. Coat the cauliflower with sauce and serve at once.

Peter Dixon, White Moss House

Calories per serving: 160
Food value: Fibre, vitamins and minerals. Moderate fat.

SPINACH AND WALNUT SALAD

In this simple salad the warm dressing provides an interesting and unusual effect.

INGREDIENTS

4 handfuls young spinach
16 walnuts
juice of ½ lemon
1 tbs walnut oil
1 tbs olive oil
salt and pepper
4 rashers streaky bacon

GARNISH
finely chopped chives and
  chervil

SERVES 4

METHOD

Strip the spinach from its stalks, wash well and dry gently. Crack the walnuts and divide into quarters. Mix the lemon juice with both oils and season lightly.

Cut the streaky bacon into very fine strips and fry slowly to release the fat. Then place in the oven or under the grill to crisp up.

Pour the walnut oil dressing into the pan used for frying the bacon and heat very gently. Toss the spinach in the warm dressing. Sprinkle on bacon and walnuts and garnish with chopped chives and chervil.

Melanie de Blank, Shipdham Place

Calories per serving: 235
Food value: Protein, fibre, vitamins and minerals. Low fat.

CRACKED WHEAT SALAD

This salad exists in many versions throughout the Middle East, where it is called variously tabbouli, tabbouleh and tabbuil, depending on the country of origin.

INGREDIENTS

1 bunch spring onions
2 tomatoes
6 oz (180 g) fine burghul
  (cracked wheat)
4 tbs parsley
2 tbs mint
3 tbs olive oil
juice of 2 lemons
salt and freshly ground
  pepper

SERVES 4

METHOD

Chop the spring onions finely and skin and chop the tomatoes. Put the burghul in a bowl, cover it with cold water and allow it to soak for at least 15 minutes. Take it out by the handful, squeezing out the excess water as you do so. Spread it on a tea towel to dry.

Place the burghul in a clean, dry bowl, stir in the onions, tomatoes, freshly chopped parsley and mint. Add the olive oil and lemon juice, mix well, taste the salad and add more oil or lemon juice if necessary. Season with salt and freshly ground pepper to taste.

On each plate arrange a few crisp lettuce leaves with which to scoop up the salad, and serve with flat bread.

Calories per serving: 310
Food value: Fibre, vitamins and minerals. Low fat.
Note: The quantities of mint, parsley, burghul, lemon juice and oil can be varied according to preference, although opinion always seems to favour plenty of parsley.

This salad also makes a good accompaniment to grilled or barbecued chicken or lamb, especially if a dish of yogurt is provided as well.

TWO PEAR SALAD
with grapefruit mayonnaise

The two pears of the title are William pears and avocados – a combination that provides an unusual contrast in flavours.

INGREDIENTS

SALAD
1 pink grapefruit
4 tbs mayonnaise
2 ripe avocados
2 William pears
mixture of salad leaves,
  e.g. cos lettuce,
  radicchio, curly endive

DRESSING
  makes 1 pt (600 ml)
5 fl oz (150 ml) cider
  vinegar
1 dsp acacia honey
¼ tsp mustard
½ tsp salt and pepper
15 fl oz (450 ml)
  sunflower oil

SERVES 4

METHOD

First make the dressing. Put the cider vinegar, acacia honey, mustard, salt and pepper into a liquidizer and begin to blend slowly. Add the sunflower oil a little at a time until the dressing is lightly emulsified. Adjust the seasoning if necessary.

Wash the grapefruit, grate the zest and mix it with the mayonnaise. Then peel the grapefruit, removing every trace of pith, and cut into segments by inserting a knife between the membranes. Catch any juice that flows in a bowl and add it to the mayonnaise, mixing well.

Halve the avocados, remove the stones and peel. Place cut side down and make several incisions downwards, leaving the top intact. Gently press into a fan shape. Peel and halve the William pears, then scoop out the core and make a hollow with a teaspoon. Remove the fibrous stalk and cut a neat channel along the pear. Take a small slice off the rounded side of each half so it will sit securely on the plate.

Arrange the salad leaves around four plates. Carefully place half an avocado on each one and brush with a little dressing. Arrange half a William pear next to it, fill the cavity with some grapefruit mayonnaise and scatter a few grapefruit segments over the salad.
Carol Trevor-Roper, Knights Farm

Calories per serving: 400
Food value: Fibre, vitamins and minerals. Moderate fat.
Note: Any unused dressing can be stored in a sealed jar in the refrigerator.

This salad is rather high in calories mainly because of the avocados, which contain a good deal of fat (half an avocado is 250 calories). So if you are serving it as a first course, plan to have a very light, low-fat main dish without a rich sauce.

167

LA SALADE JUTEUX

A mouthwatering salad combining Charentais melon, pink grapefruit, pears, pine kernels and lovage, with a lemon and honey dressing.

INGREDIENTS

½ melon (preferably
  Charentais)
2 pink grapefruit
2 pears
2 oz (60 g) pine kernels
1 tbs chopped lovage

DRESSING
2 tbs clear honey
5 tbs groundnut oil
1 tbs lemon juice

SERVES 4

METHOD

Using a melon baller, scoop out the melon flesh into a large mixing bowl and collect any juice separately. Carefully peel all skin and pith from the grapefruit with a very sharp knife, then divide the flesh into segments, cutting against the fine inner membrane and collecting any juice that flows. Add the flesh to the melon balls. Peel and core the pears, cut into very small cubes, and mix with the melon and grapefruit.

Mix together the juices from the melon and grapefruit and add to the honey, groundnut oil and lemon juice. Blend well until amalgamated (this can be done in a screw-top glass jar).

Just before serving, add the pine kernels and chopped lovage to the salad, pour over the dressing and toss gently. Divide into individual serving glasses.

As a pretty alternative, arrange lamb's lettuce leaves like petals on a plate, pile the salad into the centre and strew with nasturtium flower petals.

Paul and Muriel Wadsworth, Pebbles Restaurant

Calories per serving: 315
Food value: Fibre, vitamins and minerals. Low fat.
Note: It's worth remembering that more than half the calories for this dish come from the dressing.

CITRUS SALAD
with crème de menthe

*An unashamedly pretty dish, constructed to look like a flower,
and perfect for a summer's evening.*

INGREDIENTS

4 pink grapefruit
4 white grapefruit
1 tsp crème de menthe
4 oranges

GARNISH
fresh mint leaves

SERVES 4

METHOD

Remove the peel and pith from the grapefruit and, using a sharp knife, carefully divide into segments. Keep the pink and white segments in separate bowls. Add a little crème de menthe to the white grapefruit to give it a pale green colour. Remove the rind from the oranges with a zesting knife and then peel and divide into segments.

Arrange the fruit on four large plates: alternate the pink and "minted" grapefruit around each plate to look like the petals of a flower. Place the orange segments in the centre and add a little orange zest to represent the flower stamens. A few leaves of fresh mint will also enhance the overall appearance of this delightful dish.

Anthony Rudge, Salisbury House

Calories per serving: 140
Food value: Vitamins. No added fat.

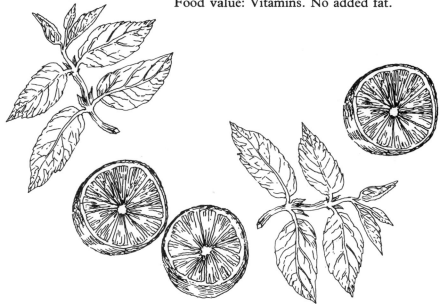

MUSHROOM AND BEAN SALAD
with croutons

Although this salad perfectly complements the Little Cheese Soufflé on p. 62, it is very versatile and can be eaten as it is.

INGREDIENTS

3 oz (90 g) button
  mushrooms
juice of ½ lemon
3 oz (90 g) Edam or
  Gruyère cheese
3 oz (90 g) French beans
6 slices brown bread
4 handfuls salad leaves,
  e.g. lettuce, curly endive

DRESSING
10 fl oz (300 ml)
  walnut oil
1 pt (600 ml) sunflower oil
5 fl oz (150 ml) white
  wine vinegar
2 turns of pepper mill

GARNISH
chopped chives

SERVES 6-8

METHOD

Wash the button mushrooms in plenty of water, dry in a cloth, slice off the bottoms of the stalks and squeeze over a little lemon juice to prevent any discoloration. Cut into thin slices and put to one side.

Cut the cheese into small cubes. Tail, wash and blanch the French beans for 3 minutes, then refresh under cold water. Prepare little croutons by cutting the slices of brown bread into cubes and roasting them in the oven until golden brown (rub them with garlic if you like).

Wash the assorted salad leaves and dry in a cloth. Then prepare the vinaigrette dressing by mixing together the walnut oil, sunflower oil, wine vinegar and black pepper.

If you intend to serve this salad with the Little Cheese Soufflé, mix the leaves with the mushrooms, French beans, cheese and a small quantity of the dressing. Place attractively around the plates and garnish with croutons and some freshly washed and finely chopped chives. Set the soufflé as the centrepiece of the dish.

Alternatively the salad can be served on its own, or as the accompaniment to another dish.
Raymond Blanc, Le Manoir aux Quat' Saisons

Calories per serving: 190
Food value: Protein, fibre and vitamins. Low fat.
Note: Gruyère has a higher fat content than Edam but produces better results for this recipe.

CHICORY AND GRUYÈRE SALAD

The best Belgian witloof, or "white leaf", chicory is excellent eaten raw and combined with other more colourful ingredients such as radicchio and watercress.

INGREDIENTS

1 large witloof chicory
1 large radicchio
1 bunch watercress
2 heaped tbs fresh shelled
  walnuts
2-3 oz (60-90 g) Gruyère
  cheese
1 tsp freshly chopped
  lovage
zest of lemon or lime
  (optional)

DRESSING

1 tbs lemon juice
1 tbs white wine vinegar
3 tbs walnut oil
salt and black pepper

SERVES 4

METHOD

Chop the chicory and radicchio into suitable pieces, and sort through the watercress, throwing out any discoloured or rotten leaves. Chop the freshly shelled walnuts lengthways and finely slice the cheese (a potato peeler is useful for this). Mix the ingredients together and add a little finely chopped lovage with some lemon or lime zest if you like.

Make up a dressing with the lemon juice, white wine vinegar and walnut oil. Season with salt and black pepper. Blend well and add to the salad just before serving.

James Kempston, Stone Green Hall

Calories per serving: 200
Food value: Protein, vitamins and minerals. Low fat.
Note: Gruyère cheese has a very distinctive flavour which goes perfectly with the strong, bitter taste of chicory. However, it is a high-fat cheese and if you are trying to keep calories to a minimum you might try substituting a low-fat alternative such as ricotta.

The balance of ingredients and nutrients in this particular salad makes it equally suitable as a side dish or – in larger quantities – as a lunchtime snack for vegetarians and non-vegetarians alike.

LETTUCE AND COURGETTE SALAD

This simple, healthy salad can be served with a main dish or as a separate course to refresh the palate. The flavour is·greatly improved by using the very best virgin olive oil.

INGREDIENTS

1 crisp lettuce
6 small courgettes
1 tbs sunflower seeds
a few leaves fresh sweet
  marjoram
2 tbs olive oil
1 tsp cider vinegar

GARNISH
4 sprigs of salad burnet

SERVES 4

METHOD

Wash the lettuce, dry and break into bite-size pieces. Slice the courgettes into thin rings and blanch very quickly in boiling water. Strain and refresh under cold running water.

Mix the lettuce and courgettes in a large bowl, toss in the sunflower seeds and some roughly chopped leaves of fresh marjoram. Combine the oil and cider vinegar very carefully but do not dress the salad until just before serving.

Divide the salad into four individual bowls and garnish each one with with a sprig of salad burnet.
Patricia Hegarty, Hope End Country House Hotel

Calories per serving: 80
Food value: Fibre, vitamins and minerals. Low fat.
Note: Although this recipe is quite specific about the necessary ingredients, there is always room for flexibility. For instance, the herbs can be varied: basil might be a good alternative to fresh marjoram, and if you are unable to obtain salad burnet, a garnish of chervil would be just as effective.

You can use any type of lettuce for this recipe, provided that it is very fresh, green and crisp.

ORANGE AND AVOCADO SALAD
with mint

INGREDIENTS

4 slices fresh pineapple
4 lettuce or curly endive
  leaves
2 avocado pears
2 oranges

DRESSING
4 oz (120 g) cream cheese
juice of 2 oranges
handful of fresh mint

GARNISH
2 tbs chopped roasted
  hazelnuts
orange and chive shreds

SERVES 4

METHOD

Place the slices of pineapple on the lettuce leaves. Peel the avocados, remove the stones and cut the flesh into fine slices. Peel the oranges and divide into segments. Arrange the avocado slices and orange segments on top of the pineapple.

To make the dressing, blend the cream cheese with the orange juice and finely chopped mint in a liquidizer until smooth. (Alternatively whisk well with a fork.) Chill before serving.

Before bringing to the table, spoon some dressing over the salad and garnish with roasted hazelnuts, and orange and chive shreds.

Calories per serving: 420
Food value: Fibre, vitamins and minerals. Low fat.

SALADE DE LANGOUSTINES
aux mangues et girolles à l'estragon

INGREDIENTS

4 girolles
2 tbs olive oil
1 clove garlic
juice of 1 lemon
1 small mango
10 fl oz (300 ml)
  vegetable fumé (made
  with white wine)
2 carrots
6 Dublin Bay prawns
knob of butter*
5 fl oz (150 ml) cream
1 tsp tarragon, chopped
oak-leafed lettuce and
  spinach leaves

SERVES 1

METHOD

Marinate the girolles in oil, garlic and lemon juice.
Cook gently in the same juice. Cut some mango into
segments and dice the rest. Cook in vegetable fumé.
Heat fleurettes of carrot in more vegetable fumé.

Remove the heads and tails from the prawns, clean
and cut in half lengthways. Fry gently in butter, then
drain. Add vegetable fumé to the pan with the cream,
lemon juice and tarragon, and cook.

Place the girolles in the centre of a plate. Surround
them with prawn sauce. Arrange the prawns over the
sauce and the lettuce and spinach leaves, topped with
carrot and mango, around the edge.
René Gaté, Les Semailles

Calories per serving: 300
Food value: Protein, vitamins and minerals. Low fat.

DESSERTS
Introduction

Traditionally desserts are the part of a meal where people indulge themselves and throw caution to the wind. A glimpse of creamy gâteaux, syllabubs and pastries often banishes all thoughts of eating healthily and sensibly. But all is not lost. It is possible to enjoy the occasional rich dessert if it is balanced by the rest of the meal, and it is also possible to enjoy exquisite desserts that don't contain cream or refined sugar.

DESSERTS OLD AND NEW
A glance through the dessert section of most recipe books or a look at the standard dishes on most restaurant sweet trolleys might lead you to think that desserts are exclusively composed of cream, pastry and sugar, supplemented – in the case of traditional English puddings – by suet and lard.

There are certainly countless dishes of this type and they are firm favourites with many people. However, there are alternatives – desserts that aim to be light, refreshing and non-fattening. Fresh fruit can be the base, not only for exotic and adventurous salads, but also for sorbets, terrines and tartlets. Fruit sauces add a new dimension to many desserts, and the natural sweetness of fruit is now replacing refined sugar.

CHOOSING DESSERTS
When deciding on a dessert, take into consideration what has gone before in the meal as well as what is available. If you have eaten lightly, then you can choose something rich to finish with; if, on the other hand, you have eaten a substantial meal, including meat and a rich sauce, it is better to have a light and simple dessert. By choosing carefully, you can eat what you like without feeling guilty.

Many people also like to eat cheese at the end of a meal. Generally it's advisable to have one or the other, although a very light dessert and a small portion of cheese (with biscuits, but no butter) will preserve the appropriate balance.

FRUIT TERRINE
with a coulis of mango

This dish – light, easy and inexpensive – represents for Raymond Blanc "the generosity of summer".

INGREDIENTS

2 bananas
4 oz (120 g) raspberries
4 oz (120 g) strawberries
4 oz (120 g) plums
4 oz (120 g) melon
4 oz (120 g) pink
 grapefruit
4 sheets gelatine
6 oranges

COULIS
2 mangoes
4 passion fruit

SERVES 8

METHOD

Take the fresh fruits, slice the bananas into four lengthways, wash the raspberries and strawberries, stone and chop the plums, cut the melon into little cubes and divide the grapefruit into segments. Pack all the fruits into a terrine dish until it is full.

Put the gelatine in water to soften. Press the oranges so that you obtain 7 fl oz (210 ml) of juice. Filter into a small pan, bring to the boil and skim off any impurities as they rise to the surface. Add the softened sheets of gelatine and whisk. While still tepid, pour over the fruit in the terrine dish so that it is completely covered. Place in a refrigerator to set for at least 2 hours.

Peel the mangoes and remove the flesh with a knife. Cut the passion fruit in half, remove the seeds and mix the flesh with that of the mangoes. Liquidize, then pass through a fine sieve and keep cool.

When ready to serve, slice the terrine into small portions, using a warm, serrated knife. Arrange on individual plates and pour a little of the coulis around each portion.

Raymond Blanc, Le Manoir aux Quat' Saisons

Calories per serving: 45
Food value: Vitamins and minerals. No added fat.
Note: This dessert relies for its effect on natural flavour and sweetness, so don't be tempted to embellish it with sugar or cream.

BROCHETTE OF TROPICAL FRUITS

In this dish, the paw-paw, kiwi fruit and strawberries are threaded on to a skewer, basted with brandy butter and grilled until golden brown.

INGREDIENTS

4 kiwi fruit
16 large strawberries
1 paw-paw

BRANDY BUTTER
6 oz (180 g) butter*
6 oz (180 g) caster sugar
3 fl oz (90 ml) brandy

SERVES 4

METHOD

First prepare the fruit. Peel and quarter the kiwis, hull the strawberries and peel and de-seed the paw-paw, cutting the flesh into uniform pieces. Thread the fruit on to skewers ready for grilling.

Soften the butter and beat together with the sugar until white and smooth. Then add the brandy very slowly and mix well.

Place the brochettes on a grilling pan and cover liberally with the brandy butter. Grill until golden brown and serve immediately.

Baba Hine, Corse Lawn House Hotel

Calories per serving: 300
Food value: Vitamins and minerals. Moderate fat.
Note: The brandy butter means that this is a rich, indulgent dish, but because the butter is used largely for basting, only a small amount is actually consumed.

This is the kind of dish where you can experiment with different kinds of fruit. Aim for a contrast in flavour, texture and colour and, for added interest, try to mix familiar and unfamiliar varieties.

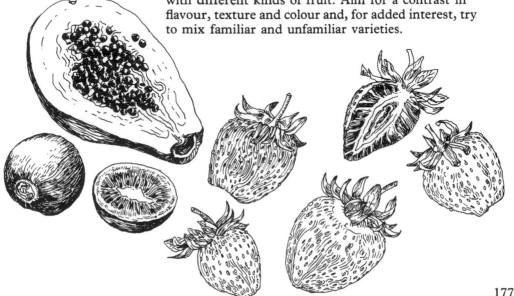

FEUILLANTINE DE FRAISES RÔTIES
crème au citron

An elegant dessert consisting of hot strawberries sandwiched between thin biscuits and served with lemon sauce.

INGREDIENTS

16 strawberries
2 tbs caster sugar
½ oz (15 g) butter*
dash of Kirsch

BISCUITS
4 oz (120 g) icing sugar
4 oz (120 g) flour
2 oz (60 g) egg white
4 oz (120 g) melted
  butter*

SAUCE
8 fl oz (240 ml) milk
4 oz (120 g) caster sugar
6 egg yolks
zest of 4 lemons
8 fl oz (240 ml) cream

GARNISH
whole strawberries

SERVES 2

METHOD

To make the biscuits, mix the icing sugar with the flour then incorporate the egg whites and the melted butter. Leave to rest for 2 hours. Cut out into thin, biscuit-sized circles and put on a lightly buttered baking sheet. Cook in a moderate oven at 350°F (180°C), Gas Mark 4, until lightly browned.

Prepare the sauce as follows. Bring the milk to the boil with half the caster sugar. At the same time whisk the egg yolks with the rest of the sugar until white. Add the lemon zest to the milk and pour on to the egg yolks. Cook slowly until the sauce coats the back of a spoon. Cool on ice.

Cut the strawberries in half and pan-fry with sugar, butter and Kirsch. Drain well. To serve the dish, put one biscuit on the centre of each plate, cover with eight strawberry halves, place another biscuit on top and slightly to one side. Add the remainder of the strawberries and top with a third biscuit. Glaze with icing sugar. Pour some of the lemon sauce around the dish and decorate with a few whole strawberries, which have been cooked as above.

This dish needs to be assembled very quickly and served hot.

René Gaté, Les Semailles

Calories per serving: 500
Food value: Protein, fibre, vitamins and minerals.
Moderate fat.
Note: The biscuits and sauce together contribute most of the calories in this dessert. The calories themselves come partly from fat, partly from carbohydrate.

PINEAPPLE AND COCONUT ROULADE

*The roulade can be prepared a day or two in advance,
although the final decoration of the dish should not be
completed until just before serving.*

INGREDIENTS

ROULADE
6 eggs, separated
5 oz (150 g) caster sugar
2 oz (60 g) cocoa powder

FILLING
8 oz (240 g) plain
 chocolate
2 tbs Malibu liqueur
2 eggs, separated
½ fresh pineapple

DECORATION
10 fl oz (300 ml) double
 cream
1 dsp icing sugar
1 tbs Malibu liqueur
toasted desiccated coconut
fresh pineapple pieces
chopped pistachio nuts

SERVES 6-8

METHOD

Separate the eggs and put the yolks into a basin.
Whisk well until they start to thicken, then add the
caster sugar and continue to whisk. Stir in the cocoa
powder.

Whisk the egg whites in a separate bowl until peaks
form, then carefully fold into the cocoa mixture. Pour
the mixture into a lightly greased rectangular baking
tin lined with greaseproof paper, and bake in the oven
at 350°F (180°C), Gas Mark 4 for 20-25 minutes until
well risen and springy. Turn out immediately on to a
large piece of baking foil and leave to cool.

To make the filling, break the chocolate into pieces
in a basin and add the liqueur. Place the basin over a
pan of simmering water and stir until the chocolate has
melted. Remove from the heat and beat until smooth.
Separate two eggs, beat the yolks slightly then add to
the chocolate, Stir well and allow to cool. Whisk the
egg whites until stiff and fold into the chocolate
mixture. Finally add the chopped and drained
pineapple, folding the pieces in lightly.

Pour the mixture on to the roulade and spread very
carefully. Leave until almost set. Roll the roulade,
peeling away the foil as you proceed. Wrap in foil and
put in the refrigerator for at least 2 hours.

To decorate, whip the cream together with the icing
sugar and liqueur until stiff. Spread over the roulade
and cover completely. Sprinkle with desiccated
coconut and decorate with fresh pineapple and
pistachio nuts.

Robert Jackson, Herbs Restaurant

Calories per serving: 550
Food value: Protein, vitamins and minerals.
Moderate fat.

ALMOND GÂTEAU
with blackcurrant and apple purée

Richness is the key to this gâteau, although the fruit purée provides a tart contrast in flavour.

INGREDIENTS

4 eggs
7 oz (210 g) caster sugar
3 oz (90 g) ground
  almonds
grated rind and juice of
  ½ lemon
4 oz (120 g) fine semolina
5 fl oz (150 ml) double
  cream

PURÉE
8 oz (240 g) blackcurrants
8 oz (240 g) apples

SERVES 4-6

METHOD

Line a deep cake tin with greaseproof paper, then dust it with sugar and flour.

Separate the eggs and beat the yolks together with the sugar until thick and white. Fold in the ground almonds, the grated rind and juice of the lemon and the semolina. Leave to stand for 3 minutes to allow the semolina to soften. Whisk the egg whites until stiff, fold in the almond mixture and spoon into the cake tin. Pre-heat the oven to 375°F (190°C), Gas Mark 5 and cook for 50 minutes until nicely brown. Allow the gâteau to get cold, then split and fill with whipped double cream.

To make the purée, sort through the blackcurrants, removing any bits of leaf and stalk, wash well and put into a large pan. Peel and core the apples, chop into small pieces and add to the blackcurrants. Simmer gently, stirring well to ensure that the fruit does not stick to the bottom of the pan. When well cooked and soft, pass through a sieve and then liquidize until you have a smooth purée. Let the purée cool, then serve separately with the gâteau.

Ann Long, The Count House Restaurant

Calories per serving: 450
Food value: Fibre and vitamins. Moderate fat.
Note: The semolina and almonds provide useful amounts of fibre, while the fruit contributes vitamin C.

When serving this dish, try to balance the quantities of gâteau and purée so that neither dominates.

REDCURRANT TART
with raspberry coulis

The contrasting shades of pink and red make this delightful dish as good to look at as it is to eat.

INGREDIENTS

12 oz (360 g) raspberries
1 tsp caster sugar
dash of framboise
juice of 1 orange
5 fl oz (150 ml)
  crème fraiche
  (or fromage blanc)
5 fl oz (150 ml) double
  cream
12 oz (360 g) ripe
  redcurrants
8 oz (240 g) redcurrant
  jelly
4 sablé pastry cases

SERVES 4

METHOD

Liquidize the raspberries, adding caster sugar, framboise and orange juice to taste. Pass through a fine sieve, and put to one side.

Whip together the *crème fraiche* (or *fromage blanc*) and the double cream. Sweeten to taste if necessary.

Sort through the redcurrants and strip them from their stalks. Melt the redcurrant jelly and carefully mix in the fruit.

To serve, spoon some of the cream into the pastry cases and pile the redcurrants on top. Serve the tarts surrounded by the raspberry coulis.

Ian Weeks, Weeks Restaurant

Calories per serving: 460
Food value: Vitamins and minerals. Moderate fat.
Note: A few whitecurrants added to the tarts will make them look even more attractive. As an alternative to the raspberry coulis, Ian Weeks suggests *crème anglais* flavoured with orange liqueur.

Crème fraiche is a type of soured double cream which is very popular in France and now widely available elsewhere. *Fromage blanc* is a good low-fat alternative, which will be particularly attractive to the health conscious.

PRUNES STUFFED WITH WALNUTS
in honey and lemon syrup

A light and nutritious dessert which is easy to make provided you have patience and agile fingers.

INGREDIENTS

16 large Californian
  prunes
15 fl oz (450 ml) tea
juice and rind of 1 lemon
1 tbs honey
4 oz (120 g) shelled
  walnuts

SERVES 4

METHOD

Cover the prunes completely with tea and simmer until soft. Top up with extra water if necessary. Strain off and reserve the juice.

Wash the lemon and pare a few strips of rind from it. Squeeze the juice, and mix with the honey and prune liquor in a pan. Boil and reduce.

When the prunes have cooled, slit them open on one side and remove the stones. Fill with walnuts so that the prunes will just close over the stuffing. Spoon over the honey and lemon syrup and serve.

Patricia Hegarty, Hope End Country House Hotel

Calories per serving: 240
Food value: Fibre, vitamins and minerals. No added fat.

HOT APPLE TARTLETS

A novel variation on the theme of apple tart, with the pastry moulded around the fruit.

INGREDIENTS

2 Coxes apples
8 oz (240 g) puff pastry
caster sugar
knob of butter

TO SERVE
Jersey cream

SERVES 4

METHOD

Peel the apples, cut in half, scoop out the cores and score lightly. Roll out the puff pastry and draw the outline of the apples with a sharp knife; include stalk and leaf for decorative effect. The pastry should be slightly larger than the fruit.

Place half an apple in the centre of each pastry shape and score. Keep in the refrigerator.

Sprinkle each tartlet with sugar and top with a knob of butter. Place in a hot oven at 450°F (225°C), Gas Mark 8 for 10 minutes. Sprinkle with sugar again and cook for another few minutes.

Melanie de Blank, Shipdham Place

Calories per serving: 270
Food value: Fibre, vitamins and minerals. Low fat.

OLD-FASHIONED CURD TART

The addition of black treacle gives an extra richness of flavour to this traditional English dessert. The recipe can be easily adapted to make individual curd tartlets.

INGREDIENTS

PASTRY
3 oz (90 g) butter*
6 oz (180 g) self-raising flour
1 egg
1 oz (30 g) sugar

FILLING
3 oz (90 g) sugar
3 oz (90 g) butter*
1 egg
4 oz (120 g) curd cheese
3 oz (90 g) mixed dried fruit
pinch of mixed spice
2 tbs black treacle

GARNISH
candied angelica

SERVES 4-6

METHOD

First make the pastry. Soften the butter and blend in the flour. Beat together the egg and sugar and add to the flour and butter. Knead until you have a smooth dough, and use it to line a large flan ring.

To prepare the filling, cream together the sugar and butter. Beat in the egg and add the curds, dried fruit, mixed spice and treacle. Blend well.

Half fill the pastry case with the curd mixture (to allow for rising), and bake in the oven at 325°F (170°C), Gas Mark 3 for 30-40 minutes. Cool, then decorate with diamonds of candied angelica.

Bronwen Nixon and Jane Binns, Rothay Manor

Calories per serving: 475
Food value: Protein, fibre, vitamins and minerals. Moderate fat.
Note: Curds are easy to make from milk that has gone sour. Simply allow the milk to drip through a muslin cloth overnight. 1 tsp rennet added to 1 pt (600 ml) milk will turn it sour.

SWEET PASTRY CASES

INGREDIENTS

1 oz (30 g) melted butter*
12 oz (360 g) puff pastry
2 oz (60 g) icing sugar

SERVES 6

METHOD

Roll out the pastry, then cut and mould into pear shapes. Transfer to a greased baking sheet, leaving space between each piece. Refrigerate for 30 minutes.

Pre-heat the oven to 425°F (220°C), Gas Mark 7 and bake the pastries for 5 minutes until golden brown. Remove and dust liberally with icing sugar.

Increase the oven heat to maximum, and put in the pastries for a few minutes until they have a caramelized, glossy appearance. Cool on a wire rack.

Barbara Deane and Jonathon Hayes, The Perfumed Conservatory

Note: This recipe is ideally suited to The Marriage of Atholl Brose and William Pear on page 192.

FRESH FRUIT CHEESECAKE

Decorate this cheesecake with fruits in season – exotic varieties, such as mangoes and kiwi fruit, or more common ones, such as peaches, apples, oranges and grapefruit.

INGREDIENTS

4 oz (120 g) butter*
8 oz (240 g) wheatmeal
  biscuits
1 lb (½ kg) curd cheese
8 oz (240 g) low-fat soft
  cheese
3 eggs
4 oz (120 g) sugar
1 tsp vanilla essence
assorted seasonal fruits

SERVES 6-8

METHOD

Gently melt the butter in a saucepan and add the finely crushed wheatmeal biscuits. Mix well.

Grease a loose-bottomed flan tin and firmly press the biscuit mixture in to form a base. Place in the refrigerator while making the filling.

Combine the curd cheese, soft cheese, beaten eggs, sugar and vanilla essence in a large bowl and beat well until completely smooth. Pour the filling on to the biscuit base and cook the cheesecake for 30 minutes at 300°F (160°C), Gas Mark 2. Turn the oven off and leave until cool. Refrigerate for at least 2 hours before carefully removing from the flan tin.

Decorate lavishly with assorted seasonal fruits sliced and prepared as required.

Robert Jackson, Herbs Restaurant

Calories per serving: 395
Food value: Protein, fibre, vitamins and minerals.
Low fat.
Note: As it stands, this is essentially a low-fat dessert. However if you want to enrich it you can pipe whipped cream around the edge of the cheesecake before serving.

MANGO WITH MANGO SORBET
and marinated lime

A colourful and exotic dessert that is extremely simple to prepare and serve.

INGREDIENTS

3 limes
1 tbs sugar
1 tbs green Chartreuse
3 mangoes

SORBET
4 oz (120 g) sugar
6 fl oz (180 ml) water
8 oz (240 g) mango flesh

GARNISH
langue de chat

SERVES 6

METHOD

To make the sorbet, dissolve the sugar in the water and allow to cool. Add the prepared mango flesh and liquidize until smooth. Pass through a sieve, then whip and freeze in the usual way.

Segment the limes and cover with sugar and Chartreuse. Allow to stand for a few hours. Peel and slice the mangoes.

To serve, place a dome of sorbet in the centre of a very cold plate and arrange slices of mango and lime around it. Add a *langue de chat* and serve.

Baba Hine, Corse Lawn House Hotel

Calories per serving: 240
Food value: Fibre, vitamins and minerals. No added fat.

WARM PEARS
in Poire William liqueur

In this recipe, the pears should have a "super-ripe" flavour – between ripe and cooked – which is accentuated by the liqueur.

INGREDIENTS

4 ripe Comice pears
5 fl oz (150 ml) fruit sugar
  syrup
5 fl oz (150 ml) Poire
  William liqueur

GARNISH
almond tuille biscuits

SERVES 4

METHOD

Peel, halve and core the pears. Warm gently until the juice just begins to flow (this can be done in a microwave). Slice and fan on to a warm plate.

Mix together the fruit sugar syrup and Poire William liqueur and warm gently. Dress each pear with a little of this warm sauce and serve with an almond tuille biscuit.

James Kempston, Stone Green Hall

Calories per serving: 195
Food value: Fibre and vitamins. No added fat.
Note: This dish has many variations, for example you might try peaches or nectarines in Maraschino or Mirabelle liqueur.

GUAVA AND LIME SYLLABUB

This dessert is a refinement of the traditional syllabub, which was originally made by milking a cow directly into a pan of wine or cider.

INGREDIENTS

10 fl oz (300 ml) double
  cream
2 oz (60 g) caster sugar
juice of 1½ limes
2 guavas
2 tbs Cointreau

GARNISH
selection of tropical fruits

SERVES 4

METHOD

Whip together the cream and sugar until fairly stiff. Then slowly add the juice of the limes, beating continuously.

Peel the guavas, liquidize and pass through a fine sieve, leaving a smooth, pipless purée. Add this to the mixture, together with the Cointreau.

Serve the syllabub in a delicate tall glass, in a biscuit cup or in a brandy snap, and garnish it with a selection of tropical fruits. A string of fresh violets will give the dish a finishing touch.

Barbara Deane and Jonathon Hayes, The Perfumed Conservatory

Calories per serving: 460
Food value: Protein, vitamins and minerals. Moderate fat.

COLD MANGO SOUFFLÉ

A light, tangy and refreshing dessert that will provide a delicate conclusion to a substantial meal.

INGREDIENTS

1 ripe mango
2 fl oz (60 ml) honey
juice of 1 lemon or lime
juice of 1 orange
1 fl oz (30 ml) Galliano
4 sheets gelatine
5 fl oz (150 ml) double
  cream
2 egg whites

GARNISH
slices of mango
slices of lime

SERVES 4

METHOD

Peel the mango and put the flesh into a liquidizer. Add the honey, lemon or lime juice, orange juice and Galliano and blend well. Then pour the contents into a stainless steel bowl and allow to cool.

Soften and melt the gelatine in water, then whisk rapidly into the mango pulp. Stir in the semi-whipped cream and finally fold in the stiffly whipped egg whites.

Spoon or pipe the soufflé into four tall glasses and garnish with slices of mango and lime.

Pauline Harrison, The Moss Nook Restaurant

Calories per serving: 260
Food value: Protein, fibre and vitamins. Low fat.

RUBELI-TORTE
with fresh apricot sauce

*A colourful and stylish variation on the theme of carrot cake,
made even more appealing with fresh apricot sauce.*

INGREDIENTS

3 oz (90 g) cake crumbs
*10 oz (300 g) grated
  carrot*
*8 oz (240 g) grated
  hazelnuts*
½ oz (15 g) baking powder
1 tbs ground cinnamon
1½ tbs rum
grated rind of 1 lemon
5 eggs, separated
8 oz (240 g) caster sugar
4 tbs hot water

SAUCE
1 lb (½ kg) fresh apricots
8 oz (240 g) sugar
10 fl oz (300 ml) water
2 tbs apricot brandy

SERVES 6

METHOD

Put the cake crumbs into a large bowl and add the grated carrot, the hazelnuts (blanched, peeled and grated) and the baking powder. Mix in the ground cinnamon, rum and grated lemon rind.

Separate the eggs and whisk the yolks with 4 oz (120 g) caster sugar and the hot water to a high ribbon stage. Fold into the carrot mixture.

Whisk the egg whites with the remaining 4 oz (120 g) sugar to a meringue consistency and fold into the carrot mixture. Blend well. Pour into a baking tin and cook for 1 hour at 300°F (160°C), Gas Mark 2.

Meanwhile, prepare the sauce. Put the apricots, sugar and water into a thick-bottomed pan and bring slowly to the boil. Simmer gently until the fruit is soft. Sieve to remove the stones, then put the apricots into the liquidizer. Finally strain off, add the apricot brandy and cool. Serve separately with the torte.
Allan Garth, Gravetye Manor

Calories per serving: 450
Food value: Fibre, vitamins and minerals. Low fat.
Note: Allan Garth points out that this recipe cannot be halved or doubled. Also he recommends grape sugar as an alternative to caster sugar.

Only fresh apricots will give the required flavour and fragrance to the sauce served with this very simple and inexpensive dessert.

FIG SOUP
with cinnamon ice cream

The "soup" in this recipe is actually a mixture of fruit and wine, which goes perfectly with the home-made ice cream.

INGREDIENTS

ICE CREAM
4 egg yolks
4 oz (120 g) caster sugar
10 fl oz (300 ml) milk
2-3 level tsp ground
cinnamon
10 fl oz (300 ml) double
cream
1½ tsp vanilla essence

SOUP
4 fresh figs
16 fl oz (480 ml) red wine

SERVES 4

METHOD

Beat the egg yolks and sugar together. Heat the milk to boiling point, then pour over the eggs and sugar, beating continuously. Return to the pan and add the ground cinnamon, stirring constantly. Heat gently until the mixture begins to thicken.

Stir in the cream and vanilla essence. Transfer to a bowl and put in the freezer, stirring at 15 minute intervals until the ice cream is frozen.

Skin and peel the figs and put into a pan with the wine. Bring to the boil, then liquidize. Transfer to a bowl and chill. Serve in tall glasses.

Peter Hollins, The Marquee Restaurant

Calories per serving: 550
Food value: Protein, fibre, vitamins and minerals. Moderate fat.

ICED HAZELNUT MOUSSE

Serve this delicious iced mousse with a raspberry sauce.

INGREDIENTS

6 egg whites
9 oz (270 g) caster sugar
10 fl oz (300 ml) single
cream
7½ fl oz (225 ml) double
cream
4 oz (120 g) hazelnut
praline (see below)

SERVES 4-6

METHOD

Whisk the egg whites with the caster sugar in a bowl over a *bain-marie* until the sugar has dissolved. Remove and continue to whisk until cool.

Blend the single and double cream together and semi-whip. Blend in the egg and sugar mixture and fold in the praline. Freeze until required.

Francis Coulson, Sharrow Bay Hotel

Calories per serving: 500
Food value: Protein, fibre, vitamins and minerals. Moderate fat.
Note: Prepare the praline by heating together 4 oz (120 g) sugar with half a vanilla pod until brown. Mix in 4 oz (120 g) roasted hazelnuts. Harden on a board, then pound as finely as possible.

RHUBARB AND GINGER YOGURT ICE

Young forced rhubarb, bought in February, gives this yogurt-based ice cream the most attractive colour. An ice cream machine isn't necessary for this recipe.

INGREDIENTS

2½ lb (1¼ kg) rhubarb
2 fl oz (60 ml) water
6-8 oz (180-240 g) caster sugar
10 fl oz (300 ml) plain low-fat yogurt
2 oz (60 g) stem ginger
2 tbs ginger syrup
5 fl oz (150 ml) double cream

SERVES 6

METHOD

Cut the rhubarb into small chunks and put into a stainless steel pan with the water and sugar. Cover and cook slowly until soft. Allow to cool, then liquidize. Mix the puréed rhubarb with the yogurt, finely chopped stem ginger and ginger syrup.

Beat the double cream until it forms stiff peaks, mix with the rhubarb and yogurt, then freeze for 1 hour. Beat well again, and refreeze for another hour. Repeat the process once more, then seal the container and freeze until required. Place in the refrigerator for 30 minutes to soften, then serve in frosted glass dishes with home-made ginger snaps.

Lin Scrannage, The Market Restaurant

Calories per serving: 290
Food value: Fibre, vitamins and minerals. Low fat.

CLARET AND GINGER JELLY

It pays to select a decent bottle of claret for this dessert, although great vintages should be reserved solely for drinking.

INGREDIENTS

4 oz (120 g) caster sugar
1 tbs ginger marmalade
1 piece stick cinnamon
3 cloves
10 fl oz (300 ml) water
10 fl oz (300 ml) claret
juice of 1 lemon
4 sheets gelatine

GARNISH
swirl of whipped cream
crystallized stem ginger

SERVES 4

METHOD

Combine the sugar, marmalade, cinnamon and cloves in the water and heat gently until the sugar has dissolved. Bring to the boil, then remove from the heat and add the claret and lemon juice.

Soften the gelatine in cold water and add to the mixture. When it has completely melted allow the spices to infuse while the jelly cools.

Strain through a fine muslin cloth into four wine glasses, and allow to set. Garnish each with a swirl of whipped cream and slices of crystallized ginger.

Liam Barr, The English House

Calories per serving: 175
Food value: Vitamins and minerals. Low fat.

PERUVIAN CHOCOLATE CUSTARDS

Victoria Stephenson recommends the best Jersey cream for this recipe, although any good quality single or whipping cream will produce excellent results.

INGREDIENTS

1 tbs coffee beans
1 pt (600 ml) cream
1 tbs coffee (instant)
4 oz (120 g) cooking
   chocolate
3 oz (90 g) caster sugar
2 tbs cold water
3 tbs hot water
1 egg
5 egg yolks
1 vanilla pod
dash of Tia Maria

GARNISH
swirl of whipped cream
grated chocolate

SERVES 8-10

METHOD

Roast the fresh coffee beans in the oven for a few minutes. Then add to the cream in a saucepan, together with the instant coffee powder. Bring almost to boiling point, then switch off the heat and leave for 30 minutes.

Melt the chocolate very gently in a double saucepan. Dissolve the sugar in the cold water in a separate pan, then boil rapidly until dark brown. Add the hot water and stir until dissolved.

Beat the egg and yolks gently to amalgamate. Strain the hot cream mixture into the melted chocolate and discard the coffee beans. Stir until smooth.

Scrape the seeds from the vanilla pod into the mixture, and add the caramelized sugar and Tia Maria to taste. Stir well. Then carefully pour on to the eggs and blend very gently. (Don't beat vigorously, otherwise the mixture will froth.)

Pour the custards into individual bowls and cook in a *bain-marie* for 35-40 minutes at 325°F (170°C), Gas Mark 3. Chill and serve decorated with a swirl of whipped cream and grated chocolate.
Victoria Stephenson, Bradfield House Restaurant

Calories per serving: 250
Food value: Vitamins and minerals. Moderate fat.

MILLE-FEUILLE DE FRAMBOISES
dans son coulis

INGREDIENTS

12 thin dessert biscuits
  (see recipe on page 178)
1 lb (½ kg) raspberries
4 fl oz (120 ml) double
  cream

GARNISH
whole raspberries
leaves of fresh mint

SERVES 4

METHOD

Prepare the thin dessert biscuits as on page 178.
Divide the raspberries into two portions (keeping
several aside for the garnish). Liquidize one portion,
then sieve until you have a smooth coulis.

Assemble the dessert as follows: cover each plate
with some of the coulis. Place one biscuit on top.
Arrange a layer of whole raspberries, as shown above,
and pour over a little of the cream. Place another
biscuit on top. Continue with a second layer of fruit
and cream, and finish with a third biscuit. Garnish
with whole raspberries and mint leaves.

Calories per serving: 300
Food value: Fibre, vitamins and minerals. Low fat.
Note: This dish is adapted from an original recipe
by Pierre Chevillard of Chewton Glen Hotel.

191

THE MARRIAGE OF ATHOLL BROSE
and *William pear*

INGREDIENTS

2 oz (60 g) oats
3 tbs caster sugar
juice of 1 orange
2 tbs whisky
1 tbs honey
½ pt (300 ml) double cream
3 William pears
¼ pt (150 ml) Champagne
juice of 1 lemon
1 cinnamon stick
1 vanilla pod
6 pastry cases

SAUCE

8 oz (240 g) caster sugar
2 fl oz (60 ml) Bailey's
* Irish Cream*
¼ pt (150 ml) double cream

SERVES 6

METHOD

Caramelize the oats and 1 tbs sugar. Remove from the heat and add the orange juice, whisky and honey. Cool, then add the whipped cream and refrigerate.

Make a caramel sauce by burning the sugar over a low heat. Add water carefully until a syrupy consistency is reached. Cool, then add the Bailey's Irish Cream and double cream.

Peel and core the pears, leaving the stalks intact. Poach in 5 fl oz (150 ml) water with the champagne and other ingredients, plus 2 tbs sugar, for 15 minutes.

Pour the sauce on to each plate, arrange half a fanned-out pear to one side. Fill a pastry case (see recipe on page 183) with brose and set beside the pear. Warm and serve with a spun sugar ball.

Barbara Deane and Jonathon Hayes, The Perfumed Conservatory

Calories per serving: 680 (Includes pastry case.)
Food value: Fibre, vitamins and minerals. Moderate fat.

MENUS
for special occasions

Many of the dishes in this book can be eaten as single courses, but to use the balance rating system to best advantage you should combine them to produce a three-course menu. As mentioned in the Introduction (page 8), an average three-course meal should have a rating of 6, although there are many ways in which this can be varied.

In this section I have put together ten imaginative three-course menus for special occasions to show how dishes can be combined in practice. With one or two exceptions they are balanced meals with a total rating of 6, and the choice of dishes reflects the seasons, as well as the social event for which the meal is devised.

Remember that extras like vegetables, bread, cheese and coffee will need to be taken into account when planning the meal. You will also need to think about the choice of drinks, and I have given a few suggestions at the end of each menu.

IN PRAISE OF SPRING

The centrepiece of this springtime meal is young, new season's lamb, cooked as simply as possible.

Scallop pâté with green peppercorns
(see page 54)

Steamed best end of lamb with rosemary
(see page 100)

Rhubarb and ginger yogurt ice
(see page 189)

To drink: A medium white wine and light to medium red wine.

FOR A SUMMER'S EVENING

A light starter and an even lighter dessert flank a rich, but delicate main course with a sumptuous sauce.

Avocado and watercress with strawberry vinaigrette
(see page 29)

Poached sea bass with courgettes and saffron
(see page 86)

Fruit terrine with a coulis of mango
(see page 176)

To drink: A white Burgundy and Champagne to follow.

A CELEBRATION OF AUTUMN

Seasonal produce – some of it from the wild – is used to good effect in this special menu.

Mushroom and chicken omelet with watercress and shallot sauce
(see page 63)

Roast duck breast with blackberry sauce
(see page 131)

Iced hazelnut mousse
(see page 188)

To drink: A warm, spicy fruit punch followed by a rich white wine.

A WINTER'S MEAL

A stylish alternative to thick, nourishing broths, wholesome stews and heavy puddings.

Mille-feuille of mussels with lemon sauce
(see page 93)

Noisettes of venison with port and cranberries
(see page 144)

Warm pears in Poirę William liqueur
(see page 185)

To drink: A rich red wine, for example a Rhône or grand Bordeaux.

NO EXPENSE SPARED

A menu for those occasions when style and elegance are important and the cost of the ingredients is not.

Chicken and lobster salad with walnut oil dressing
(see page 47)

Papillote de turbot et saumon au beurre de caviar
(see page 73)

Guava and lime syllabub
(see page 186)

To drink: A top quality white Burgundy followed by a sweet dessert wine.

THE PAUPER'S PARTY

A menu to show that good food doesn't have to cost the earth if the ingredients are fresh and well chosen.

Carrot ring with light tomato sauce
(see page 148)

Poached chicken breast with apple and clove sauce
(see page 126)

Prunes stuffed with walnuts in honey and lemon syrup
(see page 182)

To drink: A dry or medium white wine or cider.

QUICK AND EASY

The emphasis here is on simple preparation that takes the minimum of time, but produces impressive results.

Young turnips with orange and parsley
(see page 162)

Fillet of lemon sole with smoked salmon
(see page 86)

Claret and ginger jelly
(see page 189)

To drink: A white Burgundy.

FOR VEGETARIANS

A meatless menu which shows that vegetarian food can be sophisticated and imaginative.

Green pepper and fennel soup
(see page 24)

Galette d'aubergines with tomatoes and yogurt
(see page 156)

Redcurrant tart with raspberry coulis
(see page 181)

To drink: A Californian white wine or Beaujolais Nouveau.

A FEAST FROM THE EAST

This menu doesn't focus on any particular cuisine, but gives a flavour of the Orient and its different types of food.

Thai prawns
(see page 39)

Soya-braised knuckle of pork
(see page 113)

Mango with mango sorbet and marinated lime
(see page 185)

To drink: Chinese tea or saké.

FOR THE HEALTHY GOURMET

A menu that will appeal to anyone who is intent on eating healthily, but also adventurously.

Paper-thin raw beef with rock salt and Colchester oysters
(see page 45)

Steamed salmon over seaweed
(see page 70)

Citrus salad with crème de menthe
(see page 169)

To drink: A fresh fruit cocktail or sparkling mineral water.

CONTRIBUTORS

The chefs whose recipes appear in this book are listed here in alphabetical order together with the names and addresses of their restaurants.

Russell Allen
The English Garden, 10 Lincoln Street, London SW3
Liam Barr
The English House, 3 Milner Street, London SW3
Raymond Blanc
Le Manoir aux Quat' Saisons, Great Milton, Oxfordshire
Melanie de Blank
Shipdham Place, Church Close, Shipdham, Norfolk
Christopher Bradley
Mr Underhill's Restaurant, Stonham, Stowmarket, Suffolk
Jean Brunner
Le Français, 1 Paston Place, Kemp Town, Brighton, Sussex
Stephen Bull
Lichfield's, Lichfield Terrace, Sheen Road, Richmond, Surrey
Jean Butterworth and Peter Dixon
White Moss House, Rydal Water, Grasmere, Cumbria
Pierre Chevillard
Chewton Glen Hotel, New Milton, Hampshire
Francis Coulson
Sharrow Bay Hotel, Ullswater, Near Penrith, Cumbria
Michael Croft
The Royal Crescent Hotel, 16 Royal Crescent, Bath, Avon
Tim Cumming
The Hole in the Wall, 16 George Street, Bath, Avon
Barbara Deane and Jonathon Hayes
The Perfumed Conservatory, 182 Wandsworth Bridge Road, London SW6
Allan Garth and Bernard Rendler
Gravetye Manor, Sharpthorne, Near East Grinstead, Sussex
René Gaté
Les Semailles, 9 Druid Hill, Stoke Bishop, Bristol, Avon
Paul Gaylor
Inigo Jones, 14 Garrick Street, London WC2
François Huguet
Inverlochy Castle, Fort William, Scotland
Patricia Hegarty
Hope End Country House Hotel, Hope End, Ledbury, Hereford & Worcester
Baba Hine
Corse Lawn House Hotel, Corse Lawn, Near Tewkesbury, Gloucestershire
Martin Hoefkens
Tarn End Hotel, Talkin, Brampton, Near Carlisle, Cumbria
Allan Holland
Mallory Court, Bishops Tachbrook, Near Leamington Spa, Warwickshire
Peter Hollins
The Marquee Restaurant, 1 Bircherley Green, Hertford, Hertfordshire

Vincenzo Iannone
La Fiorentina, Lower Kings Road, Berkhamsted, Hertfordshire
Robert Jackson
Herbs Restaurant, Trinity House Hotel, 28 Lower Holyhead Road, Coventry, Warwickshire
Robert Jones
Ston Easton Park, Ston Easton, Near Bath, Avon
James Kempston
Stone Green Hall, Mersham, Near Ashford, Kent
John Kenward
Kenwards Restaurant, Pipe Passage, 151a High Street, Lewes, Sussex
Judy Knock
The Gentle Gardener, Long Street, Tetbury, Gloucestershire
Nico Ladenis
Chez Nico, 129 Queenstown Road, London SW8
Kenneth Lo and Kam-Po But
Ken Lo's Memories of China, 67 Ebury Street, London SW1
Ann Long
The Count House Restaurant, Botallack, Near Penzance, Cornwall
Robert Mabey
Hintlesham Hall, Hintlesham, Suffolk
Andrew Mitchell
Greywalls, Muirfield, Gullane, East Lothian, Scotland
Somerset Moore
Flitwick Manor, Church Road, Flitwick, Bedfordshire
Anton Mosimann
The Dorchester, Park Lane, London W1
Bronwen Nixon and Jane Binns
Rothay Manor, Ambleside, Cumbria
Anthony Rudge
Salisbury House, 84 Victoria Road, Diss, Norfolk
Nicolas Ryan
Crinan Hotel, Crinan, Lochgilphead, Argyll, Scotland
Richard Sandford
Milton Sandford Restaurant, Church Lane, Shinfield, Berkshire
Betty and Peter Saville
The Weavers Shed Restaurant, Golcar, Huddersfield, West Yorkshire
Lin Scrannage
The Market Restaurant, 30 Edge Street, Manchester
Victoria Stephenson
Bradfield House Restaurant, Bradfield Combust, Near Bury St Edmunds, Suffolk
Robert Thornton
The Moss Nook Restaurant, Ringway Road, Manchester
Carol Trevor-Roper
Knights Farm, Burghfield, Near Reading, Berkshire
Paul and Muriel Wadsworth
Pebbles Restaurant, 1 Pebble Lane, Aylesbury, Buckinghamshire
Ian Weeks
Weeks Restaurant, 31 Egremont Street, Glemsford, Sudbury, Suffolk
Colin White
White's Restaurant, Jews House, 15 The Strait, Lincoln, Lincolnshire
Antony Worrall-Thompson
Ménage à Trois, 15 Beauchamp Place, London SW3

FOOD VALUE AND CALORIE CHARTS
Introduction

Although this book is not intended to be a nutritional guide, I have included some general information about the calories and food value of specific dishes to help readers who want to know what their food contains.

CALORIES

The calorie is a very small unit of energy, which provides a way of measuring the amount of energy taken in as food and used up in daily living. In practice, however, the calorie (with a small "c") is so tiny that we tend to use units of 1,000 calories (kilocalories or Calories with a capital "C") for convenience.

Proteins, carbohydrates and fats all supply calories, but fat is by far the most concentrated source. So a reduction in fat is one useful way of controlling or reducing calories. Calorie counts don't tell you whether the calories come from protein, fat or carbohydrate, so they can be misleading, and at best are rough guidelines that need qualification to be really helpful.

An average person takes in and uses up around 2,000 Calories per day. Anyone leading a very active life may need as many as 4,000, while those on "calorie controlled diets" may take in as few as 1,500. Any reduction below that also means sacrificing other valuable nutrients, such as vitamins, which is not recommended. Having said that, everyone utilizes their daily food at a different rate, and some do it much quicker and more efficiently than others – so it is possible to sit at a desk all day and cope perfectly well with a high calorie intake.

The charts that follow are easy to understand; a black dot in any of the various columns indicates that that particular food contains protein, fat, fibre or vitamins.

DAIRY PRODUCE

	Calories	Chydrate	Protein	Fat	Fibre	Vitamins
Butter, 1 oz (30 g)	210	0		•		•
Cheese, Austrian smoked, 1 oz (30 g)	75	0	•	•		•
Brie, 1 oz (30 g)	85	0	•	•		•
Cream cheese, 1 oz (30 g)	120	0		•		•
Curd cheese, 1 oz (30 g)	25	0	•	•		•
Cottage cheese, plain, 1 oz (30 g)	25	0	•	•		•
Camembert, 1 oz (30 g)	85	0	•	•		•
Cheddar, 1 oz (30 g)	110	0	•	•		•
Cheshire, 1 oz (30 g)	110	0	•	•		•
Danish blue, 1 oz (30 g)	100	0	•	•		•
Dolcelatte, 1 oz (30 g)	95	0	•	•		•
Double Gloucester, 1 oz (30 g)	100	0	•	•		•
Edam, 1 oz (30 g)	85	0	•	•		•
Emmenthal, 1 oz (30 g)	110	0	•	•		•
Gorgonzola, 1 oz (30 g)	100	0	•	•		•
Gouda, 1 oz (30 g)	85	0	•	•		•
Gruyère, 1 oz (30 g)	130	0	•	•		•
Lancashire, 1 oz (30 g)	100	0	•	•		•
Leicester, 1 oz (30 g)	110	0	•	•		•
Mozzarella, 1 oz (30 g)	95	0	•	•		•
Parmesan, 1 oz (30 g)	120	0	•	•		•
Port Salut, 1 oz (30 g)	90	0	•	•		•
Ricotta, 1 oz (30 g)	70	0		•		•
Roquefort, 1 oz (30 g)	100	0	•	•		•
Stilton, blue, 1 oz (30 g)	130	0	•	•		•
Wensleydale, 1 oz (30 g)	110	0	•	•		•
Cream, single, 1 oz (30 g)	60	1		•		•
double, 1 oz (30 g)	130	1		•		•
soured, 1 oz (30 g)	55	1		•		•
clotted, 1 oz (30 g)	160	1		•		•
Eggs, raw (1)	80	0	•	•		•
boiled (1)	80	0	•	•		•
poached (1)	80	0	•	•		•
fried (1)	130	0	•	•		•
scrambled (2)	340	0	•	•		•
Duck egg, raw (1)	160	0	•	•		•
Quail's egg, raw (1)	40	0	•	•		•
Margarine, standard, 1 oz (30 g)	210	0		•		•
polyunsaturated, 1 oz (30 g)	210	0		•		•
Milk, gold top, 1 fl oz (30 ml)	20	1		•		•
silver top, 1 fl oz (30 ml)	20	1		•		•
homogenized, 1 fl oz (30 ml)	20	1		•		•
long life, 1 fl oz (30 ml)	20	1		•		•
powdered, standard, 1 oz (30 g)	140	11	•	•		•
low fat, 1 oz (30 g)	100	15	•			•
skimmed, 1 fl oz (30 ml)	75	17	•			•
evaporated, 1 fl oz (30 ml)	45	3	•	•		•
Yogurt, natural, 1 oz (30 g)	20	2		•		•
5 oz (150 g)	90	9		•		•
low fat, natural, 1 oz (30 g)	15	2		•		•
5 oz (150 g)	75	9				•

MEAT

	Calories	Chydrate	Protein	Fat	Fibre	Vitamins
Bacon, back rashers, raw (2) 3½ oz (105 g)	420	0	•	•		•
grilled, 2 oz (60 g)	230	0	•	•		•
fried, 2 oz (60 g)	260	0	•	•		•
Beef, steak, raw, 1 oz (30 g)	55	0	•	•		•
grilled, 8 oz (240 g) raw	440	0	•	•		•
fried, 8 oz (240 g) raw	500	0	•	•		•
joint, raw, 1 oz (30 g)	80	0	•	•		•
roast, 3 oz (90 g)	300	0	•	•		•
minced, lean, raw, 1 oz (30 g)	35	0	•	•		•
Chicken, raw, 1 oz (30 g)	35	0	•	•		•
roast, 4 oz (120 g)	170	0	•	•		•
grilled, 4 oz (120 g)	170	0	•	•		•
boiled, 4 oz (120 g)	210	0	•	•		•
Duck, raw, 1 oz (30 g)	120	0	•	•		•
roast, 4 oz (120 g)	380	0	•	•		•
grilled, 4 oz (120 g)	380	0	•	•		•
Guinea-fowl, on bone, roast, 1 lb (480 g) raw	490	0	•	•		•
Ham, boiled, 3 oz (90 g)	230	0	•	•		•
smoked or grilled, 3 oz (90 g)	190	0	•	•		•
baked, 3 oz (90 g)	230	0	•	•		•
Parma ham, 1 oz (30 g)	65	0	•	•		•
Hare, raw, 1 oz (30 g)	40	0	•	•		•
roast, 3 oz (90 g)	160	0	•	•		•
Kidney, raw, 1 oz (30 g)	25	0	•	•		•
Lamb, joint, raw, 1 oz (30 g)	70	0	•	•		•
roast, 3 oz (90 g)	230	0	•	•		•
chop, raw, 6 oz (180 g)	530	0	•	•		•
grilled, 6 oz (180 g)	400	0	•	•		•
Liver, all types, raw, 1 oz (30 g)	50	0	•	•		•
Oxtail, raw, 1 oz (30 g)	50	0	•	•		•
Partridge, roast, 12 oz (360 g)	270	0	•	•		•
Pheasant, roast, 12 oz (360 g) raw	330	0		•		•
Pigeon, roast, 1 lb (480 g) raw	290	0		•		•
Pork, joint, raw, 1 oz (30 g)	75	0	•	•		•
roast, 1 oz (30 g)	240	0	•	•		•
chop, raw, 6 oz (180 g)	470	0	•	•		•
grilled, 6 oz (180 g)	330	0	•	•		•
Poussin, roast, 12 oz (360 g) raw	250	0	•	•		•
Quail, roast (2), 1 lb (480 g) raw	330	0	•	•		•
Sweetbreads, raw, 1 oz (30 g)	35	0	•	•		•
Turkey, raw, 1 oz (30 g)	30	0	•			•
roast, 4 oz (120 g)	160	0	•			•
Veal, joint, raw, 1 oz (30 g)	30	0	•	•		•
roast, 4 oz (120 g)	260	0	•	•		•
chop, raw, 6 oz (180 g)	150	0	•	•		•
grilled, 6 oz (180 g)	240	0	•	•		•
escalope, raw, 4 oz (120 g)	120	0	•	•		•
grilled, 4 oz (120 g)	190	0	•	•		•
Venison, raw, 1 oz (30 g)	40	0	•	•		•
roast, 3 oz (90 g)	170	0	•	•		•

FISH

	Calories	C'hydrate	Protein	Fat	Fibre	Vitamins
Abalone, raw, 1 oz (30 g)	30	1	•			•
Anchovy, raw, 1 oz (30 g)	55	0	•	•		•
canned in oil, 1 oz (30 g)	55	0	•	•		•
canned in brine, 1 oz (30 g)	55	0	•	•		•
Bass, raw, 1 oz (30 g)	25	0	•	•		•
Bream, raw, 1 oz (30 g)	25	0	•	•		•
Carp, raw, 1 oz (30 g)	25	0	•	•		•
Caviar, red, 1 oz (30 g)	60	0	•	•		•
Clam, raw, 1 oz (30 g)	20	0	•	•		•
Cockle, shelled, raw, 1 oz (30 g)	10	0				
boiled, 1 oz (30 g)	15	0	•			•
Cod, raw, 1 oz (30 g)	20	0	•			•
Cod's roe, fried, 1 oz (30 g)	55	1	•	•		•
smoked, 1 oz (30 g)	30	0	•			•
Crab, cooked, 1 oz (30 g)	35	0	•	•		•
Crayfish (3), 6 oz (180 g)						
in shells	70	0	•			•
shelled, 2 oz (60 g)	60	0	•			•
Eel, raw, 1 oz (30 g)	50	0	•	•		•
smoked, 1 oz (30 g)	55	0	•	•		•
Haddock, raw, 1 oz (30 g)	20	0	•			•
smoked, raw, 1 oz (30 g)	20	0	•			•
Hake, raw, 1 oz (30 g)	20	0	•	•		•
Halibut, raw, 1 oz (30 g)	25	0	•	•		•
Herring fillet, raw, 1 oz (30 g)	65	0	•	•		•
salted, 1 oz (30 g)	80	0	•	•		•
pickled, 1 oz (30 g)	80	0	•	•		•
roe, fried, 1 oz (30 g)	70	1	•	•		•
Kipper fillet, raw, 1 oz (30 g)	80	0	•	•		•
fried, no breadcrumbs, 5 oz (150 g)	340	0	•	•		•
Lobster, whole, boiled, 1 lb (480 g)	190	0	•	•		•
Mackerel, raw, 1 oz (30 g)	65	0	•	•		•
smoked 5 oz (150 g)	440	0	•	•		•
Mullet, raw, 1 oz (30 g)	40	0	•	•		•
Mussels, raw (6), 3 oz (90 g)	55	0	•	•		•
Octopus, raw, 1 oz (30 g)	20	0	•			•
Oysters, raw (6), 3 oz (90 g)	45	0	•			•
smoked, 3 oz (90 g)	45	0	•			•
Plaice, raw, 1 oz (30 g)	25	0	•	•		•
Prawns, shrimps in shells, 6 oz (180 g)	65	0	•			•
shelled, 2 oz (60 g)	60	0	•			•
potted, 1 oz (30 g)	120	0	•	•		•
Salmon, raw, 1 oz (30 g)	50	0	•	•		•
smoked, 1 oz (30 g)	40	0	•	•		•
Salmon trout, raw, 1 oz (30 g)	50	0	•	•		•
Sardine, canned in oil, drained, 1 oz (30 g)	60	0	•	•		•
Scallops, raw (2), 3 oz (90 g)	90	0	•			•
Scampi, boiled, 1 oz (30 g)	30	0	•			•
Skate, raw, 1 oz (30 g)	20	0	•			•
Smelt, raw, 1 oz (30 g)	25	0	•	•		•

FISH (Continued)

	Calories	C'hydrate	Protein	Fat	Fibre	Vitamins
Sole, lemon, raw, 1 oz (30 g)	25	0	•			•
Sprats, raw, 1 oz (30 g)	25	0	•	•		•
Squid, raw, 1 oz (30 g)	20	0	•			•
Trout, raw (1), 8 oz (240 g)	200	0	•	•		•
smoked, 8 oz (240 g)	200	0	•	•		•
Tuna, canned in oil, 1 oz (30 g)	80	0	•	•		•
Turbot, raw, 1 oz (30 g)	20	0	•			•
Whelks, boiled in shell, 1 oz (30 g)	4	0				
shelled, 3 oz (90 g)	75	0	•			•
Whitebait, raw, 1 oz (30 g)	15	0	•	•		•
deep-fried in flour, 4 oz (120 g)	590	6		•		
Winkles, boiled in shell, 1 oz (30 g)	4	0				

VEGETABLES

	Calories	C'hydrate	Protein	Fat	Fibre	Vitamins
Artichoke globe, boiled (1) 8 oz (240 g)	15	3				•
heart, boiled, 4 oz (120 g)	15	3				•
Artichoke, Jerusalem, boiled, 4 oz (120 g)	20	4				
Asparagus, raw, 1 oz (30 g)	3	0				•
Aubergine, raw, 1 oz (30 g)	4	1			•	•
Avocado (½), raw, 4 oz (120 g)	250	2	•	•		•
Bamboo shoots, canned, 1 oz (30 g)	8	1				
Beans, broad, raw, 1 oz (30 g)	15	2			•	•
French, raw, 1 oz (30 g)	2	0			•	•
haricot, dried, 1 oz (30 g)	75	13	•		•	•
boiled, 4 oz (120 g)	110	19				•
runner, raw, 1 oz (30 g)	7	1			•	•
Beansprouts, raw, 1 oz (30 g)	3	0				•
Beetroot, boiled, small, ½ oz (15 g)	6	1			•	•
pickled, small, ½ oz (15 g)	6	1			•	•
Broccoli, raw, 1 oz (30 g)	7	1			•	•
Brussels sprouts, raw, 1 oz (30 g)	7	1			•	•
Cabbage, Chinese, raw, 1 oz (30 g)	4	1				•
red, raw, 1 oz (30 g)	6	1			•	•
Savoy, raw, 1 oz (30 g)	7	1			•	•
spring, raw, 1 oz (30 g)	6	1				•
white, raw, 1 oz (30 g)	6	1			•	•
winter, raw, 1 oz (30 g)	6	1			•	•
Carrots, raw, 1 oz (30 g)	7	2			•	•
juice, 1 fl oz, (30 ml)	7	2				•
Cauliflower, raw, 1 oz (30 g)	4	0				•
Celeriac, raw, 1 oz (30 g)	7	1			•	•
Celery, raw, 1 oz (30 g)	2	0			•	•

VEGETABLES (Continued)	Calories	C'hydrate	Protein	Fat	Fibre	Vitamins
Chicory, raw, 1 oz (30 g)	3	0				•
Corn on the cob, raw, 5 in (13 cm), 5 oz (150 g)	180	34			•	•
Corn oil, 1 oz (30 g)	250	0		•		
Courgette, raw, 1 oz (30 g)	3	1				•
Cucumber, raw, 1 oz (30 g)	3	1				•
pickled, 1 oz (30 g)	3	1				
Endive, raw, 1 oz (30 g)	3	0			•	•
Garlic, 1 clove, raw	1	0				
Gherkins, pickled, medium (1)	2	0				•
Horseradish, raw, grated, 1 tsp	2	0				•
Horseradish sauce, fresh, ½ oz (15 g)	30	4	•			•
Leeks, raw, 1 oz (30 g)	9	2			•	•
Lentils, boiled, 4 oz (120 g)	110	19	•		•	•
Lettuce, raw, 1 oz (30 g)	3	0			•	•
raw, 2 oz (60 g)	7	1		•	•	•
Marrow, raw, 1 oz (30 g)	5	1				•
Mushrooms, raw, 1 oz (30 g)	4	0			•	•
Mustard and cress, 1 oz (30 g)	3	0			•	•
Okra, raw, 1 oz (30 g)	5	1			•	•
Olives, black with stones (10), 1 oz (30 g)	25	0		•		•
green with stones (10), 1 oz (30 g)	25	0		•		•
Olive oil, 1 fl oz (30 ml)	250	0		•		
Onion, raw, 1 oz (30 g)	7	1				•
pickled, 1 oz (30 g)	7	1				
Palm heart, canned, 1 oz (30 g)	30	8				
Parsley, raw, 1 oz (30 g)	6	0			•	•
Parsnips, raw, 1 oz (30 g)	15	3			•	•
Peas, raw, 1 oz (30 g)	20	3			•	•
Peppers, raw, 1 oz (30 g)	4	1			•	•
Potatoes old, raw, 1 oz (30 g)	25	6				•
baked (1) 2½ in (6 cm) diameter	110	26			•	•
mashed with milk and butter, 4oz (120 g)	130	20		•		•
new, raw, 1 oz (30 g)	25	6				•
boiled, 4 oz (120 g)	85	21				•
chips, fried, thin cut, 4 oz (120 g)	360	42		•		•
thick cut, 4 oz (120 g)	180	31		•		•
roast with fat, 4 oz (120 g)	180	31		•		•
crisps, 1 oz (30 g)	150	14		•	•	•
Pumpkin, raw, 1 oz (30 g)	4	1				•
Radishes, 1 oz (30 g)	4	1				•
Salsify, raw, 1 oz (30 g)	5	1				•
Sauerkraut, canned, 4 oz (120 g)	20	4			•	•
Split peas, dried, 1 oz (30 g)	90	16	•		•	•
boiled, 4 oz (120 g)	130	25	•		•	•
Spinach, raw, 1 oz (30 g)	10	0			•	•

VEGETABLES (Continued)	Calories	C'hydrate	Protein	Fat	Fibre	Vitamins
Spring onions (4), raw, 1 oz (30 g)	10	2			•	•
Spring greens, raw, 1 oz (30 g)	8	1			•	•
Sweet potatoes, raw, 1 oz (30 g)	25	6			•	•
Tomato, raw, 1 oz (30 g)	4	1				•
canned, 1 oz (30 g)	3	1				•
purée, 1 oz (30 g)	20	3				•
juice, 1 fl oz (30 ml)	5	1				•
Turnips, raw, 1 oz (30 g)	6	1			•	•
Vegetable lard, 1 oz (30 g)	250	0		•		
Water chestnuts, canned, 1 oz (30 g)	15	4				•
Watercress, raw, 3 oz (90 g)	10	1			•	•
Yeast, fresh, 1 oz (30 g)	15	0	•			•
dried, 1 oz (30 g)	50	1	•		•	•

FRUIT, NUTS AND SEEDS

	Calories	C'hydrate	Protein	Fat	Fibre	Vitamins
Almonds, shelled, raw 1 oz (30 g)	160	1	•	•	•	•
roasted and salted, 1 oz (30 g)	170	1	•	•	•	•
marzipan, 1 oz (30 g)	65	18		•		
Angelica, 1 oz (30 g)	80	21				
Apple, small, raw, 4 oz (120 g)	40	10				
dried, 1 oz (30 g)	65	17			•	•
juice, natural, 1 fl oz (30 ml)	10	3				
Apricot, raw (1)	9	2			•	•
dried (2), 1 oz (30 g)	50	12			•	•
Banana, small, 4½ oz (135 g)	60	15			•	•
dried, 1 oz (30 g)	65	16			•	•
Blackberries, raw, 1 oz (30 g)	8	2			•	•
Blackcurrants, raw, 1 oz (30 g)	8	2			•	•
Brazil nuts, shelled, 1 oz (30 g)	180	1	•	•	•	•
Candied peel, 1 oz (30 g)	85	22				
Cashew nuts, shelled, 1 oz (30 g)	160	8	•	•		
roasted and salted, 1 oz (30 g)	150	6	•	•		
Cherries, 1 oz (30 g)	10	3				•
Chestnuts, shelled, raw, 1 oz (30 g)	50	10		•		
dried, 1 oz (30 g)	95	20			•	•
Clementine, 2 oz (60 g)	20	5			•	•
Cob nuts, shelled, 1 oz (30 g)	110	2		•	•	•
Coconut, shelled, raw, 1 oz (30 g)	100	1		•	•	
desiccated, 1 oz (30 g)	170	2		•	•	
milk, 1 fl oz (30 ml)	6	1				
Cranberries, raw, 1 oz (30 g)	4	1			•	•
Currants, dried, 1 oz (30 g)	70	18			•	•
Damsons, raw 1 oz (30 g)	10	2			•	•
Dates, with stones 1 oz (30 g)	60	16			•	•

FRUIT, NUTS AND SEEDS (Cont.)

	Calories	C'hydrate	Protein	Fat	Fibre	Vitamins
Fig, raw (1), 1½ oz (45 g)	15	4			•	•
dried (1), ¾ oz (22.5 g)	45	11			•	
Ginger root, raw, 1 oz (30 g)	15					
crystalized, 1 oz (30 g)	100	27				
Gooseberries, raw, 1 oz (30 g)	5	1			•	•
Grapefruit, raw (½), 7 oz (210 g)	20	5				•
juice, unsweetened, 1 fl oz (30 ml)	9	2				•
Grapes, black, without stalks (6), 1 oz (30 g)	15	4				•
white, without stalks (6), 1 oz (30 g)	15	4				•
Greengage, raw, with stones, 1 oz (30 g)	15	3				•
Groundnuts, shelled, raw, 1 oz (30 g)	160	2	•	•	•	•
with shells, 1 oz (30 g)	110	2	•	•	•	•
Groundnut oil, 1 fl oz (30 ml)	250	1		•		
Hazelnuts, shelled, 1 oz (30 g)	110	2		•	•	•
Lemon, raw, 3 oz (90 g)	15	3			•	•
juice, unsweetened, 1 fl oz (30 ml)	2	0				•
Loganberries, raw, 1 oz (30 g)	5	1			•	•
Lychees, raw, 1 oz (30 g)	20	5				•
Mandarin, medium, raw (1), 2½ oz (75 g)	25	6			•	•
Mango, raw, 7 oz (210 g)	120	30			•	•
Melon, cantaloupe, 6 oz (180 g)	25	6				•
honeydew, 6 oz (180 g)	20	5				•
ogen, 6 oz (180 g)	20	5				•
watermelon, 6 oz (180 g)	20	5				•
Mulberries, raw, 1 oz (30 g)	10	2				•
Mustard powder, made up, 1 tsp	10	0	•			
Nectarine, with stone, raw, 5 oz (150 g)	65	16			•	•
Orange, medium, raw (1), 3 in (7½ cm) diameter	60	14			•	•
juice, 1 fl oz (30 ml)	9	2				•
Marmalade, 1 oz (30 g)	76	20				•
Passion fruit raw, 4 oz (120 g)	15	3			•	•
Peach, medium, raw (1) 2 in (5 cm) diameter	35	9				•
dried, 1 oz (30 g)	60	15			•	•
Peanuts, shelled, 1 oz (30 g)	160	2	•	•	•	•
Peanut butter, 1 oz (30 g)	180	4	•	•	•	•
Pear, medium (1), 6½ oz (195 g)	55	14			•	•
Pineapple, raw, 1 oz (30 g)	15	3				•
juice, unsweetened, 1 fl oz (30 ml)	15	4				•
Pistachio nuts, shelled, raw, 1 oz (30 g)	170	5	•	•		•
roasted and salted, 1 oz (30 g)	170	5	•	•		•

FRUIT, NUTS AND SEEDS (Cont.)

	Calories	C'hydrate	Protein	Fat	Fibre	Vitamins
Plums, large, raw (2), 4 oz (120 g)	40	10				•
Pomegranate, raw (1), 7 oz (210 g)	75	20				•
juice, unsweetened, 1 fl oz (30 ml)	10	3				•
Prunes, dried, with stones, 1 oz (30 g)	40	9			•	•
soaked, stewed, no sugar, 5 oz (150 g)	100	26			•	•
Raisins, 1 oz (30 g)	70	18			•	
Raspberries, raw, 1 oz (30 g)	7	2			•	•
Redcurrants, raw, 1 oz (30 g)	6	1			•	•
Rhubarb, raw, 1 oz (30 g)	2	0			•	•
stewed, no sugar, 5 oz (150 g)	8	1			•	•
Satsuma, medium (1), 3 oz (90 g)	20	5			•	•
Sesame seeds, 1 oz (30 g)	160	6	•	•	•	•
oil, 1 fl oz (30 ml)	250	0		•		
Sunflower oil, 1 fl oz (30 ml)	250	0		•		
Tangerine, medium, raw (1), 3 oz (90 g)	20	5			•	•
Walnuts, shelled, 1 oz (30 g)	150	1	•	•	•	•

CEREALS

	Calories	C'hydrate	Protein	Fat	Fibre	Vitamins
Arrowroot, 1 oz (30 g)	100	27			•	
Barley, raw, 1 oz (30 g)	100	24			•	•
Bran, 4 tbs, 1 oz (30 g)	60	8	•	•	•	•
Bap (1), 3 oz (90 g)	270	47			•	
Brown bread, 1 slice, 1 oz (30 g)	65	13	•		•	•
Brioche (1), 2½ oz (75 g)	220	25	•	•	•	•
Croissant (1), 2½ oz (75 g)	260	30		•		
French bread, 1½ in (3.75 cm), 1 oz (30 g)	80	16	•		•	•
Granary bread, 1 slice, 1 oz (30 g)	60	12	•		•	•
Pitta (1), 3 oz (90 g)	220	51				•
Matzoh, 1 oz (30 g)	110	25	•			•
Pumpernickel, 1 slice, 1 oz (30 g)	65	13			•	•
Rye bread, 1 slice, 1 oz (30 g)	65	14			•	•
Crusty roll (1), 2 oz (60 g)	160	32	•		•	•
Soft roll (1), 2 oz (60 g)	170	30	•	•	•	•
Soda bread, 1 slice, 1 oz (30 g)	75	13	•	•	•	•
Toast, 1 slice, 1 oz (30 g)	65	14	•		•	•
Bread, wholemeal, 1 slice, 1 oz (30 g)	60	12	•		•	•
wholewheat, 1 slice, 1 oz (30 g)	60	12	•		•	•
crusty white, 1 slice, 1½ oz (45 g)	100	21	•		•	•

CEREALS (Continued)	Calories	Chydrate	Protein	Fat	Fibre	Vitamins
Cornflour, 1 oz (30 g)	100	26				•
Flour, plain, 1 oz (30 g)	100	23	•		•	•
wholemeal, 1 oz (30 g)	90	19	•		•	•
Oats, raw, 1 oz (30 g)	110	21	•		•	•
Pasta (all types), cooked, 1 oz (30 g)	35	7				
Pastry, choux, raw, 1 oz (30 g)	60	6		•		•
cooked, 1 oz (30 g)	95	9	•	•		•
flaky, raw, 1 oz (30 g)	120	10		•		•
cooked, 1 oz (30 g)	160	13		•		•
puff, raw, 1 oz (30 g)	120	9		•		•
cooked, 1 oz (30 g)	150	11		•		•
shortcrust, raw, 1 oz (30 g)	130	14		•		•
cooked, 1 oz (30 g)	150	16	•	•		•
Rice, white, raw, 1 oz (30 g)	100	25		•		•
boiled, 1 oz (30 g)	35	8				
brown, raw, 1 oz (30 g)	100	24			•	•
boiled, 1 oz (30 g)	35	8				
Semolina, raw, 1 oz (30 g)	100	22	•		•	•
Wheatgerm, 1 oz (30 g)	100	13	•	•	•	•

MISCELLANEOUS

	Calories	Chydrate	Protein	Fat	Fibre	Vitamins
Sugar, white, 1 oz (30 g)	110	30				
1 tsp	30	7				
Sugar, brown, 1 oz (30 g)	110	30				
1 tsp	30	7				
Honey, 1 oz (30 g)	80	22				
Chocolate, milk, 1 oz (30 g)	150	17	•	•		•
plain, 1 oz (30 g)	150	18	•			
cooking, 1 oz (30 g)	150	9	•			

NON-ALCOHOLIC DRINKS

	Calories	Chydrate	Protein	Fat	Fibre	Vitamins
Coffee, instant, powder, 1 oz (30 g)	30	3	•			•
black, 1 cup, 7 fl oz (210 ml)	4	1				
with milk, 1 cup 7 fl oz (210 ml)	130	9	•			•
with milk and sugar, 1 cup, 7 fl oz (210 ml)	160	17	•			•
ground, beans, black, 1 cup 7 fl oz (210 ml)	4	1				
with milk, 7 fl oz (210 ml)	20	9	•			
with milk and sugar, 7 fl oz (210 ml)	50	9				
with cream and sugar 7 fl oz (210 ml)	60	8	•			
Ginger ale, 1 fl oz (30 ml)	7	2				

NON-ALCOHOLIC DRINKS (Continued)	Calories	Chydrate	Protein	Fat	Fibre	Vitamins
Lemonade, sparkling, 1 fl oz (30 ml)	6	2				
Tonic water, 1 fl oz (30 ml)	6	2				
Tea, black, 1 cup, 7 fl oz (210 ml)	2	0				
Tea, with milk, 7 fl oz (210 ml)	20	1				•
with milk, sugar, 7 fl oz (210 ml)	50	9				•

ALCOHOLIC DRINKS

	Calories	Chydrate	Protein	Fat	Fibre	Vitamins
Armagnac, 1 fl oz (30 ml)	65	0				
Beer, canned bitter, 1 fl oz (30 ml)	9	1				
1 pt (600 ml)	180	13				•
draught and keg bitter, 1 fl oz (30 ml)	9	1				
1 pt (600 ml)	180	13				•
draught mild, 1 fl oz (30 ml)	7	0				
1 pt (600 ml)	140	9				•
Benedictine, 1 fl oz (30 ml)	110	14				
Cassis, 1 fl oz (30 ml)	70	9				
Champagne, 1 fl oz (30 ml)	20	0				
Cider, dry, 1 fl oz (30 ml)	10	1				
1 pt (600 ml)	200	15				
Cognac, 1 fl oz (30 ml)	65	0				
Cointreau, 1 fl oz (30 ml)	95	9				
Crème de menthe, 1 fl oz (30 ml)	90	8				
Dry Martini cocktail, 2½ fl oz (75 ml)	140	1				
Gin, 1 fl oz (30 ml)	65	0				
Grand Marnier, 1 fl oz (30 ml)	90	8				
Irish coffee, 4 fl oz (120 ml)	160	8		•		
Lager, 1 fl oz	8	0				
1 pt (600 ml)	160	8				•
Pernod, 1 fl oz (30 ml)	70	0				
Port, 1 fl oz (30 ml)	45	3				
Rum, 1 fl oz (30 ml)	65	0				
Sherry, dry, 1 fl oz (30 ml)	35	0				
medium, 1 fl oz (30 ml)	35	1				
sweet, 1 fl oz (30 ml)	40	2				
Vermouth, dry, 1 fl oz (30 ml)	35	2				
sweet, 1 fl oz (30 ml)	45	4				
Wine, red, dry, 1 fl oz (30 ml)	20	0				
sweet, 1 fl oz (30 ml)	25	1				
white, dry, 1 fl oz (30 ml)	20	0				
medium, 1 fl oz (30 ml)	20	1				
sweet, 1 fl oz (30 ml)	25	2				
sparkling, dry, 1 fl oz (30 ml)	20	0				
medium, 1 fl oz (30 ml)	20	1				
sweet, 1 fl oz (30 ml)	25	2				

INDEX

208